The Courage

Hope and Help for Alcoholics

Personal Conversations

Robert Bauman
Sid and Florence Ceasar
Billy and Sybil Carter
Graham Chapman • Gary Crosby
Ryne Duren
The Reverend Jerry Falwell
Shecky Greene • Wilbur Mills
Elmore Leonard • Don Newcombe
Jason and Lois Robards
Doc Severinsen • Grace Slick

to Change

and Their Families

with **Dennis Wholey**

Gerry Spence • Rod Steiger
Gale Storm and Lee Bonnell
Pete Townshend • Tom Tryon
Bob Welch • Daniel J. Anderson, Ph.D.
Joan Pheney DeFer, M.S.W.
Conway Hunter, Jr., M.D.
Jean Kirkpatrick, Ph.D.
The Reverend Vaughan Quinn, O.M.I.
G. Douglas Talbott, M.D.
and members of Alcoholics Anonymous

G.K.HALL&CO.
Boston, Massachusetts
1985

Published in Large Print by arrangement with Houghton Mifflin Company.

G.K. Hall Large Print Book Series.

Set in 16 pt English Times.

Library of Congress Cataloging in Publication Data

Wholey, Dennis, 1937-
   The courage to change.

   (G.K. Hall large print book series)
   1. Alcoholics—Rehabilitation—United States—Biography. 2. Large type books. I. Bauman, Robert, 1937- . II. Title.
HV5292.8.W48 1985   362.2'928   85-17705
ISBN 0-8161-3959-8 (lg. print)

*This book is for my mother and father,
for my sisters, Ann and Nora,
and for my brothers, Tim and Skef.*

Acknowledgments

My sincere thanks go to the participants in *The Courage to Change* who gave so freely of themselves and welcomed me into their homes. It is their book as well—a collective effort.

I am also grateful to Dr. Rob Roy McGregor, who opened the door into the publishing world for me and guided me to Austin Olney at Houghton Mifflin. Michael Medved played a key role, with his enthusiasm for the project at the right time, by introducing me to Arthur and Richard Pine. Over the months I have continually leaned on Richard for his professional expertise and enthusiasm. My very good friend and confidant, Paul Kasper, has kept me on an even keel— through all the highs and lows of this book as well as life. David Dodd, who handled all of the research and checked the transcripts, has been constantly involved in the book-making process. His professionalism and good humor in taking care of a hundred and one other thankless "things to do" reflect his commitment to this book.

I have the deepest appreciation for the heroic efforts of Yvette Mandell, who transcribed thousands of pages of tapes, handled my correspondence, and coordinated the efforts of others at the word processors, especially Ray Tess, Robin Thompson, Judy Garry, and Michelle Mikulec. Mel Niser, who heads AAA Typing, let his staff meet my deadlines. Thanks also to Patty Steeby for her assistance when the crunch was on, and to Leonore Bechtel, who helped me with the original presentation. Sharon Kraft came through at the eleventh hour, and Lori Andiman made sure that Richard Pine and I always talked.

At Houghton Mifflin my sincere thanks go to all who have played a part in the creation of this book, especially Austin Olney for his commitment to the idea from the beginning. He has repeatedly placed the concept of producing a good book over selling books. I also appreciate his sensitivity to me as a first-time author, and as a human being. Larry Kessenich has made an outstanding contribution in organizational suggestions and making the book more readable. Geraldine Morse, Virginia Ehrlich, Helena Bentz, Jessie Dorin, Steve Lewers, Tira Nelson, Louise Noble, Bob Overholtzer, and Steve Pekich all helped, too. The editorial board of Houghton Mifflin should be confident that their decision to publish *The Courage to Change* will help many people. At WTVS, I appreciate the enthusiasm for this project by our boss, Bob Larson.

At "LateNight America" I want to thank Bill Pace, Dianne Hudson, Jan Zap Jungquist, Carole Gibson, Karen Melamed, Deborah Maldonado,

Clark Attebury, Jeff Kirk, Carlota Almanza, Andrea Amato, Barbara Diggs-Berry, and especially Jack Caldwell and Henrietta Fridholm, who, probably without realizing it, have helped me to grow. A special thank-you to three friends who have died along the way but contributed greatly to my sobriety—George Lahodny, Thad Gaillard, and Joe Mulqueen.

On a very personal note, I thank all of the members of my extended family for their encouragement and support, and Scott Murphy, Michael Murphy, Jack Conn, and Dr. Lonnie MacDonald. They all have an extra special place in my life.

Many other people, of course, have let me be me throughout the years and walked the journey with me. I thank them all.

Contents

Foreword

Gordon MacRae has distinguished himself in every area of show business: film, radio, television, nightclubs, recordings, and theater. He has starred in more than twenty films, including the legendary Oklahoma *and* Carousel. *He and his wife, Elizabeth, and their daughter divide their time between Lincoln, Nebraska, and Beverly Hills, California. In addition to his continuing work in theater, nightclubs, and concerts, Gordon is actively involved in alcoholism prevention and education.*

You have in your hands a very exciting and important book. What you will read will make the disease of alcoholism very real and very personal. Alcoholism affects millions of Americans—not only the drinkers but their families, close friends, and co-workers, too. This collection of firsthand experiences by the well known and the anonymous is powerful. These self-revealing stories are not only open and honest, they are inspirational.

I am an alcoholic myself, so I understand

alcoholism on a very personal level. I was there once myself, so I know the feelings of torment and despair.

All of the contributors in this book offer their hope, help, and expertise unselfishly. They do this so that others may be led out of their suffering and find happiness.

Those who have lived through the nightmare of alcoholism and come out the other side want to help others who still hurt. We know lectures, threats, and even punishments never seem to work with those caught up in alcoholism.

What has worked, and what is presented here, is one alcoholic telling his or her story to another alcoholic and one family member of an alcoholic telling his or her story to another family member of an alcoholic. This sharing at gut level is the most successful way of changing alcoholic lives, and identification plays the key role.

The message in this book to the drinking alcoholic is: Recognize yourself in these stories and get help. If you think you have a drinking problem, you do—and it will get worse.

The message to the family member or friend of the alcoholic is: You are paying a tremendous price for living with alcoholism, and you may be contributing to your alcoholic's drinking. You don't have to live the way you are living. Seek help for yourself. A change in your attitudes and behavior will ultimately affect the alcoholic, who then may seek help.

The message to the general public is: Understand that alcoholism is a physical, mental, emotional, and spiritual disease. Alcoholics are not bad or weak people. Alcoholics are sick people who desperately need to get well.

In my work for the National Council on Alcoholism I have been encouraged by recent steps forward to inform and educate the public about alcoholism and to smash away the stigma of alcoholism.

This book will help greatly in that process.

I congratulate all of the contributors to *The Courage to Change*. Their willingness to place themselves on the line—with the only motivation to offer help and hope to those who need it—is extraordinary. *The Courage to Change* brings out the very best in all of us.

It is easy to say good words about a book that will change people's lives in a dramatic and positive way.

I am proud to play a role in this effort.

Gordon MacRae
Honorary Chairman
National Council on Alcoholism

1 I'm Dennis, and I'm an Alcoholic

The Courage to Change is a celebration of life. It is about what is good in people. There is nothing negative, depressing, shameful, embarrassing, or sensational about it. It is a collective effort of many individuals to help people who suffer from alcoholism—the alcoholics themselves and their close family members. This book is also for anyone who is interested in understanding alcoholism.

The contributors to this book want to help others. Together they all say, "Recognize alcoholism and do something about it. We did and we are happier now than we ever were before."

The stigma of alcoholism and being labeled an alcoholic is the disgrace. Regardless of what America says, the truth is that the general public still knows and understands little about alcoholism and addiction. Because alcoholism is so misunderstood, it is swept under the rug and hidden in the closet. Alcoholism—a disease that directly affects more than one third of the entire population—is America's national secret. Alcoholics are still seen as modern-day lepers, and those who live in an alcoholic home are looked on as poor suffering martyrs.

The Courage to Change presents a microcosm of the alcoholic experience and medical information about alcoholism. As you read this book, all of us ask you to set aside everything you think you may know about alcoholism and read with an open mind.

Alcoholics have a disease: they are allergic to alcohol. They can't drink, but they don't know that. One drink triggers a biochemical craving that demands more drinks. No one is more confused about his drinking than the alcoholic who stops by the bar each Thursday and has three drinks, and then one night stops at the same bar and has fifteen drinks, with disastrous consequences.

Alcoholics are not bad people; they are sick people. Alcoholic behavior is bad. Mentally and emotionally alcoholics are rougher on themselves than any outsider could ever be. They miss the fact, or deny, that alcohol is at the heart of their troubled and painful lives. Alcoholics are not weak people, and not drinking for the alcoholic has nothing to do with will power. Alcoholics can quit—we all quit many, many times—but alcoholics go back and drink again, and again. The difficult thing is staying stopped. Quite often —after he has stopped for a day, a week, or a month—a small thing or false confidence will trigger the alcoholic to take "one drink"—and because of the biochemical process the merry-go-round begins again. The one drink triggers the compulsion.

Those around the alcoholic are forever asking him to "cut down." This is like asking your daughter to get only a little pregnant. The alcoholic tries, he really does. Sooner or later, he gets drunk again. Most alcoholics cannot quit drinking for good on their own.

By the time an alcoholic is an alcoholic—addicted to the drug alcohol—he has lost all perspective on life and cannot see what alcohol is doing to him. Everything else is the problem and alcohol is the blind spot because, even though it brings mental, emotional, physical, financial, and spiritual pain, it works. It does the job it is supposed to do. Alcohol blocks out the reality of life.

Alcoholics have to want to quit drinking before the miracle of happiness can occur. No one can make the alcoholic quit, but others around him, especially family and employer, can play a key role in forcing the alcoholic to face the truth. Sooner or later the alcoholic must quit drinking totally.

The Courage to Change became a book for a very simple reason. With the exception of a few books that seem to be heavy reading or specific autobiographies, the literature about alcoholism for the general public is still very weak. By collecting the expertise and personal experiences of many people who know about alcoholism, we hoped all of us together might make an impact, a real contribution.

I would not have placed my own story at the beginning of this book. However, the editors have suggested that I do so to tell you about the book and introduce myself.

My father was a lawyer and a judge who helped many people; he was also an alcoholic. We lived in the country in Rhode Island, so it was hard to escape the tensions, the unpredictability, the problems of a home life with an alcoholic.

My father would often arrive home from work after having clearly been drinking on the way. From inside the house we would watch him struggle, and debate helping him, which seemed like the charitable thing to do, or letting him stay out there to teach him a lesson. My father was not a bad person, but his alcoholic behavior was painful to all of us. My mother, my two brothers, and two sisters and I lived a continuous nightmare for years. My mother deserves credit for holding things together.

I have many painful memories of my growing-up years. I remember, one afternoon, asking my father, when he was sober, if I could use the car that night. He said yes, and I made my plans with my friends. After supper, when I wanted to leave, he wouldn't let me go. He was drunk. In my anger and frustration, and in tears, I picked up his gold pocket watch and smashed it. As another example, my father would regularly quit drinking for Lent. All of us would hope and pray that he would see the light. But he would always start

6

drinking before an early afternoon dinner on Easter Sunday.

It is not terribly important why I drank. Everybody does. Of course, having experienced what I did growing up, I was never going to be like my father, but I became an alcoholic, too. I always felt I was the outsider, I was the loner. I was the rebel without a cause. Growing up in an alcoholic home, I was emotionally damaged as a kid, and alcohol solved all that. It made me feel good. I was happier and funnier. My shyness disappeared, and alcohol helped me to fit in.

Unhappy children grow up to be unhappy adults—and for more than twenty years, I looked for the answer to my unhappiness and depression in psychology and psychiatry. I went to the very best therapists. I was a good patient, a very hard-working patient. For one stretch of several years, I logged four hours a week. Dreams were analyzed, behavior was studied, feelings were held up for examination, and Valium was prescribed. Scotch and Valium do not mix very well. In the end, I became addicted to both.

It is almost impossible to convey the relief I now have since I found out that I am an alcoholic. It's like the old joke about the man who suffered from migraine headaches and was scheduled for brain surgery. As the surgeon was about to wield the knife, the man's hospital dressing gown fell open and the doctor discovered that the patient's jockey shorts were too tight.

The problem in my life was alcohol, but I had

7

never looked there for the answer. I looked everywhere else. At one point, one of my therapists told me that I was not an alcoholic. Well, I am an alcoholic. It's really no big deal. I'm allergic to alcohol. It's that simple. I don't drink anymore.

My earliest memory of drinking involves driving a car while drunk, with the wheels anchored on either side of the white line so I wouldn't drive off the road. I was sixteen.

When I went off to college I was scared. I was only seventeen and drinking helped me to fit in.

Early in my freshman year, my brother Skef, who was president of the student council, asked me to emcee the Homecoming festivities. I wore white tie and tails, and my performance was a great success. I got smashed afterward. It was not the last time.

Sometime during my sophomore year, a priest friend asked if I would be willing to see a psychiatrist if he paid the bill. He had observed, he told me, that I lived life in a series of extreme highs and lows. The psychiatrist's recommendation, after two sessions in the office and some take-home testing, was that I should begin therapy immediately. The diagnosis was that I might commit suicide if I didn't. I may be exaggerating, but that's how I remember it. I did a lot of drinking in college.

I taught high school for two years after college in order to continue therapy. I remember once asking the students to rate me as a teacher

8

anonymously. I must have been twenty-one or twenty-two at the time. They gave me good marks except for Mondays, when I was usually hung over.

Anywhere and everywhere I went, I managed to hook up with other drinkers. I loved to drink. In my twenties, I was able to bounce back quickly. Actually, alcoholics can almost always function the next day; that's a clear sign of the disease. Normal drinkers, when they drink too much, stay in bed for two days and stay away from alcohol for three months. Alcoholics get drunk at night and want to get up the next morning and play softball. For the alcoholic, the party never ends.

In New York City I got a job at NBC as a guide conducting tours. Later I became a guide trainer, a radio director for NBC, and an assistant to the producer of a film documentary series. As I progressed up the ladder, I also progressed in my drinking career.

I began interviewing on FM radio and got my television break hosting, ironically enough, a series on narcotics addiction for the PBS television station in New York City; I stayed on staff there for two years as a producer and host. There were quite a few drunken incidents. I'm told that one night in a bar I told Edward Albee how to write plays. To sit down in those days and have four or five ''double Black and Whites'' on the rocks was usual for me. Alcoholics seem to drink doubles.

9

WKRC-TV in Cincinnati, where I was host of a daily morning talk show, was my entry into commercial television. My star was rising. ABC tapped me to host a game show, "The Generation Gap," and some brass at Westinghouse were in my camp to replace Merv Griffin—a job that eventually went to David Frost.

Taft Broadcasting put together a talk show for syndication, which I hosted. One of my producers at the time spotted my drinking problem. He made it clear that the best way to throw away a career was to get arrested for drunk driving or make a fool out of yourself in public.

I became a closet drinker. In public, I controlled my drinking most of the time. Drinking never interfered with my work, or so I told myself, but I know now it held me back from moving ahead more quickly. I could turn it off on Sunday night and not pick up a drink until Friday afternoon. The truth of the matter is that one drink was never enough for me, so I would do without. This disciplined drinking was very self-deceiving because I kidded myself that I could stop. And I stopped often.

When the Taft show folded, I went back to New York, where I drank for two years. I justified it by saying I couldn't find a job, but of course I didn't look very hard. I was terrified of auditions and avoided them. During the time I was out of work, well-meaning friends kept me financially afloat after I used up the money from Taft. I'd managed to run myself into fifty thousand dollars' worth of debt.

In May of 1973, I came to do a week's worth of shows in Detroit and when, at the end of the second day, they asked me to do a second week, I knew I had the job. That Friday I took the entire staff to lunch at the London Chop House to put the job on ice.

Celebrating a sure thing, I got royally drunk on the plane, drank through a Friday night poker game, and was arrested at three o'clock in the morning for disturbing the peace—no small task in New York. A junior partner in the law firm that handled my contracts bailed me out at 7:00 A.M. He wondered why I had done this to myself, since I had to be back on the air in Detroit at 7:00 A.M. on Monday morning. I wondered, too. Alcoholics drink at the most inopportune times. The incident so frightened me—after being so long without work—that I didn't drink for six months.

Throughout my entire life I had been totally career oriented. But when I went to Detroit, I became involved in two relationships, both with women who had children. Those "family" relationships put a lid on my drinking, except when I drank alone or occasionally when I was out with drinking friends.

After more than four years in Detroit, I moved to Washington, D.C. The first year on the air was terrible. The second year—the contract was not renewed—I lived off the money from some stock investments. I drank an awful lot that second

11

year and seriously thought about quitting television for good.

I returned to Detroit to host a local telephone-and-audience talk show on the PBS station. When I returned, I did a phone interview with a newspaper columnist who said, "Dennis, in the early seventies you were one of the bright young interviewers on television—Tom Snyder, Phil Donahue, and you. What happened? Why aren't you at the top like they are?" I knew the answer.

I was just barely hanging on to life. Throughout those last few years I often isolated myself and drank. I could not sleep without Valium, and the thought of running out of it scared me. For the last five years before quitting, I drank only beer and took Valium. My tolerance was shot—and a few beers would put me away. Alcoholics kid themselves when they switch from the hard stuff to beer or wine.

Blackouts were common to me for many years. I once threw a party for five hundred people in New York City. To this day, I can remember only one person who was there.

Drunk one night in the early 1970s, I called a very close friend and told him I wanted to check into a hospital. He told me to have another drink and he'd be down to escort me there. We went to Saint Vincent's Hospital in New York City. He walked and I lurched.

You haven't lived until you've been in a New York City hospital emergency room on a Saturday night. I was about fiftieth in line, with assorted bodies strewn around, arms falling off, blood dripping from faces, and people lying on cots, moaning. It was mayhem and nothing was happening.

Of course, an essential part of my personality as a drinking alcoholic was a strong "me" orientation. If I were number fifty, checking in was going to take a long time. I approached the first woman, who had blood streaming down the side of her face. "What's wrong?" I said. "My boyfriend cut me," she answered. I turned and hollered, "Get someone over here to take care of this woman." And someone came. I went to the next person and asked, "How long have you been here?" "Three hours," he replied. "Nurse," I hollered again, "Let's help this man, now!"

It must have appeared to my friend Jeane that he was watching a speeded-up movie. Suddenly nurses came and went, stretchers appeared, and people disappeared. X-rays were taken and bandages applied. Badly damaged people were checked in, and not so badly damaged ones were patched up and released. I recall hours later standing there with Jeane and his asking, "What are you going to do now?" I said, "Check in, that's what I came for." He said, "Are you crazy? These people think you're running the hospital. They think you're the head resident. You're the reason everybody's been taken care of."

I can still see that first woman. The rest of those hours were spent in a blackout. I did go back the next day and checked in after the shift change. I spent about a week there "drying out," with a technician standing by my side when I wanted to shave. No matches, no razors, nothing dangerous.

I do remember being arrested at a peace march in Washington, D.C. After a good deal of scotch, I invited fifty college students for free hamburgers at a White Castle not far from the Peace Corps building. The owner of the White Castle panicked and called the cops. The police asked me to move along three times, and a normal person would have. Not me. The charge was attempting to incite a riot. Sounds a little heavy to me. We never did make it to the site of the rally the next day. We found some new drinking friends along the way.

In December 1980 I went to California and went through a series of business meetings and personal get-togethers with old friends. I never touched a drink. On my way to the airport, I dropped off my rental car and bought a bottle of vodka. I got smashed on the plane to Detroit. Someone gave me a ride home. To this day, I don't know who it was.

In the end I felt hopeless because I had worked so hard at the therapy, but was still so unhappy.

I vividly recall the following scene. I was in the office of Jack Caldwell, who was the boss of WTVS in Detroit. "Jack, I'm thinking of quitting." It was a surprise to both of us. "Personally and professionally, nothing in my life is working," I continued. "I'm sorry to hear that,"

14

he replied. "We're about ready to launch a new show for you. Whatever you decide is best for you, let me know." I was surprised by his humane attitude. From a selfish point of view he could easily have pushed me to continue. We talked for a while. "Is the problem alcohol?" Jack asked. "No," I said. I meant it.

That evening I made a number of desperate calls to family and friends. I was looking for emotional and financial support. I had decided to enter a hospital. I couldn't get off the merry-go-round. I needed some rest. I needed to quit drinking. But I continued to drink as the evening wore on. Finally I talked with Father Vaughan Quinn. He runs the Sacred Heart Rehabilitation Center in Detroit, and I had interviewed him on television. We made an appointment for the next afternoon.

Father Quinn and I talked for three hours. The conversation was frank. I put my life on the table. All the loneliness, the depression, the anger, frustration with people and jobs, thoughts of suicide, and fears. Quinn listened to all of it without interruption. Finally it was his turn. There was no hesitation. He said it quietly but forcefully, "The problem in your life is alcohol." He was right.

Father Quinn also told me about a group of nondrinking alcoholic friends he wanted me to meet. They were the ones who helped me quit drinking. I couldn't do it on my own.

At the same time, Father Quinn teamed me up with a psychologist named Jack Gregory. Jack is terrific and has worked with hundreds of alcoholics. It was Jack who finally convinced me that the Valium had to go, along with the drinking. With his urging I tapered myself off over a period of time, and that was that.

Then Dennis had to look at Dennis real hard.

The last three and a half years have been exciting and positive—rewarding beyond my wildest dreams and expectations. Everything has changed, and changed for the better. Professionally, with "LateNight America," I have never been more successful. "LateNight" is carried by stations in almost one hundred cities, with a nightly audience of one and a half million people. On a personal level, I am at peace.

I certainly don't beat myself for being an alcoholic. I didn't have much to do with it at all. My drinking days are behind me, and it's not very hard not to drink. I've learned that nobody cares, either, except me.

Not drinking has made all the difference in the world. I have never been happier in my life.

I am somewhat embarrassed when I look back and realize I was so self-centered. I had gone through life thinking that I was better than everyone else and, at the same time, being afraid of everyone. I was afraid to be me. That has changed dramatically.

I am learning I am very human. I have many faults. I am not the center of the universe. I'm just like everybody else. I have some unique talents that I take no credit for, that I try to use to earn a living and benefit other people.

I have stopped trying to get people to always do things my way and I try to fit into the process more. Most of the time I can see the positive in people and situations. People are special unto themselves. More confidence and more tolerance have come my way. I've learned that if I put in my best effort and know that I've done as much as I can, most things seem to work out fine. Action and acceptance are both important to me. I don't try to impress people, as I did in the past, and I try to put myself into other people's shoes. I'm no doormat anymore, and I'm trying to rid myself of the aspect of my personality that centers around people-pleasing. I still do that. If I'm angry, I know I'm doing something wrong. Depression and unhappiness are no longer a part of my life, and self-pity rarely engulfs me.

I certainly know that I cannot drink or use drugs, and that doesn't seem very difficult. Not drinking is very much a part of my life, and I stick very close to my nondrinking alcoholic friends. They are responsible for my sobriety and happiness. My aunt is a diabetic and must watch her diet. I'm an alcoholic and must watch mine. I can't drink. I know that, and so far, so good. Not to drink, for me, is a gift. The compulsion is gone. God has a very special place in my life today. A friend of mine says, "If you're going to worry, don't pray, and if you're going to pray, don't worry."

It is so much easier this way. Basically, I never

grew up. I started cutting off uncomfortable feelings when I was a teenager by drinking. I've had to experience some of those feelings and work my way through them. I'm learning, and it's a great adventure. I'm growing up.

This book is part of my adventure. It has been fun, and I have learned not only about alcoholism, but also about life. I have had the rare opportunity to travel many miles and sit and talk with the contributors to the book. I have done the interviews in offices, homes, cars, and on planes.

When I began to put the book together in print, it seemed that my questions got in the way, so I have edited them out. The voices in this book are powerful; they don't need any intrusion from me. Those who tell their own stories and offer their expertise have traveled on their personal *Titanic* and been saved. They do not suggest they did anything heroic. They will tell you their survival was at stake: sink or swim, now or never. They all possessed the courage to change. I thank them all.

2　The Beginning

Alcoholics are night watchmen and rock stars, housewives and millionaires, newspaper columnists and bank executives, college students and secretaries, baseball players and first ladies, nuns and priests, models and teachers, blue-collar workers and actresses, company owners and cab drivers. Fewer than 3 percent of all alcoholics are skid-row bums.

Everyone knows an alcoholic whose drinking behavior sometimes causes embarrassment to others. Alcoholics get into arguments or fights, run into financial difficulties, have blackouts, and make light of the fact that they drank too much the night before. They are unpredictable and irresponsible. Friends and family worry about their drinking.

Inside, the alcoholic is afraid of the world, a loner who doesn't feel he belongs. Alcoholics are shy and look to alcohol for self-confidence; then they feel guilt and shame after drinking. They resent others who talk to them about their drinking. They run at half speed because of hangovers, and others around them walk on eggshells.

There are no rules, however; every alcoholic is an exception.

At the beginning of his drinking career, the alcoholic drinks to feel good. Right from the start the alcoholic likes what liquor does for him; he likes the effect. Alcohol may release his inhibitions, solve his problems, or help him fit in. Alcohol does the job.

Alcohol is a drug. We haven't come to grips with that simple fact yet. If we are to understand alcoholism, it is essential to understand that millions of Americans become addicted to the drug alcohol, and it destroys their lives and the lives of those around them. No one wakes up one morning and decides to become an alcoholic. It is a slow process that may take years. So insidious is the disease of alcoholism that people become addicted without realizing what is happening. A variety of factors play a role in alcoholism —genetic predisposition, family background, personality, social environment, and, of course, using alcohol.

Dr. Doug Talbott makes understanding alcoholism vividly clear with his comparison to ether. Normal drinkers, using his example, have a sniff or two and go about their business of enjoying life and one another. Alcoholics go through life isolated, with the ether mask tied around their faces, pushing people away.

G. Douglas Talbott, M.D., is an alcoholic. He is the director of the Ridgeview Institute Alcohol and Drug Program in Smyrna, Geor-

gia. The Medical Association of Georgia has designated the Ridgeview Institute as headquarters for its Impaired Physicians Program.

G. Douglas Talbott, M.D.

Alcohol is a drug, and if you are addicted to alcohol, you are an alcoholic. Alcohol is a compound—C_2H_5OH—an etherlike substance, a sedative hypnotic drug. At the Ridgeview Institute I don't let the nurses talk about anybody being drunk or intoxicated. They have to say, "Dr. Talbott, you have a drug O.D. out front."

Your brain has no more idea than a pussycat's does whether you O.D.'d on alcohol, meprobamate, Miltown, Equanil, Phenobarbital, Valium, Librium, or any one of dozens of other sedative hypnotic drugs. The brain gets the same message from sleeping pills and tranquilizers as it does from the beverage alcohol. But America isn't ready to look at that yet.

If you take a bottle of beer or wine or any kind of alcoholic beverage—scotch, bourbon, after-dinner liqueurs, gin, vodka—whatever alcoholic beverage you want—take away the color and the taste, stick in a spigot, and drip off the water, you have ether. The body and the brain have no idea whether you're in an operating room, breathing ether from a mask on your face, or in a field drinking beer. The chemical message to the body and brain is the same.

The majority of Americans drink because America's culture is a drinking one. Probably 140

23

to 150 million people in this country drink.

Approximately 22 million Americans, one out of seven, are drinking alcoholically. This figure is based on my own research with the Baltimore Alcohol Program and our research at the Ridgeview Institute. Other studies agree with this figure.

The old figure was 10 million alcoholics. I was interested in where that figure came from and found it was thought up one night in Washington when the first alcohol support bill was presented to Congress. Senator Harold Hughes asked his staff what a good number was. They said 10 million, and that figure got frozen into literature. It is way beyond that now, and, as far as we are concerned, 22 million people have an alcohol problem related to the disease of alcoholism.

An alcoholic is an individual who compulsively uses alcohol as it destroys his or her life and who displays other symptoms, such as withdrawal, blackouts, and changing tolerance.

The ultimate consequences for a drinking alcoholic are these three: he or she will end up in a jail, in a hospital, or in a graveyard. These consequences will always threaten.

Alcoholism is a chronic, progressive disease, the same way that tuberculosis and diabetes are chronic, progressive diseases. We talk of alcoholism in four stages: first using, then abusing, then crossing the wall, then developing the disease.

The disease is manifested by the compulsion to

use even as the using destroys your life. In this country, it normally takes anywhere from ten to fifteen years to go through the stages. People generally use for five or seven years, abuse for three to five years, and take two years to cross the wall.

You can't become an alcoholic overnight any more than you can contract any of the other progressive diseases overnight. A person with rheumatoid arthritis doesn't end up in a wheel-chair a week after developing some vague pains in the joints. It may take years. The loss of control that signals alcoholism may start when a person overdrinks at one party and then continues to do that for several years.

In their early teens, people begin to go to parties and make plans for the next day. They realize the next morning that they can't pursue those plans because they drank more than they meant to. So, for the first time, they begin to impose limits on themselves: "I'm not going to drink as much tonight because I couldn't go to the movie today."

They try to impose limits on themselves, but they are not successful. They try to impose tighter and tighter limits, saying such things as, "I'm not going to drink whiskey, I'm just going to drink beer." As they continue to try to put constraints on their drinking, it doesn't work. Therefore, they begin to lie about their drinking. They lie first to themselves and then to other people. At the same time, they begin to develop feelings of shame and embarrassment. They begin to hide their drinking. They do such things as drinking before going to parties, so that people won't realize they're drinking so much. The lying, the hiding, the shame—the phenomenon of denial begins to creep in. They begin to change brands and pretty soon they go to extremes of subterfuge and deceit, hiding their liquor.

Now they begin to feel really guilty about their drinking. By this time, the progression, which may have taken place over months or years, is finished. The full-blown feelings of the alcoholic are present, predominantly feelings of loneliness and loss of self-respect and self-worth.

There aren't any lonelier people in the world than alcoholics. Lots of them have pain from the physical trauma of minor falls, which result in broken bones or from withdrawal, but there is no pain more devastating, more excruciating than the pain of loneliness and loss of self-respect. I can remember reading Saint-Exupéry's *Little Prince* a thousand times because I, too, felt as if I was wandering on a desert.

At that point the disease usually manifests itself in a way that begins to affect the individual's life. It begins to affect his family. Unlike heart disease and cancer, which are our two greatest killers, this disease affects the family tremendously. I've never seen an alcoholic without a spousaholic or childaholics or parentaholics. So the family begins to get terribly sick. As the disease progresses it produces blackouts, which are true drug amnesia.

The impact on the kids, wife, husband, parents is just tremendous. Very soon it will begin to affect the community. The alcoholic will draw away from the church. The disease will begin to affect the job through absenteeism, injury, or lack of quality work. The individual will begin to fall behind in performance. He may be affected to the point of being fired. This is what I call the target syndrome.

Show me an alcoholic, and I'll show you an individual who has the target syndrome. I named this after the .22 target I used to fire at when I was a child. Regard a target as the skins of an onion. Alcoholics begin to peel off layers. First goes the activity in the church; second goes the activity in the community; third goes the activity with friends, the hobbies and leisure-time activity; fourth goes the activity with peers, people at work, fellow housewives, and so on—people the alcoholic interacts with during an average work day; fifth goes the distant family; sixth goes the nuclear family. Then, suddenly, the alcoholic is in the middle of the target, completely isolated. The only friend he or she can rely on is the bottle. Standing in the center of that target, he is completely de-peoplized. He has layered off every person around like skins of an onion and hc is alone. The alcoholic continues to drink because of compulsivity and he fails to recognize the presence of the disease or the consequences of his drinking because of denial. Denial is part of the disease. Denying is different from lying. Denial is self-deception brought about by the lack of self-respect and self-growth. Alcoholics cannot see the nature of the disease as long as denial is there, and the disease itself presents the dilemma that it does because of the compulsion. They continue to drink and the denial gets worse. The combination of the biogenetic compulsion to drink, along with the denial, keeps them in the center of the target. Alcoholics drive other people away because the hostility and anger and fear they project won't permit people to come near them. They continually isolate themselves.

Alcoholism is the disease of loneliness, the disease of aloneness, and until you get the alcoholic out of the center of that target, he or she is never going to recover. Recovery, of course, is not merely taking away the drug. You have to start there. You take away the drug and lead the alcoholic out of the target syndrome. There is no longer any question that the most effective modality of treatment is not treatment centers. Treatment centers are important, detoxification is important, physicians are important, and nurses are important, but the most therapeutic weapon we've got was started fifty years ago by a physician and a stockbroker and it's called Alcoholics Anonymous (AA). The blueprint to recovery is in the Twelve Steps of AA. There's a pathway spelled out there that helps the alcoholic to come out of the target syndrome, to re-peoplize, and to live in peace and serenity without drugs.

There is almost no way to move out of the center of the target without re-peoplization. The Twelve Steps of AA are a re-peoplization blueprint.

What is recovery from alcoholism or drug addiction? It's three things: honesty, sharing, and love. These deal with re-peoplization, and to recover from alcoholism and other drug addictions you have to trust people, be honest with people, share with people, and love people. That will get you away from chemical dependence and give you personal accountability.

Whether you become an alcoholic or not depends on genetic predisposition. We know the reason the compulsivity exists is because of a change in the endorphin and cephalin systems in a primitive portion of the brain. The reason for the disturbance in the biochemistry of the primitive brain is a predisposition. Nobody talks any longer about becoming an alcoholic. You don't become an alcoholic—you are born an alcoholic. You're an alcoholic the day you get out of the uterus. You are like the *Titanic,* waiting till time and circumstance present the iceberg, and then you sink. The days that the alcoholic with the genetic predisposition abuses start his journey toward that iceberg.

It's the genetic predisposition that, if stimulated, causes the compulsion—not volume, dose, or duration of drinking.

It is probably not a single gene that is responsible, but a number of genes. We don't know at this point. America does not look on alcohol as a drug—a lethal addictive drug—and it certainly does not look on alcoholism as a disease. It looks on it as a bad habit, something caused by a lack of will power, a moral or ethical issue. At best, it is seen as symptomatic of an underlying emotional or psychiatric disorder.

But to say that alcoholism is a symptom of an underlying disorder is simply not true. Alcoholics do have severe secondary emotional problems. Of the thousands I've seen, I have practically never seen one who didn't have depression, who didn't have anxiety, anger, grief, who wasn't very lonely, who didn't have tremendous nervousness and insomnia—a tapestry of emotional feelings. But many studies utilizing exquisite psychiatric triage have shown that 90 percent of alcoholics do not have underlying psychiatric disease. We no longer hold to the premise that people who drink too much do so because of underlying psychiatric disorder. Just the opposite is true. Alcoholism is a primary biogenetic disease, and psychiatrists over the past fifty years have traditionally done very badly with it.

Disease is an abnormal state of health characterized by specific signs and symptoms. Alcoholism has that. Disease has a chronic, progressive course. Alcoholism has that. We don't know the causes of alcoholism yet. We don't know the causes of heart attacks, diabetes, or cancer, either, but we call them diseases. These diseases cause biochemical and anatomical changes. Alcoholism does that. It is a primary symptom, not a secondary one. We know that to be true. When anybody says, "Well, disease is a cop-out, it's not really a disease," then I say, "Fine. Let's have it your way and say it's not a disease. Here at Ridgeview Institute for Impaired Physicians, I have five psychiatrists as patients, as alcoholics. Tell me why those five psychiatrists continued to drink compulsively as it destroyed their lives. I can assure you that those five psychiatrists have exquisitely normal psychiatric profiles and yet they continued to drink. Now tell me why. You say it's not a disease and I'm saying, O.K. it's not a disease. Then give me a reason. There has to be one. If not, then they're bad, dumb, evil, weak. Of course, none of those fit."

Endorphin and cephalin metabolism in the hypothalamic primitive brain center is responsible for the compulsive drinking. Alcoholism is a biogenetic disease with a psychosocial background. Of course you have to abuse. That is where the emotional psychosocial factors come into the disease, but the disease itself is biogenetic.

The medical professional has not recognized alcoholism as a disease until very recently. I had only an hour's lecture on alcoholism in my entire medical school career. We're just getting it into the medical school curriculum. The rate of alcoholism is thirty-five times higher among medical

31

people than among laymen. If you choose to be a physician, dentist, pharmacist, or nurse, it's an occupational hazard. So there is an element of denial in the medical professional. We're talking about ignorance of the disease, denial that it exists. The medical professional has been threatened by AA, even though a physician cofounded the organization. We're trying to educate the medical profession about the importance of using AA as a treatment modality. Because alcoholism is a medical disease, we need physicians to be involved and we need detoxification centers. We often need churches, too, because it's important to have a strong spiritual program. We need treatment facilities and holistic treatment teams. We need to use all of the modalities that we can to help bring about recovery.

Alcoholism is the most treatable untreated disease in this country.

In their early years, alcoholics have an incredible tolerance for alcohol. This tolerance is deceptive and leads the alcoholic to believe that he can "handle his liquor."

At a young age, Doc Severinsen was fascinated with alcohol. As a teenager in the company of adults in bands on the road, he drank a lot regularly. During his army days he knew he was drinking too much too often, and his first marriage heavily involved alcohol. When Doc examined his drinking back then, he realized how much alcohol had held him back.

Doc Severinsen is an alcoholic. He is the conductor of "The Tonight Show" band and plays concerts with major symphony orchestras around the country. He has his own rock/jazz group, Xebron.

Doc Severinsen

I was three or four years old, maybe six— somewhere in that age bracket. It was during the depression. I remember that for a good time on Saturday night my folks would have a party at the house. We had a piano and they would get out the sheet music, and somehow a jug, like a fifth of whiskey, would show up. I was attracted to the sight of that bottle in the kitchen, and while they were all banging on the piano and singing "Somebody Else Is Taking My Place" I would sneak into the kitchen, pull down the jug, and take a snort for myself. I can even recall now; it tasted good. I liked it. There was more attraction to it as time went on. That happens to a lot of kids, but with me it was a little more serious.

Alcohol was very hard to get because, in a small town such as Arlington, Oregon, population 600, who is going to give booze to kids? They used to have dances, and the guys would take their jugs to the dance and hide them out behind the dance hall. When they got boozed up

33

to a certain degree, they'd forget where the jugs were. So, if you got down there on Sunday morning, you could find them and pour all the liquor together and manage to get enough for a few drinks. I did that.

In my family background there were some people with drinking problems, but it was all kept pretty quiet. Neither my mother nor my father was an alcoholic, but other family members were. I had a brother who was an alcoholic. He died of cancer. But the question was, what was going to get there first, the cancer or the booze? I have a sister, too. She's a teetotaler.

I started working around older musicians at a dance hall when I was sixteen. They thought nothing of giving me booze to drink. At seventeen I went on the road with a band. I was a bit of a smart aleck at that point, a young kid, traveling all over the United States, mailing in my lessons while the rest of my class was back in Arlington attending high school. Whenever the opportunity presented itself to have something to drink, which was quite often, I would.

We played at nightclubs, dance halls, army bases, and lots of gambling clubs. I was at an age when I shouldn't have been around that much booze, but there it was. I was in a very independent position, and I took advantage of it. I didn't do it all the time because I was not a graceful drinker. With me it was a serious proposition.

From there I went into the army and it was no

holds barred. I belonged to the Sergeant's Club. Lord, you're talking about some serious drinkers there. I was drinking to excess at all times. When I got out, I went back on the road with bands and again booze was around all the time. I can remember being in Tommy Dorsey's band when I was still very young. I would drink a pint a day, and eventually I worked my way up to about a fifth a day. As strange as it may seem, from what I can recall about that time and until the time I quit, it never immobilized me on the job. Let's face it, sometimes I didn't do nearly as well as I could have. I didn't take advantage of my talents or of the time I had to improve myself, but I sat down and I played. I did my job. As I look back at it now, I wonder how much more I could have accomplished at an earlier age if I had not been all wound up with booze.

Eventually, I settled in New York to start playing in studio orchestras. It was a lot of responsibility and I always managed to take care of the job very nicely. I got to be a better player. I studied a lot. I took a lot of lessons. I worked at my career. Some of the real raucous hard drinking took place in the traveling years, although when I was doing studio work I can remember getting pretty blasted, too.

I was about twenty when I got married the first time, to a woman I met in a bar, who, incidentally, probably had a problem herself, had I only known it. She subsequently died of alcoholism complications. I wound up living in the suburbs and belonging to the church and the PTA. I did your typical suburban drinking in addition to your musicians' drinking.

My wife and I didn't do much of anything together, although we did have three children. It was very unpleasant. I did plenty of drinking on my own at that point. The fact that she was a tremendous boozer made it easier for me. In our little circle of friends, I think there were a lot of candidates for AA. My wife was a pretty bad drunk, so I did most of the raising of the kids, the gardening, the whole works. You might not have thought I had any problem at all, by comparison.

My wife was really in pretty tough shape, always in and out of hospitals. One day it had gotten to the point where it was beginning to have a bad effect on the children and I said, "O.K., I've got to do something—today." I picked up the phone book and looked under Alcohol. I thought there had to be something under Alcoholism. I think what I found was the Alcoholism Abuse Center in White Plains, New York. I went up there and told them my story, and they said, "You sound like you need a lawyer." Finally I went to a lawyer, but nowhere I turned was there any real help. I went to the Society for the Prevention of Cruelty to Children and said, "Help me." Their idea of helping was to try to take the children away from both of us. I had to enter a plea to prevent them from doing that, and it was just a hideous mess in our household.

She had mental problems, I suppose, underneath it all. I mean, the children and the home counted for nothing at all to her. It was a bad situation. I was too young and naive to know what to do. I can remember one time when the family doctor said, "Well, I'll tell you what. She needs to be hospitalized. We'll put her in a hospital room with this woman I know who is dying of cirrhosis of the liver—and if that doesn't stop her, nothing will." She was so angry being incarcerated that way, but she lay there and watched this woman die of cirrhosis of the liver. It's a ghastly death to see, but that experience didn't stop her either. They say alcoholics don't have will power. But if you ever want to see a demonstration of will power, just watch a drunk trying to get his next drink. You'll see will power.

I was looking for help for my wife. I don't remember exactly how it all happened, but I remember going out on Long Island for a weekend at a beach colony where there were two married couples, both musicians and their wives, who were members of AA. I told the sad story about my wife, and they all agreed it was a pretty tragic situation. Then they asked, "How much are you drinking? Have you ever thought that maybe you might have a problem?" Which really took me by surprise. I started thinking about it. "Gee, do you suppose I really am an alcoholic? I don't know. Do I really have a problem?" Then, of course, my friends from AA gave me the test, which I flunked miserably.

They were looking to set me straight and spent the weekend talking to me very seriously. By this time I realized I did have a problem. Nevertheless, on the way home I stopped and picked up a six-pack of Budweiser.

By this time, drinking was no fun for me anymore. There was no more yah ha and paper hats and climbing up on furniture. I never felt good when I drank. Never. There was never a pleasant moment of it.

I had a hangover that never stopped. Think of the worst hangover you've ever had, then imagine having to pick up a trumpet in that condition and blow a high F. I mean, you turn around and vomit and break out in a cold sweat. Now you realize another reason I joined AA. But I bought that six-pack of beer. I went down in the basement with my six-pack to practice. I opened up the first can of beer, took a few sips out of it, and threw out the whole six-pack. I have never had a drink since and it's been, well—I stopped counting at twenty-five years.

I realized that booze was really holding me back from achieving my potential. It was simply an assessment. I have this much talent and this is how good I am. Here's what I've done with it. At the time I quit drinking there were a lot of drugs around. Marijuana was available. It was always there. I went to AA and was very successful at stopping drinking, but the use of marijuana was a handy crutch. I found that if you have an addictive personality that manifests itself in alcohol and you quit the alcohol, you may still run into a problem with other things.

I used marijuana and I've had my run-ins with cocaine. I even tried LSD a couple of times, too, just to see what it was. An addictive personality was there, but I wanted to believe there was something that I could use moderately.

I'll never forget one doctor I went to when I lived in Larchmont, New York. He was a well-meaning fellow, no doubt. I was not healthy. I was not feeling well. I was an alcoholic. Do you know what he prescribed for me? Dexedrine to get up in the morning, Valium to go to bed at night, and golf. All the bad guys are not in prison; some of them wear white smocks.

Finally I found myself interested in some other things in life, and I realized that if I wanted to be successful in my pursuit of those things that the drugs could not be allowed to get in the way. I went to Silva Mind Control. When you go to Silva Mind Control, they don't say, "Hey, you have to give this up." There's none of that. It's not a religious organization, and it doesn't have any guidelines that tell you not to do this, not to do that. I suppose some people who go there can and do drink successfully. What I found was that that sort of thing was totally unacceptable for me anymore.

Now, when I look back at myself, I cringe. Why I never killed anybody while behind the wheel of a car I will never know. I would wake up every single morning in Larchmont—about a thirty-five- to forty-mile drive from New York City—and I wouldn't remember getting my car out of the parking lot in New York, or negotiating through midtown traffic on to the superhighway, or driving to my home. But I didn't run over anybody. And I didn't get into a fist fight with a policeman. And I was never fired from my job for being a drunk. But those things didn't have to happen to me to make me know that I'm an alcoholic.

Alcoholics are frequently shy and very sensitive. Alcohol has a dramatic effect on the personality. Talking about his own insecurities, Pete Townshend classified himself as an either/or person for whom things have to be a great success or a total disaster. Pete says that alcohol allowed him to deal with the intensity of his feelings. Pete felt the good feelings in drinking from his very earliest days of The Who, when making music and drinking became linked together.

Pete Townshend is an alcoholic. He achieved world stardom as the writer, guitarist/singer, and spokesman for The Who, one of the most successful bands in rock music. Today he pursues a solo recording career and is involved in book publishing as a writer and editor.

Pete Townshend

I think my behavioral propensities are either toward excess or total rejection. That applies to the way I work on the stage. I either let go completely and become the person whom the public sees as the successful performing Pete Townshend, or I go into a mood and don't communicate at all. So I perform very, very well or very, very badly. When I write songs I think I open up completely, or I throw out a load of flack to disguise what I'm really doing. From the beginning, as a young person, as soon as I started to drink, I realized that alcohol changed me. It brought about a change in the way I thought. It was like a door opening to make me more of an animal than I already was.

Anybody who has an alcohol problem stands in a door frame, trying to maintain his balance. He is either going to feel that he is achieving his best or that he is not achieving at all. This applies particularly in social situations, where we all have insecurities. If you're the kind of individual who feels that something big always has to happen, that each party has to be either the kind you can walk out of in disgust or a great success, you've got a problem. This is the kind of problem I think I had. I think I carry it with me today. I've only not been drinking for two years, so I'm still getting used to the fact that when I go to a party or to a restaurant now, I have to sit and say, "Remember, Pete, this doesn't have to be the greatest night of your life. It doesn't matter. If you just have dinner, that's what restaurants are for. We go into them and have dinner and then we go home. It doesn't matter if you don't meet anybody you knew years ago. If these things don't happen, it doesn't necessarily mean that you have to get suicidal.''

Most people for whom alcohol becomes a problem are running away from something. I have to generalize from my own experience and that of people I've known who have had drinking problems. Usually what they are running away from are feelings and their inability to deal with the intensity of their feelings. Now, when you come across seasoned drinkers, one of the things you'll find is that they're often greatly sentimental. They have a tendency to be uproariously happy one minute, and maudlin the next. When they talk about deceased friends, they genuinely cry. These people are extremely emotional and alcohol allows them to live with the intense emotions that are really a part of their makeup. I have this idea of myself as being a classic English poet, which is bullshit really, but I carry the idea around and wear it like a hat. A lot of people buy it. I'm really a sentimental person. I'm really very weepy. If I'm alone in a room, watching some soap opera on the TV, even if it's halfway sad, I'll cry. On the other hand, I don't mind laughing at bad jokes.

Most people can't even deal with the emotional level of daily living. But you give them an exciting life and they go crazy. Life is very different, much quieter for me now, for the last two years in particular, and that's difficult, in a way. I'm out of the honeymoon period of sobriety and I'm having to face up to the fact that I've got to make it alone. Eventually, I've got to deal with the way I am.

My first experience with heavy drinking was when I was the bottle boy in my dad's band, watching the musicians in the band drinking at parties. I realized that if I stood by the beer-crates and handed the guys their beer and put the empty ones away, somewhat discreetly, I became a kind of hero. This is when I was eight years old.

Then, later on with my own band, The Who, when we used to play the pubs in our local area, I experienced this same drinking camaraderie. Whenever the band worked in the studio, in rehearsal, or on the road, I would assume that I had carte blanche. If I was with my family, the kids—or even my mom and dad, who were part of a heavy drinking crowd—I wouldn't drink as much. I certainly wouldn't compete with my father or his friends. But with The Who, the old brandy bottle would come out and I would start knocking it back limitlessly. I drank heavily for fifteen years, but only when I was working. It lasted until something gave out somewhere. I don't know what gave out first, my physique or my brain. There are a lot of people in the music business, in rock, who don't do that, but people unfortunately exploit the rock-'n'-roll myth, which brings in the audience. It all turns into a great conspiracy. Some say the fans want you to walk the tightrope. They lead boring, depressed lives, and they want their heros to go crazy. It's a vicarious kick. To some extent I expect that's true, but nobody wants dead heroes. What good is a hero if he's dead? People build up heroes in order to examine them. There isn't much you can do with a corpse.

My mother had a drinking problem and she dealt with it. My dad hasn't really got the same problem. He is a heavy drinker, but he manages. I don't think I ever used my parents' drinking as an excuse. I always confused the glamour of the life of a musician with being a heavy drinker. Well, there is nothing glamorous about any of the musicians who have drunk themselves to death. There was nothing glamorous about their lives, if the truth be told, certainly not the periods in which they were putting the people close to them through hell.

I suppose it was ten years ago that the hell started for my family and me. My wife, Karen, began feeling that there was a potential problem, while I felt it was just the way I was and the way I lived. So we'd have lots of conversations. I would try to justify the way that I ingested alcohol by saying it was part of being a successful person. She didn't buy that at all. What's really peculiar is that I *did*. I was saying, more or less, "This isn't me, this is some mechanism that drives me on. This is some ambition quotient." My wife doesn't like my suggesting that my drinking problem was a result of our relationship falling apart. She feels our relationship became more difficult because of my drinking problem. The two are bound up together, from my point of view. I always felt that drinking and work were tied together in a totally appropriate and proper way. This was despite the fact that my great partner, Roger Daltrey, never drank to excess, not from the beginning of our career to the end, and still doesn't. I don't think I've ever seen him drunk, yet we were always on the same stage, in the same airplane, in the same places. But I felt that I had a bigger responsibility because I was writing songs and was the spokesman for the band. And I wasn't allowed to bring those pressures home. This was the conspiracy that my wife and I carried together. We were accomplices. When I got home, family life was sacrosanct, but it got to the point where that charade could go on no longer.

I had a big, big problem because I had been the big rock idealist and now it was all letting me down. The industry hadn't fulfilled its promise. Rock 'n' roll had changed the length of men's hair and very little else. I felt like a fool because I'd waved the banner so aggressively. And what was really worse, I felt that I was being used by journalists.

I hated the feeling that I was in a band on the downward slide that was killing people in Cincinnati, killing off its own members, killing its manager. We were into making big money and anybody who got in the way or had a problem, we dropped. Nobody seemed to notice. Nobody seemed to think this was a particularly bad thing, or we pretended it wasn't, anyway. I felt it start to kill me. Something was getting its teeth into me. I should have stopped doing what I really didn't want to go on doing. I should have stopped working with the band. I should have stopped and had another look at rock 'n' roll, the thing that I loved and cared about so much, which I held above all other things.

I had so many great hopes. I could see that the band wasn't doing what I wanted it to do. I cared about doing it for all the wrong reasons. I carried on doing it for Roger. I carried on doing it for John Entwistle. I carried on doing it for the fans. I carried on doing it because I had a contract. I carried on doing it because I had thirty employees. I carried on doing it, and I shouldn't have. I should have stopped and taken a hard, hard look at the music business and myself and come to the conclusion, which a lot of other people had come to, that the best years of The Who were the early years. With a few successful excursions into commercialism, particularly with *Tommy,* we'd just been a pretty middle-of-the-road, successful, gung-ho megastar rock band, with a few others coming up and down.

But the passionate way that I felt about rock had nothing to do with the reality. It doesn't matter how deeply you feel about football; if you're a great player, you're a great player. If you're an adequate player, you're an adequate player. I have played some great games, and I still care very, very deeply about the game, but I know I can't play the way I used to. I have to live with that. A lot of rock 'n' roll is like sports; you get to thirty-five years old and your knees give way, and you just can't do it anymore.

Karen finally said, "Listen, the drinking is starting to affect the family. I won't have that." I said, "Karen, I can't stop drinking. I can't. Particularly when I'm working." So she said, "Well, then, when you work, you stay away." That sounded reasonable, so I started to do that. If I was recording I'd check into a hotel, do some work, or maybe go to the States for a couple of weeks. I'd come back home and dry out completely, maybe just have a glass of wine with a meal on Sunday. Then I'd go away again for a couple of months and do some work and then come back again. That was a weird year. At the end of 1979 and in the early part of 1980, The Who was touring and still making records, and I did my first solo album, which I was really pleased with. But some weird things happened to me. My wife and I became estranged. We were seeing less of each other and we weren't sharing the problem.

Eventually, I started to find social solace elsewhere. I dropped a lot of our mutual friends. I found a few others. I started to get involved with temporary girlfriends. I could go into a nightclub anywhere in London and everybody in the building would know who I was. I spent very little time at home. That's when it all began. Around that time, Karen and I decided that it would be best if I took my problems elsewhere, permanently.

I adjusted to what was happening in the world, and what was happening was that people weren't drinking quite as much as they used to—certainly not as much as I was. They were using cocaine in the music business—at the dentist, the hairdresser, the lawyer's office, the record company, the recording studio, on the bus, in the taxi. They were using coke everywhere, and I quickly got into this routine, too. Having plenty of money, I was able to supply myself and also about fifty other people who followed me around London. Luckily, among that crowd of people were a few who did care about me. In retrospect, it's important. My old friends are quick to say, "It was that sick bunch of assholes you hung around with that screwed you up." Well, I sought them out, they didn't find me. But a couple of them were very unwilling to take part in my destruction and said so. They said, "Listen, I don't mind killing me, but I don't want to kill you. You are somebody I care about." I've got good memories of some of those people. At the same time, it was a cycle. It was a way of getting out of something, of getting away from the band. It was a way of getting away from rock 'n' roll. The only way I could face the work was by destroying myself. I didn't have the guts to stand up and say, "This is a bunch of shit. I've got to go." I didn't have the guts to do it the way Keith Moon did it, to take a handful of elephant tranquilizers. I didn't have the guts to put a gun to my head. I had to make other people do it. I had to make other people responsible. I wasn't bent on self-destruction, but on having somebody else do the dirty work. That's what I think is so incredibly evil.

When we were recording, "Who Are You," a friend of my dad's, who works in AA over here, talked to Keith and he later said, "Keith isn't really an alcoholic. He's a very strange man, but he's got survival written all over him. He is not the kind of guy who fits into AA. I don't know how to help him, but I could help you." "Me?" I said. "I haven't got a drinking problem. I stopped two weeks ago just so I wouldn't be drinking around Keith." He said, "Well, just remember I said that." I thought this guy was a crazy man. I do remember stopping drinking for two to four weeks to make life easier for Keith. But at the end of each working day I was apparently drinking half a bottle of vodka just before I went home. Later Glyn Johns, our producer, confirmed this. I was just stopping drinking until we'd finished the session.

When Keith died, I think I took on his role for a while. I felt I had a bit more space to move. I felt, well, he's gone; that means I've got a bit more license. Obviously, his death had very little to do with my stability, but I imagined I was freer somehow. He was still playing a lot better than a lot of other people, but he wasn't the genius that he used to be. I suppose I jumped on that. I jumped on another aspect, too. I felt the freedom to be more me. Later, right in the middle of a period when I was in New York, in early 1981, Kit Lambert, our ex-manager, died. There had been no contact for a long time, but I still adored him. I felt I had even more space then. I felt I could get away with more. I had even more license.

For me, the nightmare took about two years. Throughout that whole period I was seeing my family, spending vacations and weekends with them. At the end of 1981 I started to get into real difficulties and I missed my family a lot. I suddenly realized that I couldn't live without my wife, and she was falling right out of love with me. I couldn't handle that. I also felt that I was really hurting the other women I came across because I was such a pathetic mess. Really great people were coming into my life at that time. I'd wake up in the morning and there would be a beautiful twenty-year-old woman running around. And I would think, What am I doing to this person? She should be out finding a young man. (I loved the fact that my wife and I met when we were young and were growing together and would grow old together.)

What happened to arrest me was that the money ran out. If there was an act of God in this whole thing, which I call a miracle, it was that. I was selling records. I sold a lot of copies of

"Empty Glass," my first solo album, and The Who's first album for Warner Brothers, "Face Dances." I had money coming in, of course, because a song writer is buffered. The record was selling in 1979 and I'd be getting money in 1984. I certainly didn't need to steal an old lady's handbag to get my bottle of Remy or my drugs. But then my book publishing company went to the wolves, and it took every penny I had with it—about a million dollars. I had not supervised the company and it had no separate bank of its own. It was badly managed, overstaffed, over-invested, and contracts were too generous to authors; on the other hand, we did some good stuff and I'm very proud of it. But the company collapsed.

I was halfway through recording my second solo album when I ran out of money. I went to the bank and said, "Listen, I've got to get this record finished." They said, "No, you can't have any more money." I said, "Come on, I've been at this branch since I was seventeen years old and all I have to do is deliver the record and they'll give me two million dollars. So If we can just finish the record . . ." "No, we're not going to give you any more money." So I had to start to sell things. I had to go back to Karen and say, "Can we raise money on the house? Can you sign this piece of paper, which allows the bank to do this and that? Can we sell our country home? Can we at least borrow against our country home?" And she said, "Before I sign this piece of paper, maybe we could talk about us."

On it went until the middle of October 1981, when I gave up. I went to Chris Thomas, my producer, and said, "Stop the record. I'm going to take three months off." It was crazy, but I was tired. I had worked very hard and done a lot of writing and I wasn't very healthy. There was a doctor looking after me and I was doing a lot of exercise, so I was alive by the skin of my teeth. I was in reasonably good shape, but I was drinking a hell of a lot and not eating very well, staying out late and fucking people around. I felt the best thing to do was stop and regroup. I went to New York and spent a week there. I came back. I got in with a guy who was deeply into free-basing cocaine, and I started to dabble in that, still drinking very heavily all the time.

Then I went to work with Elton John in November 1981. I went to Paris. I took my mother and father and a girl I was seeing at the time and a few friends. I would go to the studio at nine o'clock in the morning, run through a tune with the guys in the band, and Elton would come about midday. We'd work until nine. Then I'd go out to a club, come back to the hotel, and spend some time with this unbelievable woman. God only knows what she was doing there. About five A.M. I would get the energy from somewhere to get out of bed and go and say hello to the minibar. I would drink the soft drinks, the tomato juice, the Perrier, that horrible French lemon juice, then go through the brandy, the wine, and think, Fuck it, the grain; let's have some of the grain. In the end, there would be nothing in the fridge. It would be about seven or eight A.M., and I had drunk everything. So I would ring up and get some breakfast. The next day I would do the same thing. I don't think I have ever, ever, ever been quite that bad, and yet I didn't feel any remorse about what I was doing. I didn't know that what I was doing was particularly exceptional.

Six months before, I had started to have a glass of brandy in the morning because it was the only thing that would make me feel normal. Wouldn't make me high, wouldn't make me low, just make me feel normal. It would stop my feeling sick.

We did a week's work and I had this incredible sensation on the plane coming back. It was Halloween night. We got off the plane and I said, "Take me to a pub. I've got to get some beer." We went in and there were all these people in funny fucking outfits. I drank about five pints of beer, and I still felt sick. I got out to the country and I said to this girl, "Listen, I'll give you a piece of advice—abandon me. Just go back to wherever you came from." I drank two bottles of brandy, and I was still having D.T.'s. I was in a condition where, like a heroin addict, I needed so much alcohol to balance out the bad reaction I was getting that it would kill me if I drank it all. So, after a couple of days of the shakes, I rang up my doctor and said, "Can you help me?" He said another doctor, who now works in a well-known clinic, was treating people privately. I went to see him and told him I was using hard drugs, too. He said, "Let's deal with the booze first."

So I went into a quiet little clinic. I spent five days there and had sleeping pills. I had quit drinking a week before I went into the clinic, so I had two weeks of sobriety. Then I went to New York and used a lot of straight heroin and free-based cocaine because I was still in bits. I needed something. I just replaced the booze with drug abuse. I was still very, very fucked up. I came back and went to my doctor and said, "I've got a serious problem with drugs. I'm getting more into drugs. I'm not drinking, but I've got to do something about the other drugs." I mentioned I might go to Meg Patterson, a British therapist living in California. The doctor had prescribed for me a pill called Ativan in quite high doses. I was using the whole prescription at once. Then I would get another supply from a dealer. I wasn't drinking, but I was still using coke, free-basing it. I was smoking heroin, too, quite a lot of it, which I was buying privately and doing completely in secret. Nobody knew except me. I would take two or three Ativan tablets when the heroin wore off, plus sleeping pills. I remember going to see my parents around Christmastime, and my dad said to me, "You say you're not drinking." I said, "No, no, no. I haven't had a drink for a month now." He said, "You're on something and it's a damn sight worse, in my opinion." And he got up and walked out. He was the only person who seemed to know that something was fatally wrong.

Christmas took me back to my kids and my wife. I just suddenly decided to tell Karen what was happening. I said I had stopped drinking but that I had a drug problem now and I was going to deal with it. I was going to see Meg Patterson. I rang her up and she said, "Get on the plane." I said, "I'll come over next Tuesday." She said, "No, you get on a plane now." So I said, "Tomorrow I'll come." She said, "No, now." Well, in fact, the earliest I could get on a plane was the next day. I arrived in California and had a month's treatment with her; then I came back detoxified.

Karen said I could stay in the family house in the basement. I stayed there for a couple of weeks and eventually we got close enough together to be able to rebuild the family atmosphere very quickly.

It was hard for Karen, but the kids were able to erase the problems completely. I just hope that, over a period of years, it hasn't left them with any scars. But, certainly, as far as my being there, they made me know it was great "to have you back, Dad." They made a big fuss over me and made it clear that they really enjoyed having me around. The terrible, terrible nightmare turned back into normality.

And yet the adjustment to normality was a pretty tricky affair. The best is yet to come, I am convinced. Things are still fitting into place. I'm still becoming accustomed to this middle ground and trying not to see it as a middle ground. I am experiencing this constant feeling of growth. I'm getting really bigger. In other words, it's not grandiosity, it's a feeling of largeness that I'm getting, a feeling of being a more whole, complete person. What I want to do is attend to the growth I feel.

Two years of waiting is a long time, but I've started to realize that waiting is an art, that waiting achieves things. Waiting can be very, very powerful. Time is a valuable thing. If you can wait two years, you can sometimes achieve something that you could not achieve today, however hard you worked, however much money you threw up in the air, however many times you banged your head against the wall. But it's the waiting that I'm getting bored with. I've just made a decision to take on a few things. I won't put my stability or my family at risk, but I have to do something with some risk attached. So far, I've turned away from all big chances and all big risks.

I think there is a point where the individual who is involved in the rehabilitation process has to start to run. Up to now, I've felt very much as if I'd been stuck in the middle. One has to test the water. It's not really going to do any harm. What I want to do is make use of the growth that I feel, the potential that I feel. I really feel that I'm doing something for the first time again, and

I'm afraid of failing in a new way, I suppose. But I feel at this point I can't really continue to leave myself in other people's hands all the time. Maybe I've balanced on the coals a little bit too long for my own good. Somewhere along the line I learned that I had a knack of doing a particular job. I have to try that job again in order to know what I've got, to know what I am, to know what, perhaps, I have become.

Somebody said to me the other day, "Wouldn't you prefer to be poor and happy?" I said, "Well, I don't know. I've been pretty content being miserable and rich." I think that's it. I've been quite happy being miserable. I enjoy depression. I enjoy confusion. I enjoy emotional conflict. I still look for it where it isn't. The emotional conflict game has been very profitable for me. I put it into words and make millions of dollars out of it. Maybe there are a lot of people who are only happy when they're miserable. Maybe I've been feeding them a lot of stuff. I can't do that anymore. I mustn't do that anymore. So when I write a song like "Eminence Front," I think, Well, that's about the right balance.

I'm forty years old, and if it's too late to grow, then so be it. Karen said to me the other day, "You're not involved in song-writing; how do you feel about that?" I said, "I don't think I really mind that much. I obviously have to get used to the feeling, but I would prefer to feel the way I feel today. I would prefer to be balanced and gently happy with occasional moments of euphoria and occasional depressions and write nothing ever again, rather than ending up where I nearly ended up, and having people tell me I'm a genius." What Pete Townshend, the songwriter, has done for a number of years is to make people who are shit feel pretty good. I don't want to be part of that conspiracy anymore, and those people don't want me to be a part of that conspiracy, either, because a lot of them have written to me to say, "It's great that you managed to pull yourself out." It's helping them to pull themselves out.

I'm trying to find a way to be a positive human being.

"The first time I asked a girl out, I had been drinking," says Ryne Duren, "and once the use of alcohol helped me through that, it was destined to help me through a lot of things—the night of the class play, my first open disagreement with my father, my first sexual involvement."

Most alcoholics begin drinking as teenagers. Alcohol enables the drinker to handle feelings —good and bad. Rather than deal with those uncomfortable feelings, the teenage drinker becomes dependent on alcohol to smooth things over.

Ryne believes that he was a social alcoholic at a very early age. Looking back at how much he drank, he says that tolerance was seen as a mark of manhood, not as a symptom of alcoholism. "If a person fifteen, sixteen, or seventeen years old is drinking, he is certainly leaving himself at risk of having a drinking problem, because if he's using alcohol to be social, he's not giving himself a chance to grow up." Ryne was almost forty when he quit alcohol for good and believes, "I was still fifteen."

Ryne Duren is an alcoholic. He is a former star pitcher for the New York Yankees. Today he is actively involved in promoting alcohol awareness and alcoholism prevention and is a consultant to the Atlanta Braves.

Ryne Duren

When I came up to the Yankees I had to pinch myself to believe that I was there. At twenty-nine I was, emotionally, fifteen years old—a fifteen-year-old full of self-doubt. In spite of the fact that I had outstanding talent for throwing the baseball hard, it wasn't backed up with much maturity at all. Alcohol was bombarding my central nervous system to the point where I was never able to control my eye/hand coordination sufficiently. I was lucky to be there. I never thought that I had refined my talent enough to be very competent. I couldn't necessarily throw a strike when I wanted to. It was always a percentage thing with me. I could just as well walk a man as strike him out. I was a very vulnerable person on the mound, in spite of the fact that I put together some pretty impressive innings pitched.

After hard drinking and many ball clubs, on the way down, I lost everything I had—my job, my house, my family—and maybe proved an old theory that I don't believe in: You can't help somebody until he wants help. I wanted help when I went to the first Catholic priest, to the first psychiatrist, to the first marriage counselor. I wanted help, but these people didn't understand what they were dealing with. The psychiatrist said I was passive/aggressive. The marriage counselor may have said, "Maybe you drink too much," as though it could be controlled. The priests usually asked whether I was in a state of grace, and on one occasion I was told that I was possessed by a demon. I presented myself for help to many professionals without getting the results people can get today because enlightening things have happened in the last few years.

The Angels had me in the hospital for nervous exhaustion. And I had been going to AA in the off-season. I had been at Starlight Village in the hill country on two different occasions. I was going to doctors or to psychiatrists. I was always searching for a way out.

The fact that I was told I might be an alcoholic clouded the issue for me. I don't think that until I got into De Paul Hospital—and that was the seventh time I was hospitalized, the third time I was in rehabilitation—that I actually had someone

60

say, in no uncertain terms, "Gentlemen, we have a simple problem. We're drug addicts just as surely as if we were hooked on heroin." That was the first time I really had anybody tell me what was wrong with me. Everybody had been trying to explain what an alcoholic is, but that was the wrong approach, because nobody explained what alcohol is. It's a drug.

I never saw any daylight until that time in De Paul, when I found out I was a drug addict. I swear to God, that was the magic button as far as I was concerned. I was a drug addict. Well, hell, I thought if a guy is a drug addict, there has to be a way to beat that.

According to my impression at that time, if you were an alcoholic, you were a lesser person. You were a sicko. You were weird. You were possessed. Nobody ever defined it scientifically. I never knew what alcohol was or how it could affect you. When the guy said I was a drug addict, I could understand that a drug addict might do anything, and I had been doing it all. So my behavior was now understandable. I was a drug addict, not a lesser human being. Why the hell didn't somebody tell me sooner that I was a drug addict? I could have done something about it.

I never enjoyed life when I was drinking. Today I enjoy. I see. I smell. I sense. I interact. I choose. Back in those days, I did none of those things. I existed. I went from one drink to planning the next drink; my life revolved around that. I can do almost anything now and enjoy it. I can trust what I am thinking because I know that at the bottom of what I am thinking is not to drink. An awful lot of things came to me after a while of sobriety: being tolerant and being accepting; allowing other people to be themselves; not having to have a situation change before I could be a part of it. I am very flexible today. In the past I lived a very rigid life because it had to be centered around alcohol.

I was a notorious drunk, so coming to know myself as an alcoholic really helped me to become a legitimate person.

3 The Progression

An alcoholic's life follows a pattern of joy (he likes alcohol and what it does for him), frequency (he drinks often, but not necessarily every day), tolerance (he can drink and function the next day without serious illness), and pain (he experiences crises).

In the early years of drinking, the alcoholic's tolerance level increases, and he needs more alcohol to feel good or to block out negative feelings. His body chemistry changes, and he becomes addicted. He cannot predict the number of drinks he will have, how they will affect him, or the results of his drinking.

The alcoholic knows something is wrong, but instead of looking at himself or at the alcohol as the source of his problems, he denies the true causes of his unhappiness and blames everyone and everything around him for his life's not working.

Placing the blame outside of himself, the alcoholic never has to look inward. In truth, alcohol is at the core of his ego-centered personality. The alcoholic sees liquor as an ally, not as the enemy. In the midst of the wreckage of his life, alcohol provides temporary good feelings and a shelter from his internal and external life's storm. To quit drinking would never cross his mind. Just the opposite—drinking becomes an obsession, even though he may continue to function on the job or at home. Alcohol enables the alcoholic to deal with life and the facets of his alcoholic personality: oversensitivity, low tolerance for frustration, anger and resentment, fear, failure to have immediate ego satisfaction, overdependence on others, inability to handle disappointments and failures, lack of confidence, and low self-esteem.

Tolerance decreases with continued drinking and with age. Less alcohol does the job. When this starts happening, predictable disaster is on the horizon. Once the alcoholic becomes an alcoholic and continues to drink, few options are left. Some crisis is on the way: personal, marital, financial, legal, social, or medical.

It's a matter of time. Often the crises are repeated, or new ones surface. In some cases, it is no one thing. Instead, it is a downward spiral of hopelessness. The alcoholic knows he has a drinking problem, but he cannot conceive of a life without alcohol.

He truly believes that he is all-powerful, all-knowing, the center of the universe—God—and it is impossible for him to imagine that he can't do something that everyone else can do—drink.

The alcoholic's life is one of anger, worry, self-pity, and depression. The alcoholic loses his ambition and finally his hope.

"Alcoholics are different in so many ways, it makes no difference." According to Dr. Dan Anderson, they model the general population. However, when the illness takes over, there is stereotyped, repetitive, and negative behavior —easily identified. Because of denial, the alcoholic can exhibit all of the progressive symptoms and still feel he is in control. Middle-stage alcoholism may include some or all of the following behaviors: drinking before a party, preoccupation with alcohol, hiding liquor, lying about drinking, guilt feelings, blackouts, loss of ambition, trying to quit drinking, failing to quit, financial, family, and job problems, drinking alone. To admit alcoholism, according to Dan Anderson, is to admit to being human.

Daniel J. Anderson, Ph.D., is the president and director of the Hazelden Foundation in Center City, Minnesota, which is recognized as one of the most successful alcoholism treatment centers in the United States.

Daniel J. Anderson, Ph.D.

Alcoholism is a chronic disease, and in the developed countries of the Western world we don't handle any chronic disease very well.

With an acute illness, you're impaired for a little while, but it's a temporary disability. You don't mind. With a chronic illness, you have a permanent impairment. That's one of the definitions of alcoholism. It's an involuntary chronic disability. It ain't gonna go away.

What do people characteristically do when they have a chronic illness? They don't want to believe it. No, not me. There is denial, rationalization, minimization, the search for another opinion. People say, "I'm really pseudoneurotic schizophrenic, not alcoholic." If you get a cold, you know you got it because you didn't dress right, you haven't been exercising, or you haven't been eating right. With a cold, an outside agent invaded your body and gave you that bloody cold. You ain't responsible. But what's the real cause of alcoholism? It's multiply determined: it's physical, its psychological, it's social, and it's spiritual. How responsible am I? Are my parents? Is my genealogy? It's hard to find something to blame it on. Explanations aren't easy.

We live in a prideful culture and cover up our human nature. We make believe we can handle anything. We eat too much. We drink too much. We use too many mood-altering substances. We work too hard. We work under too much stress. We smoke too much. We don't get enough exercise. We act as if we're invulnerable. Science is always going to fix it up. But nobody gets out of this world alive.

Let me give you an example. A diabetic is a person with a chronic condition. What's one of the things a diabetic wants to do? Beat the diet. "The hell with that. I can make it." Then he'll literally overdose on sugar and go into a diabetic coma. "What are you doing?" the doctor says. "You're a diabetic. Don't you know better?" "Oh, yes, Doctor. I promise I'll never do it again. I'll go back on my diet."

What is the first thing people with cancer do? They ignore the symptoms. "How long have you had that lump in your breast?" "Oh, about five thousand years." "Why didn't you come in sooner?" "I thought maybe it was a gland." That's stupid. Do you know what percentage of women actually perform breast self-examination? Less than 20 percent. We all deny chronic illness. None of us wants to face up to it.

Denial. Ambivalence. Resentment. Self-pity. Our culture doesn't handle any chronic deficiency well. With alcoholism you've got all these terrible feelings. I'm a no-good. I'm a worm. What the hell, I might as well have a drink. She's going to leave me anyway. So they fire me; I gave them my best years.

An alcoholic is a person who drinks excessively and/or inappropriately and experiences harmful consequences, but despite those harmful consequences is unable or unwilling to change. It becomes a chronic condition. At the same time, he seems to build up the illusion of personal freedom. "I can change. I will change. I know I've had three drunk-driving accidents but, by God, that won't happen again. I'm not going to quit drinking entirely. I'm going to have a couple of beers. I'll be able to drive. Don't worry." He tries but he still can't do it. Over and over again,

69

alcoholics lose control either of the quantity they drink or the time they spend drinking, and yet they have the illusion of freedom. "I know what happened, but remember, my wife is going through menopause. If you had that kind of wife, you might drink that much yourself." There's rationalization, justification, and the illusion of freedom. The essence of the problem is the loss of control, yet alcoholics spend more time controlling their drinking than anybody. Normal social drinkers really don't control their drinking, but they occasionally do something that I call sloppy social drinking. They have one or two or three and maybe another one, and you look at them and say, "That dumb shit." But they don't make a big thing out of it. Alcoholics think, "Now, here we go. I've got to control this thing. I'm going to go to that party and I'm going to have one drink. I'm going to walk around and talk to everybody." The alcoholic does just exactly that and is so damn proud of himself that after the party is over he goes home with a jug all by himself and really gets drunk. That ain't social drinking. That's something else. In a fit of grandiosity he says, "I did it." He rewards himself by slopping over.

The greatest tragedy of it is the loss of control, in the psychological sense. The illness is in control. I want to manage my thinking and my feelings and my behavior but at any time the illness can take over. I get so damned mad. Why do I have to be restricted and controlled? I'm a limited human being. What did I do to deserve this? It is the unpredictability that is difficult, the fact that at any time the chronic disease can rear up and take over. One of the tragic characteristics of alcoholism is that the irrational urge to get drunk can come along at any time. I don't care how sober, how long you have been sober, it can come. That irrational urge. You can just have given one of your best talks on staying sober. People shake your hand. Suddenly you've got this terrible feeling you'd love to have a drink. It doesn't mean you have to act on the impulse, but the impulse is irrational. It can come anytime—that's the way chronic illnesses are.

Alcoholism, like many other illnesses, comes and goes. "My arthritis is terribly bad this week, yet I have no symptoms the next week. Maybe it's gone. I don't have to keep taking my meds anymore." In some people, it clears up spontaneously. "I haven't had a drink now for nine months and eight days and thirty-seven hours and two minutes. Maybe all the cells in my body have changed. Maybe I'm not an alcoholic any longer. I had better find out." In chronic illness, the symptoms can go away completely, but you still have the illness.

Once you've got active alcoholism, you're operating with one hand tied behind your back. You're limited in terms of freedom to function. At times you may do an outstanding job; another time you'll fall on your face. As the illness continues to progress and take over, you lose more and more freedom, even though you try to pretend to still have as much. "Sure she left me. I don't care. Don't want to be married to her anyway. Well, sure they picked me up for drunken driving . . ." You hear these rationalizations. The grandiosity is terrible.

After alcoholism sets in, the common denominators are grandiosity, inadequacy, exaggerated dependency, exaggerated independence, and absence of humility.

There is something about all chronic illness that creates selfishness. You have a real bad cold. It's hard to think about other people's needs. When you're an alcoholic and you have to think ahead about your next drink or how you're going to explain this or that to all of the people interfering with your life, it's very difficult to look kindly upon the mass of inept, unthinking humanity out there because of your selfishness.

Resentment and self-pity just keep on developing as part of the illness. It's not the cause of the illness, but it goes along with it. We don't know what causes it. Once you're in it and that stuff is working, it really becomes a psycho-bio-social kind of retardation. You really get pounded down in terms of functioning and terrible feelings of inadequacy are created. You do feel inadequate and a drink helps you to do something. Alcoholism becomes autonomous. It not only fixes up dancing, it fixes up everything.

To me, the essence of the illness concept is an involuntary disablement. The essential feature is loss of control. It shows up by excessive, inappropriate drinking and experiencing harmful consequences. The behavior becomes more and more stereotyped and more and more repetitive. All of this is an indication that the person is not in control. So by admitting alcoholism, we're admitting we're human.

This chronic illness, this terrible devastating thing, can also be a pathway to wholeness and health. You don't get your teeth fixed until you sober up. You don't start really developing a health maintenance program until you sober up. You know you need to adjust your life to remain sober, so you want to improve your marriage. You want to improve the quality of different things in your life. The general population isn't doing that.

Someone asked Justice Oliver Wendell Holmes how to live to a ripe old age and he said, "Get a chronic illness and take very good care of it." Paul Dudley White, President Eisenhower's cardiologist, who rode a bicycle when he was ninety-nine years old or something, used to say, "Give me a room full of cardiacs; they'll live longer." I don't believe that entirely, but I'm told he had an old Greek saying hung in his office or his home—remember, it goes back over two thousand years. It said, "The cracked vase lasts longest." That makes sense. I've got an idea that people with chronic illnesses may someday show the rest of us how to live appropriately.

Alcoholism is a progressive disease. Wilbur Mills says he never had any problem with it for many years, drank when he wanted to, and didn't drink if he didn't want to. But, he recalls, he always drank it down and never sipped it, right from the first drink he had from a still back home. "The first drink I took, I took straight down," he says. "I did it under orders. A man stood with a rifle in his hand and told me to sample his homemade stuff." At the end of his drinking career Wilbur was taking 500 mg of Librium a day and drinking two quarts of 100-proof vodka at night when he got home. "The doctors say you can't live and do that, but I did. I was in a total blackout during all of 1974."

Wilbur Mills is an alcoholic. He is a former nineteen-term U.S. congressman from Arkansas who was chairman of the House Ways and Means Committee from 1958 to 1975. He is now an attorney associated with the law firm of Shea and Gould in Washington, D.C.

Wilbur Mills

The progression of my drinking is quite interesting, I think. Way back, I didn't drink anything but bourbon, and I always wanted sparkling water with it. Later on, a friend of mine down home decided I would be more sophisticated if I drank scotch. He sent me a case of twenty-five-year-old Haig & Haig. He told me to quit drinking bourbon and drink scotch. I still wanted sparkling water in it, though. Whatever I drank, I had to have some kind of water or something in it.

Then I decided that the darn sparkling water was doing something to my mind, so I quit using that, and for years I used tap water. Then I suddenly became aware of the fact that the tap water was taking space in my glass that could otherwise be used for alcohol, so I quit using the water. But I always wanted the alcohol cold, so I could never keep a bottle in my desk or in the car. It had to be cold, so I always had to have ice cubes in it. Toward the end of my drinking, it occurred to me one night, what would happen to me if I swallowed one of those ice cubes? Might strangle. So I quit using ice cubes. I put my bottles in the icebox to keep them cold and not run the risk of swallowing ice cubes. The way I drank, I could easily have swallowed them. My mouth was wide open. I used a peanut butter glass, and it didn't take me many swallows to take it down.

Lieutenant Commander Michael Bohan at the Bethesda Naval Hospital was the one who had the unmitigated gall to tell me I was an alcoholic. The first thing that flashed in my mind was, I don't know how the hell a man like that could ever have been admitted to medical school. How could he ever have graduated? Why would the navy ever commission him as a doctor? One thing certain, he would never get to be a captain in the navy. I would see to that myself. I knew he was no good, because across the way there was an admiral who, Dr. Bohan had said, was an alcoholic, too. The admiral didn't drink anything but beer, so in his opinion he couldn't be an alcoholic. He was mad as a wet hen at the doctor. Well, that just helped me feel more correct about my own diagnosis of Dr. Bohan.

I had been told, when I was in the hospital a short time before, that there was one way I could tell whether I was an alcoholic or not. If I could take a drink and didn't have to have another one, in all probability I wasn't an alcoholic. But if I took one drink and had to have another, then in all probability I was an alcoholic. Well, I knew I could pass that test. I wanted to pass it and show that incompetent doctor and another person who'd suggested I was an alcoholic that I could. I had to prove to those two and some others that I wasn't an alcoholic, so I subjected myself to this test that I knew I could pass.

Never in my life had I ever had to have a drink. I just took a drink because I wanted to. I loved the taste of it, and I still can't think of anything that tastes as good as Jack Daniel's or Old Fitzgerald. But I failed the test. I got drunk again. I drank two quarts of hundred-proof vodka that night, and more. They found me in New York and drove me back. I came to in the hospital and there were people at the foot of the bed, grinning, and here I was dying. I have often said that if you're around a fellow coming out from under a drunk, for God's sake don't have a smile on your face when he opens his eyes. Bohan and that other person, both now my good friends, wanted to know what I thought I was. I said, "Well, if it will do you any good, I'll say I'm an alcoholic." "It's not what does us good, it's what does you good. Now, what are you?" I admitted it then and began the process of accepting the fact that I was an alcoholic. At that time, my concept of an alcoholic was such that I felt lowered in my own estimation. I was the lowest thing that God let live. I was lower than a snake that crawled on its belly, because I was an alcoholic. I didn't want to live the rest of my life and have to say I was an alcoholic. But I didn't want to kill myself. I wanted to be sober. I just had that desire.

I think one has got to want to be sober in order to ever get sober. You have to want it in your gut. You really have to have an intense feeling of wanting to be sober. And when you want that, you can get sober, with help.

Since I've been sober I've found out I'm a human being. It's a great feeling just to be a human being, not having to be God. You don't have all that burden on you. In that respect, it's been a great deal different and a great deal better. I jokingly say that sometimes I just make a mistake on purpose to show that I don't have to be right all the time. I do make a lot of mistakes. I made them before, but I wouldn't admit it. I thought I had to be right all the time. If I made a mistake, I thought, the country would suffer or the world would suffer. That is an awful position to put yourself in, having to be right all the time.

My whole life has changed. I used to be very much interested in sports. I'm not anymore. I used to have season tickets to the baseball games and football games. I don't anymore. I just don't seem to care about things like that anymore. I read a lot. I never did do that much before. I never had time for anything except tax and Social Security law. Now I enjoy being with my wife. There were years when we never said anything to each other; now we go out to dinner and we socialize. It's hard to describe the difference, but it's the difference between heaven and hell.

"I was a bad drunk," says Gary Crosby. "I couldn't commit suicide, otherwise I wouldn't get into heaven; so I fought with some bad people. I wanted somebody to kill me."

Gary grew up with an unpredictable alcoholic mother and a strict disciplinarian for a father. With the exception of athletics, he had little self-confidence. Faced with the disappointment of no longer being able to play sports because of an injury, he drank to handle his resentments. Many alcoholics are angry. Years after he quit drinking, Gary finally dealt with his anger.

Gary Crosby is an alcoholic. The eldest of the four sons of the late Bing and Dixie Lee Crosby, he works in the entertainment business as an actor, singer, and writer.

Gary Crosby

Mom was an alcoholic. She was a very sensitive, gentle soul who was in show business for a while, but it terrified the hell out of her. She only wanted to get married, to get out of it. She was really happy being a wife. She needed an over-abundance of overt affection. She needed coaxing to do anything. She wanted Dad to come home at night and say, "Party tonight, honey, you want to go?" And she would say, "I can't go." And he would say, "Oh, please, come on, you have to go." And she would say, "Well, my hair is not right." And he would say, "We'll fix the hair. We'll buy you a dress. We'll get good makeup." He was supposed to fight his way through all these objections until she finally went and had a good time.

But he would come home and say, "Great party tonight. Want to go?" She'd say, "No." He'd say, "I'll see you later," and go. He figured he had fulfilled his duty. He couldn't give. He couldn't show a normal amount of affection, and she needed a superabundance of affection. That was the chasm that divided the two of them. He would go to the party, and she would sit home and feel lonely and hurt because he didn't coax her. She'd get angry at herself because she needed that much coaxing and feel stupid because she didn't go in the first place. And she would drink. She'd drink six, eight, ten weeks at a time, and then the doctor would come over and she would try to stay sober for a couple of weeks. Then she would get back on it again. When she was sober, she would shake and twitch and have a real tough time.

She was real shy, a real homebody, but she was a wonderful woman. During the Second World War, she saved more soldiers than the USO. She gave unstintingly of her time and efforts. She loved everybody.

Later on she always managed to keep her finger on things. I don't know how she did it. She always knew what was going on in town, the latest sayings, the hits, slick and cool. She knew about everybody's love life, too, and she never left her bedroom.

Mom was unpredictable. When you came into the house you always had to go into her bedroom to kiss her hello. You had to make up your mind if she was drinking. If she was, how drunk was she? When you crossed the room, when you leaned down to kiss her, were you going to get slapped or were you going to get kissed? You'd be trying to make up your mind all the way up the stairs. It was a contest every day. I loved my mother one day and hated her the next. When I was a kid, I didn't know she couldn't control it. I thought, Why the hell does she have to be this way? There are days when she doesn't drink. Why can't she be like that all the time? I thought she just wanted to do that. It would make me mad because she could be really vicious when she was drinking.

I remember Dad making rules and handing out punishments if the rules weren't kept. There were so many rules I couldn't keep them all. I didn't have a chance. There wasn't any way I was going to keep them all, not for a week. I never felt I could please this man. I felt I was a disappointment to him. I never did turn out the way he wanted, and I didn't seem to be doing the things he wanted me to do. I went to military schools. Kids gave demerits to other kids. If you got demerits you had to go on Saturday. When Dad got the notice I had to go Saturday, I got a licking Friday night.

I built up a self-picture in the early years of a person with no ability in anything except sports. I knew I was good at that. I really built all my hopes on a career in sports. To make a long story short, my high school lied to me when I asked if I could have another year of eligibility when I transferred from the military school. They said yes, I could. They waited until my senior year and then took my eligibility away, which was like chopping your head off if you were any kind of a high school football player. That is the year to build your rep.

I really started to drink when I lost my senior-year eligibility. I felt, What's the use? I just went out and got bombed every chance I could. It felt good. I didn't hate myself so much. I didn't come down on myself so hard. I could stand life when I was ripped.

I got to Stanford, which means I've got a pretty good head on my shoulders. All I did there was drink when I couldn't play ball anymore. It was a physical thing. It happened to other guys, too. Every day at three o'clock, when practice time came around and we couldn't play, the walking wounded, the guys with the bad knees and shoulders, wound up at a beer garden with eighteen pitchers of beer. We'd tell lies about how great we were and swap stories when we should have been out there practicing. Instead we'd be getting ripped. Then we'd go back and try to study, or go to a movie, or go drink some more. There was a hole in our lives, and that was how we filled it up.

I finally quit college. I got into show business with my dad. I did a lot of his radio shows. I sang and acted and did some movies with him. I liked show business. It was fun and I liked singing. I liked acting. I loved comics and musicians. I loved the lifestyle. I said, "O.K., I want to do that," but I always felt as if I was on Mars. People constantly talked to me as though I was supposed to know all this wonderful stuff. Dad had never told me anything. He wanted me to be a lawyer, doctor, or some damned thing. That just wasn't me. I couldn't be that. When I came into show business, he said, "Just show up and don't run into the furniture." That's all I got from him. But people constantly looked at me as if I was a thirty-year vet. They'd say things to me and I'd run home and try to figure out what the hell they meant. I would call people and ask them. Or else I'd go back in there, not knowing. Then I'd just walk out and do it. Most of the time, I was right. That scared me, because of the low self-esteem that had been built into me during my early years. Dad was always calling me Sap or Dumb or referring to my terrible temper.

When I had seven or eight drinks I thought a lot more of myself than I usually did. Then it started to take more. It took eight or ten. It took ten or twelve. I started blacking out. One night I'd have six drinks; the next night I wouldn't have any. The next night I would have two; the next night twelve. Sometimes during that period I would have a three-day-and-three-night blackout, when I'd just be gone. I'd wind up in some other town, in bed with somebody I had never seen before, in a room I had never been in before. I would have to go over to the desk, pull out the Gideon Bible, see the name of the hotel and the town stamped on it. I couldn't just call downstairs and ask, "Where am I?" Other times, I'd be walking down the street somewhere in LA with my nose busted open, my face all fucked up, looking for a can to puke in. I became a total lush. I was also taking speed. I got into that because I couldn't stand listening to my old man screaming at me anymore about my weight. I started going to weight doctors at a very early age. I have done everything to control weight that you can possibly think of. I just had this picture of myself that life wasn't worth a shit and I wasn't going anywhere. Whatever career I had going, I was sure I wasn't going to have it very long. People were going to get wise to me pretty quick, I thought, and I'd be out of the business. I acted like a guy who had no future.

Then I got into the army. We were great together. Once you get past basic training you can stay loaded as long as you want. There is that percentage of guys in every outfit. Whenever there's inspection the officers know these guys can't do anything, so they send them to the movies or on leave. I was one of them. I got the shirt that was too small and pants that were too long and the hat that didn't fit and two left boots. I just put them on and wore them. I created havoc wherever I went, without doing anything. They couldn't stick me in the jug. I wasn't doing any bad time. They couldn't put me in the crowbar hotel. I was a fucking drunk. I did no more than the exact order said to do. If you do that in the army, you'll drive them crazy. I had them crazy. But I was scared of them, too. They had me crazy. We were both crazy.

There was a wonderful WAC sergeant who saved me. Otherwise, I'd never have gotten through there. They finally put me in Special Services and we would go around to places and sing, places where they hated you. So we'd just get bombed. I don't remember half of those shows. They led me around by the nose for 730 days. I didn't know where I was.

They would have inspections. That means that the post would close down. You couldn't get any booze. I never knew when inspections were coming because I was always so drunk I never heard anybody talk about them. Boom, here comes the day. I was the guy they always sent away. They always hid me out someplace. I didn't have to stand these inspections because they knew I never could pass them anyway. Sometimes I would go into a seizure. I would be talking to somebody and the next thing I knew, somebody would be leaning over me. They would take me to the hospital and give me an EKG, or blow dye up in my brain and photograph it. They decided I was an epileptic. So they put me in the hospital, in the neuropsychiatric ward. I was in there with the crazies, where they take the belt away and you wear paper slippers. You lie there at night and listen to the crazies scream and cry and carry on. I figured I had epilepsy. They started me on Dilantin. I was taking that and still, every time there would be an inspection or I couldn't get booze for twenty-four hours, I'd go off my head. Finally I came out of the army.

I had lost my driver's license. I was out about six months when I went to the doctor, and he said, "You haven't got epilepsy; you're an alcoholic. Every time you can't get enough booze in your system, you short out. That's what's happening to you." So I went and got my license back by telling them I was an alcoholic. They said, "Well, that's O.K. Here's your license; don't worry about it."

Later on, in show business, I was doing a club act. I had been up to Vegas twice, once to see my brothers and once to see Don Rickles. Both times, at the end of the show, I went to stand up from the chair and couldn't move from the waist down. So I would just kind of hang on to the table and the paralysis would pass and I would go on about my business. I didn't do anything about it. Finally, I was preparing my own act for Vegas. I rehearsed one day and then came home and lay down on the couch. I was watching television and tried to reach for the phone, and I couldn't move from my neck down. They got me to the hospital and the doctor asked if I was taking any digitalis. I said no. He said, "What *are* you taking?" I told him about the succession of weight pills and the drinking. He got the weight pills and looked at them and found they were loaded with digitalis, which had caused a partial head block. He said, "You have to lie down for six months." I said, "I can't lie down for six months; I've got to go to Vegas. You don't tell those guys you want to lie down because you're sick." He said, "O.K., here's what I'll do. I'll give you a shot of B_{12}. You get a prescription for a shot of B_{12} and a shot of Dexedrine for every show, but in between shows there can be no drinking, no using; you've got to go to your room and sit down or you'll die."

So I went out there and, by God, I did it. I didn't drink and I didn't use, and I would go back to my room and sit down between shows. I got real friendly with one girl in the show and we fell in love. This girl fell in love with me at the time I couldn't take a drink. She never knew I had a drinking problem. We got married and it wasn't until twenty-three months later that I could drink again. Then the shit hit the fan. I was off and running. I was gone again: three days and three nights here, three days and three nights there. I was drinking in between, too, scaring my wife and child to death with the D.T.'s, screaming crazy things like, "The vampires are coming!" I was picking fights, once with a one-armed man in a bar—I'll never forget that. That's one thing that sticks in my craw to this day. Finally, my wife took our kid and moved out, and two weeks later I got a letter from a lawyer. I went to see her with my lawyer and she said, "You go away, dry out, and never take another drink or I'm leaving." I didn't want to lose her, so I went away. I went to this place and dried out.

For the next nineteen years, I didn't have anything to drink. I didn't use speed, got real straight at the church, and was always straight with my wife. I never cheated on her. I was playing the good father. But everything I wanted, really reached for, I never got, and the little jobs that I did get, I never wanted. I was ungrateful as hell because I couldn't get the ones I wanted. God was handing me things in my left hand, and I didn't even look because I was busy reaching with my right.

Now you've got a real mad alcoholic. What you've got on your hands is a guy who has quit using, quit drinking, and turned to God, and nothing is working. I couldn't figure out what was wrong. There was nothing but sheer rage. I finally got demented, toward the end. What I figured out was that God was paying me back in the second half of my life for the things I did in the first half. He was making me pay, ironically, by making me reach for the big things that I wanted so badly, and then punching me in the belly, not giving them to me. I finally said, "Well, screw that; I'm not going to reach anymore." I slammed the door and stayed in the house. I'd go out for readings and stuff, but I knew I'd never get the jobs. I'd go half salty, half mean. They would always start out by asking me about my father. You walk in there crusty like that, and they ain't gonna hire you.

So for nineteen years, man, I sat and just raved to God and my fellow man. I didn't like me, I didn't like them, I didn't like anything. Finally, my wife couldn't take it anymore. She was a very positive person when I met her, and she just couldn't handle it. She gave me my walking papers. The only thing that I was successful at in my life was being a family man, being a husband and a father, and here I was, busted. Now I'm sitting with nothing and I still don't get the message. I finally wound up with a triple bypass. Because I had fallen in love with another girl, because I loved her, I listened to the doctor when he said, "You need an operation." He said, "Do you want to live?" And I said yes, because I loved this girl. I wanted to marry her. I went and had the operation. The night before the operation, the doctor said to me, "You have no triglyceride problem, no cholesterol problem; you are here for two reasons—smoking and anger. If you can stop smoking and change your attitude, maybe you can live another thirty years. Will you buy that?" I was ready to buy that to live tomorrow. I said, "Sure, Doc, I'll try," and he did the operation on me.

I quit smoking because of that and came back down to LA and started going to a shrink, a lady gestalt therapist who had worked with alcoholics for thirty-five years at the Long Beach Naval Hospital. I had been going to her before I moved away to Vegas. I told her about the bypass and the anger. "Well, it's true," she said. "You've been angry all your life. You've got to go to AA." I said, "Come on, who are you kidding? I haven't been a drinker now for nineteen years. What are they going to teach me down there?" "I can't tell you," she said. "You've got to go find out. Either you go, or you don't come back here."

Now, I had been sending people to AA for the whole nineteen years I had been clean and dry and talking about being a former drunk. I'd talk to youth groups and older people, who'd ask, "How do you stay sober?" I'd say, "Don't do it my way; go to AA." Finally I had to phone them. I said, "What's going on down there?" "We can't tell you," they said, "You've got to come and find out." I said, "You've been talking to my shrink." I went down there and I wasn't in the room thirty seconds before I knew that was where I should have been the whole time.

Nineteen years I had been out there trying to do it on my own. Mr. Willpower. I can lick this by myself. I'm wonderful. I can handle this whole thing. All of a sudden, for the first time in my life, I felt I was with a bunch of people who knew exactly what was going on with me and I knew what was going on with them. It was the funniest feeling. When I walked through the door, for the first time in my life I didn't put up defenses. I didn't feel the need to put up a wall and be that funny character that I usually put out there when I first met strangers. I didn't feel I needed any defenses. I felt accepted for just what I was, a drunk.

I sat down and started listening and sharing and I wasn't there a week before I found out what I had been doing wrong for nineteen years. I had been praying and going to church and confession and Communion and begging God for what I wanted. It took three or four days at AA to realize it's what He wants, not what you want. You pray for what He wants. And it made sense. Made perfect sense. When I first went away and dried out, I bought that part about "I have no control over alcohol," but I decided to manage my life. I thought, As soon as I get sober I'll have everything. When I got to AA, I found out I could say, "My life's unmanageable." I looked back and it always had been. It had been unmanageable when I was drinking, and using, and it was unmanageable when I was clean and dry. I felt like a big rock had been lifted off me. There's a power that will restore you to sanity if you will let Him. And I said, "I'll let Him." I can turn my will and my life over to Him. Every time there is something I can't handle, I can turn to God and say, "Here, take this." I did it and it worked. The first couple of times I did it, and it worked, I said, "Oh, this is what life's about." And I just went on from there.

No one single outside pressure has changed. The career hasn't gotten any better. There's no more money coming in than there was before. As far as the things that used to drive me crazy, they're all still there. I've just done a turnaround inside my skin; I've learned to accept things. Little things very seldom drive me up the wall anymore, like they used to. I don't get mad twenty-five times a day anymore. I've got a purpose in life. Before, whenever I didn't get a job I wanted, I acted just like what they thought I was, a rich man's kid with no talent, no ability, no desire to work, just wanting to be a bum. That drove me nuts. If there was anything I wasn't, that was it. It used to drive me nuts when

I didn't have a job. Now, if I don't have a job, I know it's because the Man upstairs has something else for me to do this day, so I lean back and try to find out what it is. If the phone rings, it will take me someplace and I'll run into somebody. Or I'll go to a meeting and somebody will be there and I'll say something that will help him for that day. That's what my life is now. I just live it from day to day. I don't worry about what I can't handle. I don't worry about tomorrow. I don't live anymore in the wreckage of my past or the disaster that can be my future. I just live today because that's all I've got. I know I sound like a walking cliché, but that's how clichés become clichés. They're true. I just live it the way the program tells me to and I do fine. I'm happier now than I have ever been in my life.

It is not necessary for an alcoholic to drink every day. Shecky Greene was a periodic drinker, but like so many alcoholics, he could not predict the number of drinks he would have or his behavior after drinking. Shecky experienced many of the classic signs of alcoholism: frequent blackouts, loss of ambition, car accidents, guilt feelings, unhappy home life, and loss of reputation. The solution for the alcoholic is to stay away from the first drink, but that goes against what being an alcoholic is. For as much trouble as Shecky got himself into, it took hospitalization for an

unrelated illness to convince him he didn't want
to end up the way he was headed.

*Shecky Greene is an alcoholic. He is the
favorite comedian of many of the biggest
stars in show business. He has appeared at
most of the major hotels in Las Vegas and
in nightclubs throughout the country and co-
starred in the television series "Combat."*

Shecky Greene

Good times? I never had any good times
drinking. I wasn't that type of drinker. I would
only drink to destroy myself. It was much easier
to drink than to commit suicide with a gun or a
knife or pills.

I had a tremendous amount of success in show
business, but I was lying to myself about being
satisfied with what I was doing. Although I was
making a lot of money, I should have been doing
more. I didn't really have the confidence to go on
to movies, television, and things like that. So I
hid out in the success I had in Las Vegas. I was
working twenty weeks a year. I could live the way
I wanted to live and do the things I wanted to do.
But eventually it would have caught up with me if
I hadn't stopped drinking.

Driving back to Lake Tahoe from San Francisco once, I went off the side of a mountain.
That could have been the end. Another time, in
Las Vegas, I was driving down the strip about
ninety miles an hour and I hit a brand new lamp.

Thank God, they had changed lamps the week before—they called the new ones breakaway lamps—othewise it could have been over. Maybe in that state of mind I would have been happier that it would have been over.

I went to college to become a coach, but never finished. If I had continued in that direction, I don't think I would ever have tasted alcohol, but I may have destroyed myself in another way because I didn't like myself.

I never drank until I was twenty-eight years old. I was not that type. As a matter of fact, I was just the opposite; I looked down on people who drank. I was an athlete. I think my alcoholism has a lot to do with my childhood, but if you looked at it you would say it was a happy childhood. I grew up during the depression and my mother went to work. Maybe it was her not being in the house, her lack of involvement with us kids, despite the fact that she loved us. Maybe it wasn't that. Maybe it was something else. Maybe it was a genetic situation. Maybe I was born with it.

My father bets horses. Race book every day of his life. I went the same route and I hated it. I hated to watch him do that. I hated what it did to my mother. I hated what it did to us. But I went the same route. My mother was always worried about money. I think that's probably why I began gambling. Money was a terrible issue. We had terrible arguments in the family about it.

I can go back and blame my alcoholism on my

mother's going to work, but that's a cop-out. My mother had her own problems. She didn't use alcohol much, but my grandfather was an alcoholic. And when my mother did have a drink (and anyone who knows my mother would never think that she drank) she would be out of it—silly.

I had a cousin, Henry Salinger, who discovered Amos and Andy. He was the sweetest, nicest man whom God put on this earth. Once my mother was talking to him about my drinking problem, and he said in a very gentle voice, "I'm an alcoholic. All these years you people didn't know." So what constitutes alcoholism? Is it chemistry? Heredity? I guess it's a combination of many things.

My drinking was condoned when I was working in Las Vegas because I was doing such a tremendous business. If I had owned the Riviera Hotel at that time and an entertainer did some of the things that I did there, I would have thrown him out and said, "That's it." Pardon my using the word *whore,* but that's the whore aspect of our society. If somebody—no matter if he's an alcoholic or what—if somebody's good for making money, we turn our backs on his problem. I went and talked to people. I tried to explain to the bosses at the Riviera that I was an alcoholic, that I needed help, and they all laughed. I had one boss I am still very close to who is a successful businessman, but he's the type of guy who buries his head. If he's got a friend, he

95

doesn't want that friend to have any weaknesses. He can't accept it.

I would intentionally do outrageous things at the hotel. I really wanted to be fired and nobody would do it. I wanted the easy way out. I was hoping somebody would say, "You're out of show business. That's it."

I went to a psychiatrist and discussed my problem, but I still went out and drank. That was the lie I was living. I was still self-destructive.

Basically, I was an animal. Steve Lawrence once told me that if he walked into a room and heard I was there, he would hide behind a post to see what condition I was in. I never drank every day. I was a periodic drinker. People don't understand that there are many forms of alcoholism. There are hundreds. I was a periodic drunk. I would drink maybe every three months, maybe once every six months. Maybe once a year. But when I drank, forget it. I mean, if I started off with scotch, I would stay with scotch. If I started with beer, I'd stay with beer. If I started with wine, I would stay with wine. But I wouldn't stop until I was either arrested or something terrible happened. It's frightening to remember. I look back and have nightmares about some of the things I did, because that's not really me and it never was. There is a Jewish word, *dybbuk*. My mother said, "There's a dybbuk inside of you." It's like in *The Exorcist*. Something was inside of me and I couldn't control it. I always hated drinking. I knew that one drink would set it off, but I would drink.

I didn't drink that much on the stage, but when I did, it was over.

A successful period, a down period, anything could trigger it. I think I did a lot of things out of fear and lack of confidence. I was like a little kid, punishing myself and the people around me.

Working these places, I gambled and lost; then I drank. And when I drank, I would gamble. So one led to the other. I can't tell you which came first, the chicken or the egg, but I did both. I would punish myself. A lot of times, I would finish work and drink, then that monster inside me would take over, and all of a sudden I would go and gamble. I had no control. The next morning, I hated myself for drinking. Forget the next morning; it went on for a week, and then I hated myself for a month and I just said, "Let me get out of this before I kill somebody." I thought about suicide many, many times.

After these binges, there was bad depression. I couldn't face anybody later on because I didn't know what I'd done. I was having a tremendous number of blackouts—just about every time I drank. I drank until I had a blackout. Lots of times near the end I would see somebody after a drinking session and I'd say, "Hi, Charlie, how are you?" And he'd say, "You got the guts to talk to me, after what you did, you dirty rat? You used to be a nice guy." Then I would get into saying, "What did I do?" I would come back into the hotel and somebody else would say, "Boy, did you tie one on last night. You know what you did? You tore the telephone out of the wall." I had a thing about telephones. I went around tearing telephones out of walls. I did a lot of things in my life that were self-destructive, like two marriages. Both women, who I thought were exactly the opposite, were very much alike and very foreign to my life and culture. I think that, from the time I was a child, I was searching for something. I was very family-oriented and I think I was searching for the right type of family.

I attended only one AA meeting, and for me that was not the answer, but I know many, many people who have been helped by AA.

I would not be sitting here if I hadn't gotten ill. Out of bad sometimes comes good. I had a parathyroid operation, which damaged the laryngeal nerve. It paralyzed the vocal cord and I lost my voice. They put me on a pill and with the pill you couldn't drink, so it was a forced cleaning-up. I think if it wasn't for those circumstances, I would have gone on the way I was going until I was dead—and I would have been dead. I look back at it now and it's a frightening thing. I had to get ill to awaken to the fact that I didn't want to die that way.

I look back now and I think, If that Strip was crowded, like it's crowded today in Las Vegas, and I was driving on it at ninety miles to a hundred miles an hour like I did, I could kill a hundred people.

Let me tell you, the joy of my life right now is that I can wake up every morning and remember what happened yesterday. Whether it was the best day in the world or not, at least I can remember it. I can face myself in the mirror and go out and face the world. I can look at people and not be afraid. I don't have to say, "Did I see you last night? Did I offend you in any way?" I have a great respect for myself now. And it's getting better, even to the point where my career is getting back to where it was. I'm working and I'm enjoying the freedom I've got. The creativity is there again. For a long time it was lost. I was just frightened. Alcohol made that happen. I used to question myself. I don't question myself anymore. I was never meant to be an alcoholic. I turned out to be one. There are a lot of people, I'm sure, in the same situation that I am.

I can't go back and say alcohol screwed up my life. I screwed up my life. I'm the one who took that drink. I'm the one who did that. How can I blame it on a bottle? A bottle is an inanimate object. It stays there on the table. But I reached for that thing.

I don't want to kill myself anymore. I want to work and make enough money. I want to enjoy me. I want to enjoy the people around me, and I want the people around me to enjoy me. I think that's the thing—to find out who you are, what you are, and what you want to be.

I don't worry about other people as much now. I'm concerned about myself, and by straightening myself out, I've made the people around me happier.

This is a wonderful world. There are things to see and places to go and people are really wonderful. They really are. I have more of a sense of peace. Peace. That's getting better. I just want to go day by day. Don't project this. Don't look back. The worst thing that happens to alcoholics and compulsive people is that they look back. We cannot correct the past. The only thing we can do is develop our future, and that is the reason we have to live day by day. In living day by day and seeking happiness, you can give others happiness.

4 Quitting

Many drinking alcoholics have not experienced any kind of pain. Unless they stop drinking, they will. Unless they stop drinking, they will hit bottom.

The crisis or bottom may be real or appear to be real. It can actually happen or appear to be close at hand. The alcoholic may lose his job, or he can be threatened with its loss. He can lose his wife and family through divorce, or he may be faced with that threat. He may have a car accident and kill someone, or he may be stopped and ticketed by the police for drunk driving.

The crisis may also be manufactured. The alcoholic can be confronted with his behavior by family, friends, and coworkers in an intervention. This intervention should be handled by an alcoholism expert. The goal is to force the alcoholic to seek treatment.

The crises may be totally emotional and mental, but the pain is real. Every drinking alcoholic must quit drinking, or hit bottom first and then quit drinking.

He tries to control his drinking to no avail. He tries to stop and cannot. He is at the lowest point of a totally unhappy life. He is faced with four choices: insanity, death, jail, or quitting alcohol.

The alcoholic has hit bottom. It is at this point he cries out to himself and perhaps to others: "I need help. I must stop or I will kill myself or die." He is a beaten man. Reaching out for help and admitting total defeat is a humbling experience that goes against the very nature of the alcoholic.

Graham Chapman knew all about quitting. He had "quit" drinking before. Alcoholics quit drinking all the time, only to start again. Trained and licensed as a doctor himself, Graham knew the medical symptoms of alcoholism. Although it is not recommended or necessary today, Graham made the decision to quit "cold turkey" to make an impression on himself. Even once the decision had been made, it took him two years to finally act.

Ten to fifteen percent of alcoholics quit drinking on their own. Graham's description of the mental and physical aspects of withdrawal demonstrate the powerful impact of liquor on the alcoholic.

Graham Chapman is an alcoholic. In addition to his own projects, he is a writer/performer in the British comedy troupe "Monty Python's Flying Circus" on television and in films.

Graham Chapman

Drinking didn't become a heavy part of the routine until the second series of "Python." At the same time, I was working on two other projects, two other television series. One was "Doctor in the House" and the other a situation comedy with Ronnie Corbett called "No, That's Me Over There." We had done a series of each of those programs, and they were all successful. In that one year, with thirteen Python programs to do, I had a lot of other writing to do. I needn't have done it all, but I took it all on. They brought in a lot of money, of course—and gave me a first-rate excuse for drinking.

At that point I began drinking at lunchtime. I would work in the morning and drink quite heavily at lunch. Then I'd go to the bar at the television studios and have quite a lot to drink before the afternoon writing session, which was for a different program from the session I had been involved with in the morning. I would take a couple of drinks with me to see me through the afternoon and be the first one in the bar in the evening. I felt a lot of pressure to be creative, certainly, and the drink helped to extend me, I thought, getting everything to flow out.

I think that was really the key period with me. Before that, it had been more of an extreme social type of drinking, but in control, and it certainly wasn't a necessity. If I went on a climbing holiday, which I used to do a lot, I would be off it completely, no problem. If we were in Scotland and happened to cross a pub in the wilds that had a lot of different brands of malt whiskey, we would try them, but that was quite different. It wasn't necessary. I didn't normally use it during the day or feel I needed it. Perhaps it was because of my training in anesthetics that I managed to keep it at about the right level. I would go overboard in the evening, but during the day I would cut myself off at a reasonable point.

I could get away with it because I was a professional loony. You can hide behind that a little or a lot. I could be quite outrageous and people would shrug it off by saying, "Oh, it's him, he's loony and he's a bit pissed." I must have insulted a lot of people dreadfully and even assaulted quite a few. I went through a period of feeling women's breasts at the bar, using the excuse, "It's all right, I'm a doctor." It did get me punched on one occasion. I didn't realize there was a boyfriend there. He didn't know that I was a loony. He was fresh to the country, an American guy, actually. Punched me straight in the face. Obviously, I did overstep the mark. My success fed this attitude, and I felt I could get away with more. The BBC light-entertainment party that year, for instance, was a rather boring occasion where everyone turned up in moth-eaten dinner jackets and stood around sipping sherry. Very boring. I was quite happily crawling around on the floor most of the time. No one else was doing it, so I thought, why not do it? Make the occasion less socially acceptable for everyone.

I certainly had the reputation of being very close to stepping over that point of reasonable behavior. I was living life very near to the edge. Still, even then, though heavy, my drinking was not really a problem during the day. I kept it at the kind of level at which I could function; I could work. That was not the case in the evening. I became very good at dealing with the problem to an extent during the day, pacing my drinking and holding back just before going over the top.

I never hid the fact that I was drinking. I was always very overt about that. I suppose that's from having been truthful and open at age twenty-five about the homosexual aspect of my life. I never kept a secret bottle somewhere. I would take it with me—openly, if not outrageously so. I didn't drive until I was thirty-seven because I would have been too drunk most of the time. I would sit in the back of the car with a bottle of gin, which I topped off with tonic.

I was always careful to use my knowledge of medicine. I took a lot of yeast tablets and multivitamins, which weren't popular in those days. I was aware of conceivable damage to my liver and my brain, and that was at least some kind of precaution. I was aware that I was drinking too much, certainly, but took as many precautions as I could to remain healthy. I managed to exercise and I ate well, which probably avoided some of the excesses of alcohol addiction in terms of the cells of my body. I was also quite reasonable about monitoring the progression of physical signs.

When the liver is shot to pieces, the pressure in the blood system builds up to the extent that you get varices, like varicose veins, around the base of the esophagus, which can bleed into the stomach, producing a massive hemorrhage that can kill you. Quite often, that is the way a cirrhotic dies, literally throwing out three or four pints of blood by projectile vomiting. I had been schooled in all the signs: the hypothymic flush, the reddening on the fleshy part of the hand just below the little finger, and spider nevi, which are little dilated blood vessels that look like little red spiders. If you press in the middle of these little red blemishes with a pointed object, the redness disappears. It is characteristic of them and differentiates them from regular little red spots that you get with age. These spider nevi appear with liver problems, cirrhosis in particular. They can occur in pregnancy, too, but they fade away very quickly. They also seem to fade with a reduction in intake of alcohol. When I was drinking, I allowed myself three of those and got rather worried about them if I got more. I also enjoyed my work and didn't want it to suffer too much from my drinking, obviously. Keeping an eye on things like that helped me to monitor it to an extent. So I probably drank a lot for a longer period than many people could have or would have. It was amazing, really. I knew exactly what was going on. I knew I was drinking too much.

Yet still there was this idea—this is not me, I'm not the alcoholic. I think I was mentally obsessed with it from quite early on, but being physically addicted is a difficult point to define. I didn't really give withdrawal symptoms a chance for a few years. I would make sure that I got some alcohol to drink.

The most startling moment for me was the first day of filming *The Holy Grail,* which would have been in 1974 or 1975. My addiction and withdrawal symptoms were becoming so noticeable that I had to admit them. We were in the Glencoe region of Scotland, and I was out on a Scottish mountainside at 7:00 A.M. I hadn't taken any precautions, having arrived by train the night before. I hadn't a hip flask; I hadn't access to any alcohol that I knew of. We were filming some considerable way from the hotel. We were halfway up the mountainside, a long way from the road, and none of the crew had any alcohol. At that time in my life, I would usually have a coffee with a stiff brandy in it in the morning —that kind of "not drinking." I began to get D.T.'s for the first time. I got very cold and we were in a very cold place. It was wet and rainy, and I got a terrible tremor that I could control only with great effort. It was definitely that, and I had nausea, too. I really felt dreadful.

Sitting there, shaking, on the mountainside, I had to admit that drinking was beginning to affect my work. I was not being fair to the other people in the group. At the same time, it was not fair to me. It's not fair to me? I thought. That is a bit silly. That thought literally went through my head. Stupid. Then I thought, It isn't fair to me because I have to perform in a few moments and I'm not well. I won't be able to give my best. This is stupid. I'm supposed to be working in movies, and I'm not able to do my job properly. Somehow I managed to get through that day and that scene. It wasn't a terribly difficult one; it was actually the scene where King Arthur goes across the Bridge of Eternal Death, over the Gorge of Eternal Peril. I couldn't have gotten a bigger sign from heaven. The director, Terry Jones, thought it rather odd that an ex-mountaineer should apparently be afraid of heights. He thought that was why I was shivering. Of course, that wasn't the reason I was shivering. I got through it somehow. At that point I remember resolving that when I could, I would stop. When I had a couple of months free, that is what I would do. It was two years before I found those two months.

I felt I would need two months, certainly. I knew I would have a week of extreme unpleasantness in terms of withdrawal symptoms. Then it would take me some time to recover psychologically, to get to know the new me, the sober me. I was thinking in terms of being able to work again, and I thought it would take me probably a couple of months to be able to think of that. There was every possible reason for putting off that two months. I thought, I've got my work to do, I need to earn this, I've got to do that; or just while this little bit of tension is on. Perhaps I'll carry on, not too much. I was fooling myself, really.

I had always been able to stop. But I had noticed that I would very quickly get back to the same level of drinking. I used to make a point of trying to stop for a couple of weeks a year, at least. In fact, the first time I stopped for a month, and the next year it was two weeks, and the next year it was less than a week. Each time I'd quit I'd eventually think, Well, I can get back to social drinking now. Which, of course, I couldn't. I was very quickly back to the same sort of excesses I had been on previously.

Alcohol was affecting my work and my personal relationships, too. There were a lot more arguments, a lot more recriminations. Minor things would start off an argument. Sometimes I threw things around in fits of anger, rage. It was a very selfish sort of period, in many ways, with David and also with John. We all drank too much. I was certainly the leader in that respect. It did lead to a lot of arguments. At the same time, there must have been a great deal of love there because we got over those appalling rows. A lot of them were heart-rending sessions, and quite frequently there were tears.

There was a great deal of self-pity during that period. I think the situation improved with the realization that I had while filming *The Holy Grail*. At that point I began to admit that maybe I was the cause of a lot of unrest at home. Things were better for a time, once I admitted that to myself.

There were periods of incredible joy and depression, but out of proportion to the cause. A small thing would give a tremendous amount of elation or a tremendous amount of depression. Just as a tiny slight might be a cause for anxiety and depression or anger, so, too, any little thing that could be construed as praise or any small accomplishment would be a cause for tremendous elation, a reason to go out and celebrate.

At that point, I didn't really see myself living as long as I have. I thought, It might be another two years. That seemed to be quite long enough. Frightening, really. It never, at that stage, occurred to me to go for psychiatric help, because I felt, I'm supposed to be a doctor and I'm failing on that level. I ought to be able to deal with it. I am dealing with it. Am I dealing with it? I had plenty of friends I could have talked to quite easily about it, and AA was for patients, not for me.

The last year or so—certainly the last year of my drinking—I would have to have a drink first thing, as soon as I woke up. I began to keep a bottle by the bedside because if I didn't have a couple of shots of gin in the first half-hour of waking up, I would get withdrawal symptoms, the dry heaves, cold sweats, and a really appalling nauseated feeling. I didn't want to go through that every day. It became an appalling routine, waking up in the morning, needing to get a couple of drinks down me within the first half-hour or otherwise face the unpleasantness of withdrawal. That unpleasantness began to outweigh the supposed advantages of drinking. The pleasant side of it, the joyous side of it, was no longer sufficient to counteract that unpleasantness every morning. It wasn't worth it. I had to admit that I was dependent on it and needed it the first thing in the morning. Obviously I was an addict. And I began to resent the fact that I was being weak. I was having to admit to myself that I was not strong, not a hard-drinking man about town. I was weak to the point that I couldn't last a day, couldn't last the first half-hour of the day, without drinking, which restricted my life considerably. I had to go everywhere with a drink, I felt. And I did.

So after the two years of not doing anything about it, I got into a situation where two films were set up to be done the next year. Remembering that moment in *The Holy Grail,* I thought I ought to be responsible to myself as a performer. They were quite important films. I had the lead part in *Life of Brian,* and the other was a production of my own, my first effort, *The Odd Job.* Really quite a big moment. With that in mind, I decided to stick by my promise of being responsible toward my work. Those films gave me financial security for that period, too. There was work for that year, and it would pay quite well, thank you. So that removed any nagging aspects of worry there. It became a very propitious time for me to do something about my drinking.

I decided that Christmas would be the time, and again that was grandiosity, because that would be the most difficult time. I would do it then; I would show myself. I arranged that there would be no one else around. I'd told the family that I would be going away, although I knew I wasn't, and I told friends, too. I stopped on Boxing Day, the day after Christmas, and that was it.

Once the decision was made, it was either that or, quite frankly, death. That's the way it looked to me at that time, particularly because of my experience with my friend Keith Moon of The Who. I sat with him on a couple of occasions when he was withdrawing. On one of them, he had thrown a little fit. Knowing that I was drinking the same sort of quantities, I knew I would have to go through that, too, at some point. I stopped quite a few months before Keith died. Keith was more advanced than I, but I definitely did see a parallel. We became kind of soul mates because of the drink, I suppose. We both knew we had a problem and were talking about it. I was trying to help him, and he would have helped me, too. I got him to see a Harley Street psychiatrist who was a contemporary of mine at medical school, a very good man. He had a session with Keith and said that, unfortunately, Keith didn't actually want to stop, deep down. Keith had seen quite a few psychiatrists in his time because of this problem. The group was worried about him, too. I said, "We must be able to do something. I'll stay with him every moment of the day, if you want. We must be able to stop him somehow. He has withdrawn on a few occasions; he can do it." The psychiatrist seemed to think that Keith's life span from that standpoint would be somewhere in the region of six months to two years. It was, in fact, about six months.

I remember Keith was very pleased that I was no longer drinking. In that last year, in fact, he had withdrawn and had not been drinking for about six months. Then he went out one night and saw a movie, the first screening in England of *The Last Waltz*. I wasn't there. He found himself a bottle of brandy that evening. An old friend turned up in the audience. He started drinking. I think that was the first he had had for about six months. He felt very guilty about that, I suspect. He went home and took a handful of pills that he had for preventing withdrawal symptoms, which was a very bad mixture with the alcohol. Those pills and the alcohol did it. He was dead. The death of a very close friend had a tremendous effect in terms of re-enforcing my will not to return to alcohol.

At my peak, I had begun to buy booze in bulk. I had a cellar in my house, which must have contained about fifteen crates of gin and about six crates of scotch. It was an amazing sight. Buying in bulk was more cost effective and these were larger bottles than normal, pub-sized bottles.

I was drinking sixty fluid ounces a day, we estimated. That's three British pints of gin—about two quarts American.

The day after Christmas I just stayed in bed and didn't drink. Because I hadn't had the usual loading of alcohol the night before, I began to get withdrawal symptoms, which lasted for about three days. It was the single most unpleasant experience of my life. I have had worse pain, but it was extremely unpleasant in terms of the lack of control of my body, the tremors, the hallucinations—auditory and visual ones—visually getting the impression that objects were attacking me. As I was looking at something, I would move, and something else would appear to move and make a lunge for me. Objects became the most unfriendly things, things that could leap out and take a swipe at me. I did not know whether I had been asleep or whether I was asleep now, and dreaming. This appalling thing was happening, and I felt maybe it would all stop if I went to sleep. Or maybe I was already asleep. Terribly confusing. There were cold sweats and tingling sensations on the skin, like ants crawling all over me.

I had thought of going to a hospital. Prior to that, on two or three occasions when I had withdrawn, I had taken medication to help me withdraw. In some ways, mentally, I attributed my failure to stay withdrawn to the smoothness of those withdrawals. This time, there was going to be no medication. I suppose the trigger for that was an experience many years before of a friend who was a heroin addict. I attempted to treat him. Eventually, all I could do for him was show him how to shoot up in a clean way, and provide him with clean needles and disposable syringes. He went on a working trip to Germany, and the firm that he was working for discovered that he was an addict, took him away for a period, and didn't give him anything. That was the treatment and it worked. He was O.K. after that. He had been in conventional therapy here and had had methadone substitution, but always went back. That sort of registered. So it was going to be without any aid this time, and it certainly showed me what I had been doing to my body.

It was a monstrous three-day king of a hangover, worse than I had anticipated. The worst aspect was the psychological one, the disorientation. It was an unknown experience. Although I knew that I should pull through, there was quite an element of fear there. About the third day, I woke up feeling really quite clear mentally and physically, the shaking finished. I could dress myself, whereas the previous three days I couldn't have borne to wear any clothes. It would have been too much of an irritation to me. I dressed and got up and was really feeling on top of the world. I had done it.

I called a couple of friends, and invited them around for a celebratory drink while I had a tonic. It was while pouring them a drink that something happened I'm still not exactly sure about. My version of the story is that I knocked over a Christmas card and was trying to stand it up again on the mantle shelf when the shakes came back. I concentrated very hard in order to try to perform this simple act in front of my friends, who were there to observe the new, well Graham. Suddenly, I went into total spasms and collapsed. That was a little epileptic fit, basically just like Keith had had. I possibly voided a certain amount of urine, too. Next thing I remember, I was in an ambulance. It was probably partially the three days of not eating, the loss of blood sugar—a little hypoglycemic fit. Actually, prognostically, it was rather a good sign for something as dramatic as that to happen. It was another good re-enforcement for not getting involved again with alcohol because it really was a frightener. It really scared me. The thought went through my head, Maybe I'm dying. It was a tremendous relief when I found that I hadn't, I must admit. Very close call, I felt. It wasn't, actually, but it scared the piss out of me anyway.

Thereafter, it was all rather pleasant. I mean, it was so positive. I knew that I had licked it in the sense that I wouldn't have to go through that again. The actual physical side of the illness at the time was minimal. I was able to notice improvement day by day. Because of being hospitalized, I then saw the psychiatrist I had advised Keith to see. He was the first person to actually get me to say, out loud, that I had been and was an alcoholic. I was ready to admit that then. His attitude was "Well, you're right, you've gotten over the big one now. I'm sure you'll be O.K."

The thought had occurred while I was drinking —and it was one of the reasons to carry on drinking—that I needed it for my work. Immediately after I had quit, I knew that that had been a lie. Mentally, I felt so much more in control, I knew that wasn't going to be a problem. In fact, everything is so much easier and more fun. That really does re-enforce your decision. Another thing was the speedy return of reasonable liver function tests. That was very gratifying to me. One of the tests that was very popular then, and I suppose still is, is the Gamma GT; it measures enzyme level, which is raised in alcoholics. Mine was three hundred when first measured, after I was admitted to the hospital. That went down to eighty after a month, and then was down to tests that was very popular then, and I suppose still is, is the Gamma GT; it measures enzyme level, which is raised in alcoholics. Mine was three hundred when first measured, after I was admitted to the hospital. That went down to eighty after a month, and then was down to twenty after two months. Amazing recuperative powers the liver has. That removed the worry about cirrhosis.

It's amazing, actually, when a bit of truth does creep in and one realizes, I'm an alcoholic or I'm an addict. Then you can begin to do something about it. It's not that difficult once you've gotten to that point. But admitting it—that's the difficult part.

I think the decision not to drink again was probably the biggest moment to me. Once that decision had been made, I was surprised how easy everything else was from that point on, despite the unpleasant physical aspects of withdrawal. That was much easier to take than getting to the point of saying, "I'm an alcoholic and I must not drink." It was easy to say, "I'm going to stop drinking," but to mean it, absolutely mean it, was the most crucial decision on my part.

One of the most effective ways of forcing the alcoholic to look at his drinking is intervention. In Bob Welch's situation, the Los Angeles Dodgers confronted him and offered him support and options. The purpose of an intervention is to get the alcoholic to seek treatment. Bob had tried to quit drinking on his own and couldn't. He chose to go to The Meadows, a treatment facility in Wickenburg, Arizona. With the help of staff and fellow alcoholics, Bob finally faced the fact that he wasn't too young to be an alcoholic and accepted his alcoholism. During his thirty-six-day stay at The Meadows, he learned to trust other people for the first time in his life and get honest with himself.

Bob Welch is an alcoholic. He is a starting pitcher for the Los Angeles Dodgers. Off-season he is actively involved in promoting

alcohol awareness among teenagers and col-
lege students.

Bob Welch

I thought an individual who had a problem with alcohol could not be successful, especially as a major league pitcher who could purchase any-thing he wanted at a very young age, as I could. I thought an alcoholic had to be lying on a street corner on skid row. That was my definition of an alcoholic. I didn't believe I was one. When someone would raise the question and say, "Well, I think you're an alcoholic," he'd grab my atten-tion, but he'd pissed me off more than anything. "Maybe I have a little problem with drinking," I said to myself many times, but there was no way I could be an alcoholic. I didn't believe it until I got over to the treatment center and saw what it was like for someone at my young age to have the characteristics of an alcoholic. By the time I got there, I was well on my way to drinking a fifth or a quart a day. That was three or four years ago.

My girlfriend, Mary Ellen, had no idea. She wasn't knowledgeable. She didn't know about the disease, what an alcoholic was. And I never paid attention to the fact that I might be causing my mother and father and my girlfriend some pain.

When I was fifteen years old some friends and I went out to a park, and I drank a bottle of Mogen David blackberry wine. I liked it. I liked what it did for me because I was able to speak with girls a lot more easily. That was important to me at that time. After the first time, I didn't need anyone to pull on me and say, "Hey, let's go have a beer." It just snowballed.

I was shy. I was scared to death of girls. But when I got drunk I could tell a girl I liked her. I couldn't wait for the weekend because I thought maybe I'd get a chance to talk to a girl and even kiss her. I also thought that if you didn't like a girl and she didn't like you, you could drink to cover it up. Very early on, I started running from my feelings, hiding instead of talking. I covered up my feelings by drinking.

As I look back now, I see that the friends with whom I first started drinking at fifteen were heavy drinkers. I started choosing such friends even before I started going to college. They had to be people who drank and acted and talked the same way I did. But whether it was in class or on a baseball team, if my friends didn't want to go get drunk with me, I'd go to a bar alone. I did that from the time I started drinking. I didn't go out to drink socially. I went out to drink for the effect, for what it gave me. I knew what I was going to be able to do after I drank—go to the football games, be able to talk a lot more, maybe even go to a party and dance with a girl.

I built up a reputation as both a great baseball player and a very good drinker at a young age.

In college I wanted to prove to people that I was the best baseball player, and when I was done playing, I wanted to show them that I was the best drinker. My mother told me at the treatment center that when I left to go to college the one thing she was worried about was that I was going to turn into an alcoholic. She had this insight when I was seventeen.

When I got to college, I was away from my mother and father and didn't have to worry about coming home, sneaking in the back room, or driving their car. It was a perfect setup for someone who enjoyed drinking. I had some friends there with whom I played baseball in the summertime, and I knew exactly which ones would drink like I did. Then I started finding people over at my dormitory. When I wanted to get away from baseball players, I'd go to these individuals. At seventeen I knew exactly what I was doing. I knew the people who lived in certain bars. There is a bar up in Ypsilanti where the gentlemen are full-fledged practicing alcoholics. I knew that I could go over there and fit right in with those guys. They liked me. I used to go in there and talk about playing baseball. They're probably still sitting there. I didn't associate with people who didn't drink and I didn't want anybody to look at me and question me about how much I drank.

I didn't drink and sip it. I didn't want to see what happened. It was boom! I guzzled the thing, looking for the effect. You like it or dislike it. I happened to like it.

If I pitched a game and lost, I went out and got drunk. I drowned my sorrows or my aggravation or my anger in drinking. If we won, I could celebrate. On both ends, I always had it covered.

I got to the majors by the time I was twenty-one. I'd go out and get drunk whenever I wanted to. In baseball, you don't even have to go anywhere. They have the beer in the clubhouse. It was a perfect setup. I started pitching once every five days. You start mapping out your strategy. You know exactly when you can get drunk, and you know how much time it takes you to recover. The thing that was difficult about baseball for me was that it gave me an opportunity to drink just about every day. I could stay out until three o'clock and sleep until three o'clock. I had plenty of time to rest. There were many times I said, "I'm not going out drinking tonight," but I was right back out there.

Everybody wants to be associated with a professional baseball player. They all want to party with you and buy you drinks, and they all want to push other types of drugs on you. In Los Angeles, where I was living, I knew who was going to get drunk, just like in college.

I'd get drunk four out of five days, get sober the night before pitching, and go back out drinking that night. I didn't wake up in the morning and have a drink or drink at a definite time daily, and I didn't drink every day, but 85 to 95 percent of the times that I started to drink, I couldn't stop. I'd drink until I was drunk or passed out or there was nothing left.

I had pitched in 1978 and done very well. I played in the World Series. In 1979 I participated for about two months and hurt my arm. I knew I wasn't going to play, and I was traveling to all these towns, so I'd get drunk during the games. I'm not going to play, I thought, so let's pop a few cans of beer. Not just one or two, but three or four or five or six. I justified sitting on the bench by saying, "Hell, I'm going to have a few beers and root and at least enjoy myself." I was terribly hurt that I wasn't playing, and feeling bad because one part of the team wasn't doing so well. I wanted to put myself in there and I just couldn't. I covered that up by drinking all the time.

On the way to the park, I'd know I wasn't going to pitch, so I'd say to myself, Why not have a nice little drink on my way there? I'm going to sit in traffic and I'm going to be itchy and edgy. I've got to have a drink. I'm going to have one on the way. Toward the end of the season, I really was not taking care of myself and not being concerned too much with my occupation because I was drinking so heavily. My girlfriend was beginning to hear some whispers. Friends and family members and wives of other baseball players were saying, "Hey, do you hear what your boyfriend does?" I could barely speak to her. My family was beginning to be concerned, too. I could tell not so much by what they were saying, but when I got around them they would look at me when I was drinking. They were concerned about how much I was drinking and where I was going. My health really wasn't affected too much. Basically, I took care of myself, but my ability to prepare myself to play baseball was starting to go downhill.

There was one time in San Francisco, after I was injured, that I had a chance to pitch. They wanted me to start a couple of games at the end of the season. I went out there and my elbow was feeling terrible. It was cold and windy in San Francisco. I gave up a home run. My pitching was a disaster. I went out that night and had a few drinks, went home, and went to bed. I really didn't get drunk. I woke up the next morning and I, another player, and a gentleman we knew in San Francisco went out to this place and had lunch. I started drinking, and I must have drunk three bottles of wine at lunch. The guy on our team went home. I stayed out there and drank ten more Seven and Seven's and a few more beers. I went back to the hotel about a quarter to five. Our bus was leaving about five o'clock. I went upstairs, drank a bottle of wine, guzzled it in about five minutes, then went down and got on the bus. There were a lot of reporters. I just started raising hell. I was screaming and hollering at the manager, making an ass out of myself, embarrassing everybody. I got to the ball park and fell asleep by the stall. One of my teammates woke me up and started helping me get dressed and tried to hide it from my manager. Everybody knew I was drunk. I thought it was funny. A couple of my teammates helped me out. I went out on the field and started a few fights with the guys on the Giants. I got out there in center field and then started a couple of fights with my own teammates. My manager called me in and said, "Hey, you've got to take off your uniform and stay inside." I was never so embarrassed in my life.

Before I went home to Michigan that winter, the Dodgers called me into their office and said, "We fine you for being drunk at the park. We want you to know that we want you to be a part of this club next year, and we're not going to finish last or next to last. We want you to be ready. We want you to take a look at your drinking." I told them all to go shit in their hats and leave me alone. I told them it was their fault, anyway, that if I didn't pitch in the bullpen, I wouldn't be getting drunk, I would have been healthy. "It's your fault," I said, "so why don't you get out of my life and leave me alone? If I don't pitch here, I'll pitch somewhere else."

I came home that winter and tried to quit drinking, but couldn't do it. I stopped for about two to three weeks, until Thanksgiving. That was a deadly time, because I liked to drink and there were a lot of parties in our family. I had my first drink and then I think I was drunk until after Christmas.

A telephone call came from the Dodgers on about January tenth. "We want you to come out here and speak to some people and meet with us." I knew exactly what it was all about. They didn't have to say anything about drinking. I knew what the hell was going on. I knew what was going to happen the next day. I flew out to LA, and when I arrived I smoked a couple of joints, then stopped at a place and grabbed a six-pack. I went to the Biltmore, went to sleep, woke up the next morning, and met with a gentleman who was a recovering alcoholic.

It was really the first time that someone knew exactly how to handle me, knew exactly what to say. It wasn't "Hey, you have a problem." It was "I have a problem." He sat down and shared his story with me, the story of what it was like when he was young, how his drinking had caused great pain to his family, how he had made an ass out of himself and embarrassed himself many, many times. Boy, I could see myself in that same category. I knew this was my time. I really wanted to do something about my drinking, and this gentleman helped me out by sharing his own story, not by saying, "You have a problem. What are you going to do about it?" It was more or less, "I care. There are things you can do."

He gave me the twenty questions, and I must have nailed thirteen or fourteen of them. I found myself answering yes to a lot more than I really wanted to. Those questions, they help. It may not have been the one thing that pushed me over, but those questions helped. Then the gentleman said, "I do believe, young man, that you are in the very early stages of alcoholism. You can tell me to go shit in my hat, like you did before, or you can start attending some AA meetings, or you can try to stop on your own, which you've tried, or you can go to a treatment center. There are some things you can do to help yourself. It's more or less what you would like to do. Don't do it for the Dodgers. Don't do it for me. Really take some time and decide what you would like to do." Five minutes later I said, "Get me into a treatment center." That was on Monday. Thursday I checked into The Meadows in Arizona.

I had three days in Los Angeles to really figure out if I was an alcoholic or not. I went and spoke with the gentleman I was living with at that time, and he was tickled to death that I was going. He helped me an awful lot because he could have said, "The team is just doing that for themselves. There is no way you have a problem." But no, he was right there and said, "You know, I've been around you drinking. It may be the best thing you could do for yourself." He was very supportive. He said, "I'm not going to tell anybody, and if you need me, I'll come over to see you."

I remember calling up my girlfriend and telling her. I said, "I'm going to a loony bin to find out what the hell is going on." She was still saying, "You don't have a drinking problem, do you? You drink like everybody else." She was confused. I got into that treatment center in Wickenburg and I remember being scared to death about calling up my mom and dad and saying, "Here I am in the treatment center." When I called them, I was just busting down in tears. The nurses were giving me support and saying, "Tell them exactly where you're at. You watch how much they care for you." My parents said, "If you need anything from us, we'll be there." I was fortunate. A lot of moms and dads don't give support because they're embarrassed that their child could be an alcoholic.

At The Meadows, I started to learn that I was full of shit, really. Everything I seemed to do was to bullshit myself, to cover things up by drinking. I didn't want to be real with my mom and dad and say, "I love you." When I first got over there, I said, "This place ain't me. The people are over fifty years old. They look like alcoholics. I don't look like one." Then I ran into kids younger than me who were there for drug abuse and alcohol. The one thing you really learn when you are there is to be honest because the place is there to help you. And if you have a problem, it's O.K., you're in the right spot. All the people there are like your family.

I had always been a quiet and shy person. I didn't have a lot of friends who would talk to me about the way I felt. We just went out and drank or got high one way or the other. When I got to the treatment center I was putting some trust in people for the first time. I began to be honest with myself. I had been lying to and cheating myself for quite a long time—not only in regard to the way I felt about my girlfriend, but about my mother and father and playing baseball, too.

I was in treatment for thirty-six days. When I

first came out, I had the idea that just because I didn't drink, it was O.K. to smoke a joint or pop a few pills. I almost killed myself running into the back end of someone's car. I was on Valium. Until I eliminated everything, I really didn't get a good foundation. What helped was being in the AA program, and wanting to stay sober. I'm really just now getting to the point where I can finally give in. I don't care if I never take a drink again. I don't care if I don't get high again. It's O.K. to be right here, to be sober, not get high; that's fine. I've struggled for quite a while now. It doesn't seem hard not to drink.

There are three times I still really have a craving to drink. One of them is on an airplane. I associate it with getting drunk. When I first started flying, I always drank. Another time is after I play golf. Last, when I'm done pitching. My body at times still says, "All right, where's the fucking booze?" I'm flying after a game. My body is thinking, Where is the booze at, man? We've got to go to sleep. In those three areas it pops out like, "Am I going to drink or am I not going to drink?" But as long as I know what is going on, I can prepare myself.

I have always dreamed of marrying a particular woman. We're not together right now, but I know that I love her and that she loves me. Someday we may get married. I want that woman to be happy, whether it's with me or not, and there's no way I would have said that before I was sober. I want her to be happy, and I want her to have a very good life. Before it was always, "Well, you can have a great life but it's still got to be centered around my life. You can't have a career and be with me. You have my career and then you can do some things on the side."

Now I can also say that I love my mother and father, but it took me twenty-two years to say that. I love my mother and father, my sister, my brother. I also know that I'm going to be just fine whether I play baseball and make $800,000 a year, or whether I work in a factory. As long as I stay sober, my heart is going to be just fine. I know that now.

I think I've been able to communicate with people and share with people. I've gotten softer. I've gotten a lot softer as far as feeling. I'm able to talk and share with people. My family is a lot closer now. All we would talk about before was playing baseball. Now it's "How are you feeling?" That was never there before.

I've gotten thousands of letters from people throughout the country because of a little documentary film I've done. They say, "We've seen this film about this treatment center and we were thinking about splitting because we didn't think we were young enough to be alcoholic." I tell you, I appreciate that a lot more than money. Before, I thought you had to have a house, a Mercedes-Benz, and a boat to be happy. Now I know that my peace and serenity and sobriety are more important—ten times more powerful than pitching in the World Series or participating in any game. They really are. That's another one of the ways I've changed. That's the truth, too.

I know I will quit playing baseball someday. But sobriety will last for a lifetime. As long as I have that, everything is going to be fine, whether I'm playing baseball or not.

NOTE: *Bob and Mary Ellen were married on January 21, 1984, in Boston, Massachusetts.*

At his very first AA meeting, Elmore Leonard was able to see himself in the stories of others and admit he was an alcoholic. The only price of admission to Alcoholics Anonymous is the desire to stop drinking, and AA is the most readily available way to quit drinking. There is a difference, however, between admitting that "I am an alcoholic" and accepting it. From time to time, Elmore went back to drinking to test himself. Finally, with the encouragement of his future wife, Joan, he came to the realization it was all or nothing. Today, after accepting the AA principles, he looks at life with a sense of inner peace.

Elmore Leonard is an alcoholic. He is a novelist and screenwriter. His novels include Split Images, Cat Chaser, City Primeval *and* LaBrava. *His latest novel is* Glitz, *and he has written the screenplay for the movie* Stick, *based on his own novel.*

Elmore Leonard

When I look back now, back thirty-five or forty years, I can see I had a problem. I can see I had a problem when I was in my twenties, but it wasn't noticeable. I didn't drink that much more than anyone else. The group I was with then were all fairly hard drinkers. You'd go to a party with a case of beer or bottle of Imperial. You could buy them both for five bucks then. Drinking was always kind of a macho thing—that idea of the hard drinkers in westerns and detective stories, the shot standing at the bar. I'm sure I was influenced by that. In the service I passed out beer on an island in the Pacific for a year and drank probably six or eight cans a day. I was nineteen years old. In the Philippines we weren't allowed to drink the native beer because of the water, so we drank whiskey. Three of us would sit down with a bottle of local whiskey on the approved list and drink it. That's what you did. It was a macho thing to do. I went out and got tattooed in Seattle. You'd drink whiskey and get tattooed. It was a lot of fun. I don't regret any of it.

Drinking was always fun. We'd never go to dinner anyplace that didn't serve liquor. I always felt the conversation was more stimulating and the evening was more exciting when we drank. I got to the point, though, where I believed that I was bored when I wasn't drinking. Talking to men in business was kind of boring for me, anyway, not being business oriented. Advertising was different because there were a bunch of swinging guys in it. But with the client, the straights, the manufacturers, I felt that I would have to drink in order to sit and listen to them.

I always took pride in my capacity to drink. I remember when I was at Campbell-Ewald in 1957, I went out to Colorado. I was getting material for Chevrolet truck testimonial ads. I would call on the Chevrolet dealer, who would then introduce me to a truck owner who had some fantastic story to tell about his trucks. One time, I think it was in Alamosa, I was out for the evening with a trucker. We were drinking whiskey and we had dinner. We were drinking brandy and beer and he said, "I haven't met a lowlander yet I didn't have to put to bed." We were probably at five thousand feet. I thought, "What is this? I know skinny guys back in Detroit who drink four to five martinis for lunch. They could kill this guy sitting at a table. He wouldn't last an hour with these guys in little three-piece suits." Before that evening was over, he was chasing a waitress down the alley. The next morning, I went to see him at his office, after I had gotten a couple of beers in me for my equilibrium. He looked up, red-eyed, and said, "Oh, my God, I never want to see you again."

I went on my own after I quit Campbell-Ewald in 1961. I didn't write any fiction for four years, but that was my reason for quitting. I got into business for myself. I started writing movies for Encyclopaedia Britannica and did some industrial movies. I formed my own ad agencies, and I was successful. I learned that 50 percent of it was asking for the money, and if you couldn't ask for the money, you had no business being in business.

I never reached the point of a couple of fifths a day. Not until the very end did I drink before noon. Noon was always that magic time when it became all right. If you could just hold out until noon. Sunday morning I used to hold out and then come back from Mass and have a big bowl of chili and a couple of ice-cold beers. Hangovers never bothered me because all I had to do was drink a few ice-cold beers or a real hot, spicy bloody mary and I was back.

When I think back to my twenties, social events always had to involve drinking. If someone came by, I'd always offer him a drink. I would be happy to see people drop in because then I could have a drink. I didn't realize, until later, that I welcomed this excuse. Now I am amazed at how little people drink and that they leave a drink when dinner is ready.

I was getting more noticeably drunk. I wasn't handling it the way I used to be able to. In fact, I was two different people. There was a definite personality change, like talking louder, acting wackier, which I thought was a lot of fun. I'm being funny, I thought. This is really funny stuff. It wasn't funny at all. But everyone was always laughing. Most of the people were not too far behind me, but I had to admit that I drank more than almost anybody I knew. There were a few guys who would keep up with me, but the majority of our friends didn't drink half as much.

In the late sixties, early seventies, I was going out to Hollywood quite a lot. I would take American and sit first-class because Universal Studios was paying for it, and fly the Captain's Table. They would come down the aisles, slicing the roast beef, serving drinks before the champagne, red wine with dinner, saying afterward, "Why don't you go up to the lounge for your cognac." Whatever you wanted, and I did the whole thing. Then I would be met by somebody at the plane. We'd go out to dinner and do the whole thing all over again. I'd have twenty drinks or more in me by the time I got to the hotel and went to bed. I remember once I had a meeting with Steve McQueen, who had bought a story idea of mine. We were going to sit down and discuss the screenplay, and I was so hung over that I was absolutely dying for a beer. We had lunch in his office and he said, "What do you want, pop or beer?" I said, "Oh, I guess I'll have a beer." I couldn't wait to get it down. One day I came back from California throwing up blood. I was in the emergency room and they couldn't stop the bleeding. They said they had to look in and see what the trouble was. So I asked my doctor, the internist, "What do you think it could be?" He said, "Well, I think it's probably an ulcer. If it isn't, it might be acute gastritis, but usually you only see that in skid-row bums." So they took me in and opened me up. It was acute gastritis. But it was still seven years before I had that last drink.

I did ease off for a little bit after my surgery, but within a month I was gradually drinking again, until finally I was right back where I had been. I was beginning to disguise my drinks more. I would drink a big whiskey collins instead of my favorite, which was Early Times over shaved ice. Twice I was arrested for drunk driving. That was toward the very, very end. Once, in Malibu, when I was drivng too slow at 2:30 A.M., then a year later in Michigan. I drank for thirty years and nothing ever happened and suddenly two driving-while-under-the-influence arrests in a year. That's got to tell you something.

I remember a guy telling me that he had joined the AA program because he was always thinking of the next drink. Before he had barely started the first, he was ready to order another one. I was doing the same thing at the time. Finally, a couple of friends suggested that I look into the AA program.

All I had to do was sit at one meeting and listen to the stories to know that I was an alcoholic. I admitted it at my first meeting. I opened my mouth and it came to me, "I'm Dutch, and I'm an alcoholic." But this was admission before the acceptance. I did pretty well for a while, but about every two months I'd fall off. It took me a couple of years or more to accept.

I was afraid of getting caught drinking, so I flew off. The first time was to Marrakesh in 1974 to talk to Sean Connery and Michael Caine about a picture. They were doing *The Man Who Would Be King* at the time. The producer, John Foreman, brought me over to discuss a story idea with them. I sat around the lobby drinking for a week, waiting for the meeting. I stopped off in Paris on the way home and drank some more and came home. The same year, a few months later, I went to Israel to adapt one of my books for a film to be set in Israel, which didn't make any sense at all to me. But the producer was paying for it and it was an opportunity to see Israel. I drank as soon as I got on the plane. I drank in Tel Aviv, where there are only two honest-to-God saloons in the whole town, outside of cocktail lounges and hotels. I picked a country where nobody drinks to do my drinking. I went back to Israel a couple of more times to research my book and did more drinking.

I tried to hide my drinking from myself. I would sit in my office—actually I had three offices. I had a refrigerator in the front office and in the middle office there was a kind of lounge. I had a bottle of sherry and little glasses there on the table. I would go in there and have a little glass of sherry from the decanter, then I'd have another one. After that, I'd get out the bottle and fill up the decanter to where it had been, in case anyone noticed. Then I'd get a cold bottle of white wine out of the refrigerator and put it in my desk drawer. I'd open the drawer very, very quietly, though no one was in the office, and take the wine out and drink a big, big swig of it and put it back in. Not a soul was near enough to hear anything. I didn't want to hear it.

In 1977 I was divorced. I wonder if the booze gave me the courage to leave home, to leave the situation I was in, having been married for twenty-six years. Now that I know what I know, I'm sure I would have done it in the right way with a clear head. But I did it drinking and got away with it. There were all kinds of reasons. The drinking did enter into it, there is no question about that. My first wife doesn't have a problem that I know of, but we always drank. We always drank together. We always drank before dinner. We always had wine with dinner. Every single night, we would get into arguments, with me drunk and her part of the way, with me saying vicious things, which I couldn't believe the next day. I'd be filled with remorse. I saw some familiar things when I read the book *Games Alcoholics Play* some years ago. The month that I joined the program was the month that I left home in 1974. The year that I had my last drink, 1977, was the year I was divorced. It just happened to fall that way.

I was living alone between 1974 and 1977 in the Merrillwood Apartments and I was attending AA meetings. I had a whole cabinet full of booze,

140

which didn't tempt me much, but every once in a while I would get a craving for red wine. There is some romantic notion connected with red wine. I always started with red wine, I don't know why. I would drink a bottle of red wine and I'd be off. The next day it might be something else. Scotch or anything, though usually the next day I would disguise it. I would put scotch in something that you never put scotch in—Vernor's ginger ale or something like that. I was great at trying to disguise the booze from myself. If I'd put that in a story, nobody would believe it. I really denied I was an alcoholic. I based that on the fact that I didn't have the capacity, or my drinking wasn't as intense as that of so many others whom I talked to. I remember asking a guy, "How do you have time to drink three fifths a day?" He said, "For Christ sake, you get up early. You put the first one, that first glass of vodka, right on the toilet tank while you're taking your shower, and you reach out and get it. Then you get over to the bar quick, and you order a vodka and orange juice. You drink half of it down and you say, 'Hit it again.' He puts another shot of vodka in and, by the time you're there five minutes, you've had about four drinks without even finishing the first one."

I think my present wife, Joan, had a lot to do with my quitting. She was so supportive, without any pushing or nagging, but with sympathy—the right kind of sympathy. She'd say, "You are absolutely out of your mind." Maybe it was the way she said it. "Why are you doing this to yourself?" she'd say. I think I kind of liked the idea of the tragic figure. I think this must enter into alcoholism, playing the role of the tragic figure. But, within the same moment, I could look at it as bullshit, knowing I was playing roles, playing games. It was inevitable that if I had any intelligence at all, I had to stop. I realized that I had to quit or go all the way and forget about it, the hell with it. Good-bye brains.

It's almost inconceivable to me now, all those games I played, all those things I went through to justify drinking. The big difference nowadays is that I don't have to look forward to anything. I get up in the morning and being is enough. There isn't anything that I want to go to see or anything that I want. I try to describe this to people, and I can see by the looks on their faces that I'm not explaining it properly. They think, Well, my God, that must be boring, just not doing anything. I don't have to do anything. I am much more aware of things going on but in a very quiet way. I don't need excitement. I'm into my work now, all the way and I'm not straining. I stop at six o'clock, but I'm giving it a full shot every day. I see that I can continue to get better at it. That's an amazing thing, after thirty-two years, to know I can get better. It's happening because I'm more interested in it. I have so much more confidence in my work. I can try different things. I can experiment in different styles. I look forward to working in the morning, something I didn't used to do. It was always a chore.

My personal relationships are better, there's no question about that. Getting out of myself and seeing other people and trying not to see me is the key. I'm not going to be able to play roles if I'm not thinking about myself. I just present myself as I am, optimistically, with natural, normal confidence. Here it is. This is who I am. This is what I do. Would you like to buy this book? If you don't like it, O.K., fine. Someone else will buy it. I used to be very self-conscious. What do they think of me? Walking down the street, I felt everybody was looking at me. Not anymore. It doesn't matter. I approach people now. I never used to. I approach strangers and talk to them. I was afraid of that before. I was afraid that they wouldn't like me, that they would form a bad impression of me. The key is getting out of yourself.

Today I realize I have complete trust in God. I'm in His hands. Now what I'm going to do is try to live according to His will. God's will, I think, is misinterpreted. God's will to me means one thing—love—and if I look at this as my primary reason for being here, all the specific things fall into line. When I get up, before I get out of bed, I say, "O.K. let me be an instrument of Thy will." I want to be His agent. I want to be used any way He wants to use me. I want to do His work. This is my main reason for being. My reason is not to be a writer, it's to be with everyone else and see what happens. I see a lot of people I don't like, but I see the humanness in them. We're all pretty much in the same boat. A lot of people have ugly dispositions and are fighting life for any number of reasons. But nobody wants to be that way. Nobody really wants to be antagonistic or hard to get along with. After a while, it becomes their nature. I think there is hope for everybody.

Today I don't drink. That's all there is to it. That dismisses the problem.

I can go back to the time of my last drink, 1977. From then on I have become more and more successful. There's no question about it. I can sit down and write anytime, anywhere. It doesn't matter. I don't have to be prepared. I think I kidded myself in that. I was turning out a book in four months then. But I'm doing it with so much more pleasure now that there is no comparison.

I'm doing what I do best. I'm doing exactly what I want to do. There is no better situation. I sit and look out the window when I'm writing away, I look out, and I don't believe it. I'm sitting here all by myself, doing this story, getting all excited about it and getting paid for it—a lot of money. I'm not bending to a certain commercial way to fit a commercial need. I can't do that. I have to do it my way, and thank God, it's saleable.

5 A New Life

When the alcoholic stops drinking and seeks help, good things begin to happen quickly. He looks better and feels better. He is healthier and happier. His self-confidence and self-esteem begin to return. He begins to look at himself and the world around him differently. As time goes on, he feels more comfortable in sobriety than in drunkenness. As life continues, the alcoholic chooses not to drink because life is better than it was in his drinking days. But the sober alcoholic must forever be on guard against the temptation to drink again. At the beginning it will be a battle. New patterns and habits must be put into place, but the alcoholic is on the road to a new life.

Recovery is a discovery. It is a joyful, happy, and positive experience, a discovery of self and of the world. The alcoholic who overcomes the physical addiction and mental obsession with alcohol and begins the process of self-acceptance and self-discovery experiences a world of happiness he never thought existed or was possible for him. It is a life of freedom, peace, happiness, success, and serenity.

"There is no comparison," says Don Newcombe as he looks at his life today in contrast to his drinking years. Most important to Don is the respect he regained from his wife and children. He wonders, with justification, where his three college-attending children would be today if he had not quit drinking.

As is so often the case with recovered alcoholics, Don focuses on his work today as the most important of his life—not his baseball days, not his business days. In his work, he carries the message of alcohol and drug awareness.

Don Newcombe is an alcoholic. The former star pitcher for the Brooklyn Dodgers now represents The National Institute of Alcohol Abuse and Alcoholism in Rockville, Maryland, and is affiliated with the Los Angeles Dodgers.

Don Newcombe

I never believed I was an alcoholic. I never believed I couldn't handle my alcohol. All the problems I had—bankruptcy, loss of career, the end of my first marriage after thirteen years, the fact that my current wife was going to divorce me—was just the way my life was, I thought. I never attributed it to my alcoholism.

From the beginning, I drank as much as Don Newcombe wanted to drink. I drank as much as Don Newcombe had to drink or needed to drink. But I was a situation drinker. I drank when the situation warranted my drinking. I didn't drink before a baseball game. If I had to pitch on a given night, I did not drink anything the night before, not even a bottle of beer. I knew what my job consisted of. I knew what was required of me, and I did not drink until after the game was over. I would drink on planes, trains, in hotels, and in clubhouses. I would drink wherever I wanted to, whether I won or lost. If I won, though, it was a lot easier because the manager didn't mind us drinking in the clubhouse. If I lost, everybody was mad, so I went out and drank somewhere else, away from the players.

Drinking really had no ill effect on me, especially in my younger life. It never impaired or impinged upon my success as a baseball player. I had a history of winning seasons. In all the years I played baseball, whether it was in the sandlots, the Negro League, the minor leagues, or the major leagues, I never had a losing season, except maybe one. So I had a success factor in my life. I knew that I was good and what I had to do. No player who ever knew me will tell you that Don Newcombe didn't keep himself in shape. I ran. I ran and ran by myself in the hot sun in Florida. During the baseball season, wherever we were, I would run and run to stay in shape. If I got drunk the night before, I would go out and run and sweat and work hard to keep myself in some semblance of condition. But as time went by, I began to lose that desire. I think that's where alcohol began to play a part in my life that I didn't recognize. I began to lose my desire to run and stay in shape as I got older. I'm not talking about old. I'm talking about twenty-nine, thirty, not forty or fifty. I began to slow down, to lose my desire to keep on working hard in the hot sun for two to three hours. My ambition decreased. I probably drank as much in my big winning year, 1956, as I did in one of my worst years before I retired from baseball.

Billie and I were married in 1960. After we got married, I was playing baseball in Cincinnati, then Cleveland, then Spokane, and finally Japan. After 1962 there was no more baseball playing, no more money coming in from baseball. I went back to my business—a cocktail lounge, a liquor store, and an apartment building in New Jersey —and she went with me. With all of the things I had to do in the cocktail lounge to try to build up a business and keep the cash register ring-ing, I would drink with people around the clock, from 9:00 A.M. until 2:00 A.M. Billie wasn't drinking and here she's stuck with a guy who comes home after being in the bar all day long, smelling of nicotine and alcohol, and expects her to love him. Here is an intelligent woman, a beautiful woman who finally says, "No, I can't live like this." When I came back to the business, I had a marked increase in my intake of alcohol. I'd always had a weight problem. Beer made me gain weight, and I loved beer. So I shifted from beer to whiskey. I didn't know that I was going into the major leagues of drinking and becoming a full-fledged alcoholic.

The only one who drew my attention to it was Billie, and she's responsible for the fact that I have my life together today. She did one very specific thing. She said, eighteen years ago, "I can't live with you anymore. I'm going to divorce you. I can't sit here and watch you die. I can't let you beat me up. I can't wait for you to destroy these kids, these three babies who don't deserve it. I'm not going to wait for you to destroy yourself. I'm going to divorce you now. If you want to go your way, go your way and leave us alone, and we'll do fine. I'll work or somebody will take care of us. I'll find another man somewhere, but you just leave us alone. If you promise me that, Don, I swear to you that you'll never see these kids again, nor will you be bothered with me again. We don't want anything from you because you don't have anything." And I didn't have anything.

Vulgar, crude, physical toward my wife—that was how I acted when I drank. If I ever put my hands on that beautiful woman again, other than to love her, I want God to paralyze my hands. I haven't done that in eighteen years, but when I was drinking I would slap her around from time to time. We were married six years before I stopped drinking. I would respond to her with my hands. She's a highly educated, very bright woman, and I'm rather crude, a high school dropout. Two people like that can't mix unless something happens, unless some amazing transformation takes place in their association. There is no way they're going to get along if there is something stressful like alcoholism. But I didn't recognize my alcoholism, and my wife was not going to live her life with a person who did the things I was doing. The fact that she loved me was all we really had, but she lost that because of the lipstick on my collars, because of my slapping, because of my yelling at the kids—all the things that go with a guy who is trying to cover up for his lack of education, his lack of intelligence, by drinking. There was no talking; I would not listen. She would not be able to talk to me at all. I would respond by telling her, "Shut up or I'm going to slap your goddamned mouth." So she would either have to shut up or get slapped. She said, "I can't live like this. I'm like a prisoner."

I remember taking strong diet pills. This was one time Billie really got afraid of me, and I think it was the reason she initiated the divorce. I was still drinking alcohol. I don't remember this, but Billie said I took these pills on a Saturday afternoon. When I came home from my bar in New Jersey, she was feeding our little daughter. She said I came into the house and just stood in the kitchen where she was feeding the baby and said, "I'm going upstairs, bitch, and I'm coming downstairs to beat your ass every hour on the hour." She said she looked at me and thought, What is wrong with my husband? What is wrong with him? What did he do? He left here to go to work a couple of hours ago, and here he is now, standing before me, telling me he is going to beat my ass every hour on the hour. For no obvious reason. She told me later, "You went upstairs, and every hour on the hour you came downstairs. You didn't beat me, you just stood in the door and glared at me, with this smirk on your face, and then you went back upstairs. You did that three times." Now, that's insanity. I didn't stop drinking then, but I did stop taking those diet pills, because I'd scared that lady to death.

After deciding that she was going to divorce me in 1965, Billie devised a plan to get back to California to her family, where she could initiate a divorce action and leave me with the failing business. It was going down the tubes anyhow. In the end I lost $350,000 to $400,000 in bankruptcy. She wasn't going to stay there, because she wasn't responsible for it in the first place. I had the business long before I married her. Why should she stay there and suffer the embarrassment of going through bankruptcy proceedings? So she moved to California. I even drove the car. I didn't know what she was doing. I didn't know she was going to divorce me. In my frame of reference I thought she still loved me. I thought that I had it made with my wife. I thought I was King Tut. I thought I had everything under control.

In the end, I quit drinking with her help. The only way I could quit. Eighteen years ago, I didn't know anything about AA, and I wasn't ready to admit that I was an alcoholic. I drank too much, and because of my drinking I got into all the trouble, but I was not a dirty old alcoholic. I wasn't that, not I. I'm only recovered today because of Billie. She stuck by me, she didn't divorce me. She slept on the floor with me because we didn't have any furniture and no money to buy any. We didn't have any food. I'd had a World Series ring on my finger, but that was in the pawn shop because I'd bet once too often on the race horses. But Billie stuck by me. She said, "Look I'll try to love you again. I hate you now, but I'll try to love you again as long as you don't drink, but you drink and I'm going to leave you." It took seven years from the day I stopped drinking in 1966, seven years before she told me she loved me again. That is how much I had hurt her.

There's just no comparison between the way my life is now, since I stopped drinking, and how it was, say, twenty years ago. The most important thing is that I have my wife and the respect of my three children. They're twenty-one, nineteen, and eighteen and all in college. I have a son, Don, a daughter, Kellye, and a son, Tony—two at Howard University and one at Stanford. I think back a lot of times and wonder about where my son Don would be, now that he's twenty-one, if I'd kept on drinking? What would my son be doing? What would my daughter be doing or my younger son? I'll bet they wouldn't be at Howard and Stanford. I'll bet my life on it. If I had kept on drinking the way I was going, even if Billie had stayed with me, there is no way that we would have been able to have the kind of marriage we have, to raise the kind of kids who want to achieve in school and are willing to do what they need to do to become what they want to become. My son called me a little while ago and told me how proud he is of me. Would he have been proud of me if I'd kept on drinking and scaring him and running him ragged, forcing him to hide under the bed while I slapped his mother around? Today I'm totally in control of Don Newcombe's destiny. I was not in control of any part of my destiny back then; alcohol was. I did what alcohol wanted me to do. Now I do what Don Newcombe wants to do, which is very important. That gives me peace of mind. You've got peace of mind when you are in control of your own well-being and the well-being of the people who come into your life.

In the process, I've developed what I refer to as a legacy, the Don Newcombe legacy, outside those records I achieved when I was playing baseball. This legacy allows me to leave something on this earth for somebody else to benefit from, outside of the baseball spectrum, and that's very gratifying. I was the pioneer. I was the guinea pig. I was the one who went public years ago with his alcoholism. Nobody else was doing it. Nobody else dared to do it. I had some qualms about doing it because I was interviewing with a guy about a government job, the job I finally wound up doing. But Billie and my kids finally agreed and said, "Dad, if you're not going to be embarrassed, we're not going to be embarrassed; we're with you." I'll never forget what my son Don said: "Dad, all my friends' parents have problems with alcohol. So don't you worry about how I'm going to feel and what they're going to say to me in school. You do what you've got to do, Dad." This was a thirteen-year-old boy. To hear that from my son gave me the inspiration to go public and become a pioneer in doing something to save lives. I never saved any lives when I was playing baseball, but I save lives now that I am involved in the field of alcoholism. That's something that really surpasses the imagination, to know that you have saved lives, maybe hundreds or thousands.

Alcoholics, after quitting alcohol, often speak of living two lives—or of getting a second shot at life. To quit drinking is not an easy thing for an alcoholic to do; however it is the most important decision in an alcoholic's life. Out of that decision good things begin to happen, and life gets better and better.

Gerry Spence sees the positive results, in both his personal and professional life, for having dealt with his problem of alcohol. Peace of mind, confidence, freedom, security, contribution, and unselfishness are part of what he calls a gift.

Gerry Spence is an alcoholic. Recognized as one of America's top trial lawyers, he represented the family of the late Karen Silkwood in their successful lawsuit against Kerr-McGee. Recently he represented a small family ice cream company against McDonald's and obtained a $52-million jury verdict for breach of contract and fraud. He is in private practice in Jackson, Wyoming.

Gerry Spence

I recognized that I had a problem with alcohol, but I never had the opportunity to work with people who were experienced in dealing with alcohol problems. I lived in a little community, Riverton, Wyoming. This was about fifteen years ago. There weren't sophisticated clinics for people to go to. There weren't any Alcoholics Anonymous groups in the community, so far as I knew. I didn't know any people who had ever admitted they were alcoholics. So I was mostly left to my own devices to deal with this problem and even to recognize that I had it.

None of my friends would say, "You're an alcoholic" or "You've got an alcohol problem." To this day, I don't know of anybody who ever pointed his finger at me and said, "You are an alcoholic." I never went to any doctors about it. I was never jailed. I never missed work. But it was a problem.

As time progressed, I realized that more and more of my time was being used up in dealing

157

with alcohol. It takes a lot of time to be a good drinker. It needs to be done with a little style and around the right kind of people, so I found that I spent a lot of time drinking in the evening. Then I spent a lot of time the next day trying to recover from that. I discovered that more and more of my time, my productive time, which has always been valuable to me and which I have always seen as a sort of gift, was being utilized for drinking.

The value of life was analogized for me one time when I thought back to walking up the hill with my old grandfather Spence when I was a boy. He used to walk from the barn, where he milked the cows every day, up to the house, carrying the milk buckets. He would carry them so carefully up that steep hill. He had an old wrecked, wretched back, full of arthritis and rheumatism, and his legs were crooked and bent, so it was painful for him to walk up that hill with those heavy buckets. I used to trot along beside him, watching him, and I would see how careful he was with that milk, how he never spilled a drop. When I thought back to that I suddenly realized that my life was like Grandpa's bucket. There is only so much milk in life's bucket, and we mustn't spill it, because we can't retrieve it. It can never be gotten back. I realized that day after day I was spilling my life's milk by wasting time drinking and recovering from hangovers. So I started to become aware of the problem, myself.

Then I fell in love with a woman—Imaging, my present wife, my love. She and I were absolutely delirious with love, and when people are like that they do crazy things. We abandoned all common sense, all responsibility. But it was also very painful, because I was faced with the possibility of breaking up a marriage of twenty-one years. I had married Anna when I was nineteen, and we had raised four children together. So this was unthinkable. I couldn't believe that I could do such a thing. I had been a lawyer for all these years, had handled many divorce cases, and had looked with disdain on people who divorced each other. I thought they were silly. Why would they fight like that? Why couldn't they just treat each other decently and live on? Why would they break up? I thought they must be crazy, but then suddenly I was crazy, crazy in love with Imaging. I remember one day, in the middle of the afternoon, when she and I went up to the roof of my office building and sat there, watching the cars drive by, drinking, having a hilarious time, drunk as hell. My drinking was exacerbated in my new emotional state. I drank more because it decreased the terrible feelings of despair and hopelessness. How could I ever bring myself to leave that good woman, my wife, the mother of my children, for another woman?

I needn't tell you too much of that story, except to say that things got worse as I fell deeper and deeper in love with Imaging. I also had to face the fact that I was injuring, perhaps destroying, other lives, namely the lives of my wife and children. I couldn't bear that, yet I felt unable to do anything about it. I felt trapped. I was in a double bind. I could not give up Imaging. I would rather have died than give her up. Yet I couldn't do what I had to do. I couldn't leave my wife and those kids because I couldn't bear to hurt them.

I can remember walking in to Anna and saying, "I don't have to make a choice between the two of you; I'll keep you both." But that didn't work very long. That didn't resolve it. Then I decided to leave Imaging, to move away from Riverton and give up the law, to get out of town. I would sacrifice my greatest love for my family.

We sold our house. I sold everything we had. Besides being a lawyer, I was also a painter. I sold all my paintings, too. I sold my hunting guns. I sold my pistol collection. I sold our pillows, down to the last pillowcase. I sold every last stick of furniture. I sold my beautiful little hidden ranch at Hidden Valley up in the mountains, up on the reservation. Sold my house, my office, my practice. I sold everything. I moved all of our material possessions down to a vacant store downtown, calling it "Spence's Last Remark," and invited all my friends to come and buy up what was left of Gerry Spence. And then I left Riverton, Wyoming.

We went to San Francisco and, based only on my portfolio of paintings, I was accepted at San

Francisco State in a master of arts course. But I soon discovered that I knew more about painting than they did, or at least thought I did—and I still think so. I was there for only a few days.

I couldn't stand to be without Imaging. I went to a psychiatrist and said, "I want to hire you for one purpose." He said, "What's that?" I said, "I want you to help me get the strength to leave my wife and children." The psychiatrist said, "O.K. If that's what you want me to help you do, that's good. You at least know what you want to do. That's more than most people know." So I went to him for a while, a month or so, several times a week, and one day I knew it was time to leave. I came back to Wyoming, leaving my wife and my children in California. I came back to my darling Imaging, and we soon decided what I had to do. I had to get a divorce. She had two children, and had already divorced her husband. I decided I had to divorce Anna, and I did.

When Imaging and I decided that we were going to get married, we had a big talk, which went something like this.

"Honey, you know we have broken up two homes. We have broken up two homes for each other. What gives us the right to do that? You and I have the power to destroy these marriages and these spouses of ours and these children. We have the power to destroy the whole social foundation of those marriages, which means to leave the friends of those marriages, and the extended families. But what right do we have to do that?"

The answer came back: "Well, if we did that, would we be better people than we are? If we did that, could we make our lives in this world more meaningful? Could we make a better contribution? If we were to do that, we would really have to make our lives count." We decided that was what we wanted to do.

Now, I had a large capacity for liquor, liked liquor, and drank lots of it, and Imaging was drinking heavily, too. It would just break my heart when I saw her drunk. I couldn't stand it. I would weep when I saw her that way. But it didn't bother me that I was that way. We agreed first of all that we'd have to stop drinking, because we needed to make the marriage we were going into work.

We decided that if we were going to break up these marriages, these homes, the new marriage had to stand for something. It had to be a good marriage, a foundation from which good, decent, honorable things could come. We had to quit drinking because we needed stability to make this new marriage work. So we did.

We sort of became each other's AA. We quit together, and we hung on to each other. Although I have never attended an Alcoholics Anonymous session, we must have had the same kind of experience that people have there. Every morning we would wake up, have coffee in bed, and begin to talk about what it was like not to drink. We'd exchange information, talk to each other about how it was, about the difficult times, about how strange it felt to be with old friends and not drink around them, about how, now that we were sober, we felt very distant and unrelated to those people and didn't want to be with them any longer, about how we suddenly felt isolated because all of our friends drank. Now we were alone, just the two of us, not drinking. We were afloat out on the big ocean by ourselves. And we talked about that. But there were good things, which we also shared, that came from the experience. It was very painful for me not to drink in the evening, when I usually drank, but it was wonderful not to have the hangover in the morning. And I soon had the sense that I was replenishing my bucket with life's milk because my efficiency was so much greater. There were times when I would come home to Imaging and say, "I feel so bright, so absolutely sharp and creative and full of energy that it frightens me." I didn't know, while I was drinking, that I had all this energy, all of this insight and creative power.

Imaging had her own experience with it, which she communicated to me. Every morning, without fail, we sat in bed, talking about the issues of our lives, which were, "What can we do about our guilt feelings? How can we deal with our children?" We became closer because we no longer had to deal with alcohol. We became closer and shared our feelings, our hearts and souls, our love, our misery, our turmoil, and all the rest of each other. That took the place of alcohol. And it was a great exchange. That was a wonderful exchange—to be able to get the heart and the soul of someone you love in exchange for a bottle of booze.

We're now in our fifteenth year, and neither one of us has had a drink since then—not even one. No beer, no wine, no liquor, no alcohol of any kind. Our quitting drinking and our love are so tied up together that if I were to take a drink, it would mean to me that I was betraying her love, that it had been for naught. It would be a denial of her love and mine.

If somebody said to me, "I want you to have a drink with me and if you do I will give you a million dollars," I'd rather not have a million dollars. And if somebody said, "If you give me your whole life's fortune, I will prevent you from ever taking another drink," I would give him my life's fortune. Out of the struggle that Imaging and I went through came many good things indeed. I quit representing insurance companies and began to represent people. I quit representing banks and represented the poor. I have become even more successful doing that than I was before, without any intent. I just had to become more successful in doing that. I think I have affected the lives of many young lawyers and other people, both clients and nonclients. Those are the rewards that have been given to me as a result of having dealt with the problem of alcohol. And it is a great gift.

Blame, anger, worry, resentment, self-pity, and depression are the negatives that the drinking alcoholic deals with every day. Alcohol is as much a mental, emotional, and spiritual disease as it is physical. The alcoholic carries the world on his shoulders.

After he quit drinking, Tom Tryon discovered he had it all backward. "I thought I was drinking because of my problems," he says, "but my problems came from my drinking." Tom's joy about his discovery and his enthusiasm for life today present a dramatic testimonial to life after alcohol.

Tom Tryon is an alcoholic. He is a novelist who counts among his books the best sellers The Other *and* Crowned Heads. *A former film and television star, he is best remembered for his leading role in the movie* The Cardinal.

Tom Tryon

Only two years ago I found myself drinking all day long and all night long. I'd start as soon as I got up in the morning. It was caused by despair, enormous stress, and periods of what I think were total madness. I told myself that nothing mattered except getting the book done, deluding myself that it was going to be done tomorrow or the day after. So I allowed myself to do whatever

I thought would keep the words coming and chose to indulge myself in alcohol.

I would get up in the morning and have a glass filled with half sweet vermouth and half vodka. That would be my breakfast. Then I might have an egg. Around noon, I would move to orange juice and Myers's dark rum. I would just kind of swizzle those all afternoon until five o'clock, when I could get down to serious drinking. I would start with martinis and have two, three, four, five, six of them before dinner, then wine with dinner, then Irish coffee after dinner, then black Russians or stingers, until I would just pass out and get up the next morning and start all over again.

Then I discovered the loss of my natural resiliency, on which I had always prided myself. I was not elastic anymore. It had gone and I hadn't realized it. Hangovers would go on for days and days, and they were affecting my work and all areas of my life. My friends were shaking their heads, and I was having some near misses in the car. I was due. I was drinking very, very heavily when I stopped. I thank God that there was a domino principle in effect and that just before the last thing hit me, I stepped out of the way, so it went by me and I fell into good hands.

The biggest discovery I have made is that I had it all backward. I thought I was drinking because of my problems, but my problems came from my drinking. I think that is a very common thing with people. I thought I had all these problems and the way I could handle them best was to drink. It greased the skids. It made everything easier. When I stopped drinking the majority of my problems stopped. I was a victim of the worst anxiety attacks imaginable. I mean, they would put me to bed in a darkened room for hours. I would have to stop whatever I was doing and get into a bed—anybody's bed, anywhere—to deal with them. Most of the time I would drink to oblivion. I don't have anxiety attacks anymore, or very, very rarely, anyway.

To do an interview, I would have to drink and drink and drink. I don't think I ever did one sober. I have never been on a television talk show sober, and I have been on some when I was so drunk that I barely got away with it.

I can't stress enough the enormous disability that I was laboring under with these anxiety attacks. Anxiety attack is a phrase that is bandied around a lot. Most people don't understand exactly what it is. I have deduced myself that there is a very acute correlation between anxiety attacks and drinking. I drank to try to still those attacks.

Many things would provoke an anxiety attack. The thought of having twenty people to dinner. The thought of having to make a speech. The thought of having to make an appearance. The thought of having to hand in chapters. The thought that I was getting older and not progressing as I had hoped. I often tried to explain to people who didn't know anxiety attacks what they consist of. The physical manifestation was the tightening up of all my muscles, the pain and discomfort of that, and knowing full well that my mind was causing it. Black fear. Everything was black. I don't think in black anymore. I think in yellows and oranges and pastels.

If anyone ever picked the wrong profession, I did when I became an actor. I never drank while I was working, but for all of the concomitant things—going to the premières and being a public figure and being a celeb—for all of that, I had to grease the skids. God, what a shock it was later to find out that by stopping this one thing, drinking, all the other things suddenly ironed out.

No one told me. Goddamn it, no one ever told me the problem was alcohol. No doctor ever told me to stop drinking. And I was never dishonest. I never hid my tracks. If I went to a new physician and he asked, as all doctors do, about drinking, I was right up front. I told them I'd been a heavy drinker since about 1940. That's a long time to drink, and I had drunk continually. It became a part of my life. I was raised that way. I couldn't imagine not having it. It was just always there.

I can remember the resentment I felt as an enlisted man in the navy because the officers had booze on board and could drink. When I got out of the navy, by Jesus, I drank.

I was a country-club drunk. There were no alleys with paper bags. I came from a good family. I went to Yale. I always had a job. My drinking was of the elegant, fashionable kind. You met somebody for cocktails or you had brunch with bloody marys. Drinks were always there. If you went to a football game or the senior prom, you pocketed a flask. If you traveled, you took some with you. It didn't matter where you went. Either there would be alcohol where you were going or you took it with you. That's the way we were raised.

My mother taught me how to mix a drink. Get the party started. Give them a good drink. It's all I knew. My parents drank. Their parents drank. Every Sunday after church they came into my grandfather's house next door and sat there with their drinks. All the adults would get together at various houses and the hell with Sunday dinner, they were having a party. They loved to party. I can remember when I was a kid during Prohibition, my father would make bathtub gin in the summer.

I remember being at a dinner where the president of the bank slipped out of sight; he just slid down underneath the table. And they said, "Oh, look, Harold's out." They said, "Harold's in the bag. Harold's in the bag." That's the way I was raised. My father, a terrific guy whom I admired enormously, drank for fifty years and died an alcoholic. My mother is eighty-five years old. She's still drinking. All my friends and all the parents of all my friends drank, and if you didn't, you were square. In college, my roommates didn't drink. I used to look down on them.

Who the hell were they? They didn't have any fun. If you didn't drink, you weren't having fun. If I wasn't drunk, I wasn't really with it. I didn't know. I can only plead ignorance. If I'd known then what I have learned in the last two years . . . it's remarkable.

It's also remarkable how little it took to get me to go and do something about it in the end. I was having dinner with a friend in a restaurant. I was so drunk that I thought he was criticizing me for something so I got up and left. I just left him in the restaurant. I found out the next day, when his letter came, that he had been supporting my point of view, but I had been so drunk I didn't know it. Then he said, "Tom, please give up drinking." I still have the letter somewhere. I thought, Jesus, I guess I'd better.

All along I had thought, Well, I'm a writer, so I can be a drunk. I had lots of examples, from Faulkner on. I'm just one of those. You're a writer. You're a drunk. It's O.K.

I thought I was cute, I really did. I just thought it was nifty. What it needed was for somebody years ago to say to me, "Tom, you've got a problem." Nobody ever did.

I knew that I was occasionally coming under critical fire from friends, but no one ever came to me. I would hear it around, but always behind my back. It hurt me a great deal. I couldn't understand why they wouldn't come and say it to my face. I was obstreperous, loud in restaurants, displaying lots of unbecoming behavior all the time. I never liked the idea of being offensive to anybody for any reason. I would bend over backward not to be offensive, yet now I know, looking back, that I was offensive to a lot of people for a long time. I was loud, overbearing, demanding, highly critical—all those unattractive things that really are not part of my nature.

I had been thinking about it for some time, for years, off and on, vaguely. I'll do it someday, I thought. Like I'll quit smoking or I'll go to the gym or I'll lose that ten pounds. Whatever. It was one of those things that we say we'll do and we don't. I had a plan and this was part of it. I was going to try to rid myself of the bad habits I had picked up along the way.

I went very heavy into coke, too, for a while. I did a lot of coke. It was at the point when everybody was doing it. Everyone except my mother was doing cocaine, and I don't know about her. It was the thing to do. It kept me slim and happy, and I loved it. It made the world seem the way I wanted it to be. I felt terrific. I was operating absolutely at my top. Everything I said was bright, original, witty, profound. Interestingly enough, I cannot write at all on marijuana, but alcohol and cocaine never stopped me. With every book I've done, many, many parts were written while I was coked up or in an alcoholic miasma.

What I know now is that alcohol is a poison to me. I thought because my father said it was O.K. that it *was* O.K. I never stopped to question his

171

judgment. The only thing he said was that you were to drink like a gentleman, which meant that you didn't throw up at the table or fall down stinko. Anything else went. I drove drunk in this town for thirty years—from parties, from dances, from affairs, premières, what have you. I drove Cadillacs all over this town, drunk. Why I didn't kill myself or somebody else, I don't know. One day I said, "What's my car doing in the driveway?" The houseman said, "That's where you left it." And I said, "Oh, that's strange." He said, "You had better go out and look at it." So I did. I have a little Mercedes. The whole front of it was V'd in. I had shattered the entre windshield and it cost twenty-two hundred dollars to have the car repaired. To this day I don't know how I did it. I could see my number coming up. It's a wonder to me that something really serious didn't happen.

I truly believe that if I had not stopped when I did, I would not be alive today. It was that serious. On one occasion I tried to throw myself out of a moving car in the middle of rush-hour traffic on Wilshire Boulevard. Another time I went crazy on an airplane, 35,000 feet over Cleveland, Ohio.

I suffered when I gave up cocaine. I had to go through withdrawal from cocaine with a doctor. I nearly killed myself with cocaine. He found more than twenty pustules in my nose, little white infections. All this poison was draining back into my brain. I was falling down. I was dizzy. I would have terrible headaches. I didn't know what it was. Cocaine.

There is no place for fear as a writer or as an actor. You can't be afraid. The drinking was to cover up the fear, to hide it. To hide it from myself. To hide it from other people. To make myself more like I thought I was.

I can't find any holes in AA. I learned there that I'm a lot better person than I ever thought I was. I really lacked self-esteem. This was one of my problems. I grew up a middle son and, although I had been around and done a lot, I just couldn't seem to catch on to who I was. I don't mean to say that I think I know now, but at least I know who I'm not, which I think can be as helpful as knowing who you are, if indeed anyone does know that.

I know I am not a neurotic, the victim of terrible moods that I was before. I was just going about things ass backward. It was all I knew. It was as if I had a terrible headache and took an aspirin for it, not understanding that if I hadn't been drinking I wouldn't have had the headache in the first place. What I have learned is that I do not need alcohol to live a happy life. I just know that alcohol and I don't mix. It was as if I'd slept with a pit of vipers all my life and was constantly getting bitten and poisoned. That's all I knew.

Now I feel that I've got a clean slate. My work hasn't changed, either way. I don't know that it's gotten any better, but it certainly hasn't gotten any worse. And I sleep like a top.

I think sometimes, Why did it take so long? I kid my friends, "Why didn't you tell me?" They say, "You know how it is, you can't tell people." But I think you can. There is nothing that pleases me more than seeing somebody who has a drinking problem go after it the same way I did. I wish that people I had known in the past, who have gone out of my life, could see me today so they could know that there is another side to me.

I am a person of enormous discipline. The discipline that I was given I have turned to good account in writing. I seem to have my own valves. I had them all the time, but I didn't know it. The ritual of drinking was superimposed on my life. I came to California in 1955. I was surrounded by alcoholics. They are all either dead now or still suffering from alcoholism.

I feel, today, that I came in from a terrible storm, a tempest that I'd been in for an eternity. I suffered from madnesses that are just indescribable, and they were all in my mind. Everything seems to go back to fear. I'm not afraid anymore. I'm just not afraid. I was so afraid of people, so eager to please, to make the best impression, to be liked. Now I don't care if they don't like me. I like me. I'm a nice guy. I really am. It's such a pleasure to discover that what I thought was true about myself really is true. I just had a problem. I don't know why it took this long for me to solve it. I've seen a lot of people die of this disease, and it was never a pleasure. I accept my recovery as a great gift.

I've given up alcohol, and there is no question
I stay away from it. I don't yearn for it. I don't
long for it. People say, "Do you mind if I have a
drink?" No, I don't mind. Have a drink. Have
all you want. It doesn't bother me.

6   The Woman Alcoholic

Men go out and get drunk, and that's acceptable. Women can't do that—the stigma of alcoholism is greater for them. Most women alcoholics feel very guilty about their drinking, and many women wonder "Have I hurt my children?"

Women alcoholics in particular report that they have felt anxious their whole lives and have tried many things to counteract a low-level, nagging anxiety. Often when they drink they feel "normal."

Although an alcoholic is an alcoholic, there may be less understanding of women alcoholics than there is of men alcoholics. In addition to a different kind of physiology, women often have pre-existing depressions and histories of abuse, sexual and otherwise.

Furthermore, a wife will stand behind her husband and his drinking problem, but husbands get angry at their wives for their alcoholic behavior.

Treatment centers today are much more apt to have special treatment programs for women and specially trained counselors to work with them. Increasingly, women who are concerned about good treatment are trying to develop new ways to help the woman alcoholic. Because of their guilt and low self-esteem, it is doubly important that women alcoholics understand that they have a chronic, progressive, incurable disease, and that they are not responsible.

A list of modern-day leaders in the field of alcoholism would have to include Jean Kirkpatrick. Labeling herself as that kind of old-fashioned drunk who is almost passé, she has focused her interests, experience, and expertise on the treatment of women alcoholics.

Believing that women alcoholics are dealing with not only the problems of drinking, but of low self-image and self-esteem, Jean Kirkpatrick founded Women for Sobriety. She believes that gender plays an important role in the recovery process.

Jean Kirkpatrick, Ph.D., is an alcoholic. She is the founder and executive director of Women for Sobriety, an organization of recovery that helps alcoholic women. Women for Sobriety is located in Quakertown, Pennsylvania.

Jean Kirkpatrick, Ph.D.

Society has a tendency to say, "Oh, look at Charlie, isn't he marvelous; he gave up drinking? Look how wonderful he is. Look at the courage he shows." Then you say, "Well, Mary gave up drinking, too," and society says, "Well, it's about time. Look what she did to Bob's career and how she ruined her children." Society desperately wants women to set the trend, to have some kind of moral fortitude. Society has never been able to accept a disease concept of alcoholism applied to women. As time goes along it will get better, but we've got a long way to go.

Let's face it, there is nothing at all genteel about drinking, for either men or women. A male drunk is not nice to see, but a female drunk is just awful. I can think of myself and the situations I got into when I was drinking, and honestly, I could live to be one hundred years old and I would still feel the waves of humiliation, knowing how terrible I looked and how I displayed myself. I will never forget it. What's necessary is for society to have a forgiving and accepting attitude, not necessarily a tolerant one.

I was leading a Women for Sobriety group in Allentown, and said, "Now, let's go around the room and let's talk about alcoholism." Not a single woman would talk about it. I asked, "Why?" They said, "We're not alcoholics." "What do you think you are?" I asked. And they said, "We have a drinking problem, but we're not alcoholics." There wasn't a single woman in that group who would accept the fact and say that she was an *alcoholic*. This was six months into their having stopped drinking. That's because of the stigma of a woman alcoholic. It's much easier for a woman to say to her husband, to her family, and to herself, "Well, I have a drinking problem and I'm doing something about it," but still not accept the terrible name "alcoholic." My eyes were really opened. It's so hard for a woman to say "I am an alcoholic."

We downplay that statement now in Women for Sobriety. I know I'm frequently criticized for this, but I feel if semantics are going to keep somebody from getting help, it's stupid. It's just ludicrous for us, as an organization, to say, "You cannot come in here and use this program unless you say you're an alcoholic." So we don't make a big deal about it. If they quit drinking and accept the fact that they have a drinking problem and can't drink again, down the road they will be able to say, "I really am an alcoholic." That might be three years in the offing, but so what? It doesn't make a bit of difference. We have accomplished what we needed to do. We have stopped that woman from drinking, and she has accepted that she must never drink again.

There is a slight possibility she may try to drink again, but we pound it into everybody that they cannot handle alcohol so they are able to say, "I cannot handle alcohol, that's why I'm here."

I think the symptoms of being an alcoholic are exactly the same for men and women. We drink because we're worried, we're bored, we're tired, we're frustrated, we're angry, or we just want to get drunk. Lots of people use alcohol in that way on rare occasions, but some of us begin to depend on it. Any time we use it outside of a social gathering, we are obviously using it for some kind of crutch.

An alcoholic is somebody who drinks at inappropriate times: to help herself be popular, to help get over worry, to get over sorrow, to get over grief, to get over bills. It's somebody who depends on alcohol to get her through hard times. It's someone who drinks a lot nonsocially and someone who drinks uncontrollably at one time or another, no matter how much time intervenes.

A woman may be an alcoholic if every time she has a fight with her husband she's been drinking; every time she has an upset she drinks; every time she has a problem like a broken tooth she drinks. All these are signs.

The alcoholic woman who is at home has greater freedom. She is able to drink all day long and then has time to sober up before her family arrives. This is quite different from the pattern of the woman in the work place, who really tries to hang together during working hours and then falls apart in the evening. The loneliness and isolation for the woman at home is devastating. Working it out with a sociological timetable, we find that women alcoholics in this country adversely affect the lives of thirty-eight million children. They affect not only their own children but their children's friends. Often a child will have to say, "We can't play here. Mommy is sick again." A continued pattern of children seeing their mother in this devastation is tragic.

The woman alcoholic has almost no self-image. Almost never is she able to sit down and see herself in a clear-cut way. She sees herself as being victimized, and she usually is. She sees herself as being inordinately helpless, and she usually is. She doesn't have to be that way, but most women alcoholics are rather helpless and ill equipped for life. She is most victimized by herself because of the feeling of helplessness. "I can't do it. I'm not capable. I'm not able." She is overwhelmed by life.

Women often don't have any kind of picture of themselves. In doing workshops I have asked women to write ten positive words about themselves in twenty-five seconds. They cannot do it. When a woman talks about herself, she will say her name and something like "Well, we moved here. My children go to P.S. 74. My husband works at Bethlehem Steel." You can talk to her for ten minutes and you won't learn one single thing about that woman. She has such a low opinion of herself that she doesn't feel you are interested in her.

Often she is totally dependent on the husband who keeps her within the family unit. If that unit is shattered through divorce or separation, the woman in recovery will have great difficulty because she is alone at that point. For such women alcoholics to recover, it takes a double thrust because they must quickly grow up and learn how to be self-sufficient, to take care of themselves and their children, and to have some kind of decent feeling about themselves.

In the case of the woman alcoholic, I don't

184

think she's the last one to know. I think she's the last one to admit it. I know, even though I drank for twenty-seven years, that until the last day I didn't want to admit it. I knew it all the time, but I didn't want to admit it.

I'm really glad the old-time alcoholic that I am is almost no longer around. The women who come to Women for Sobriety groups are women who have drunk five, ten, maybe fifteen years, tops. That's terrific. It shows some kind of progress because they haven't let themselves get so run down. More and more, humiliation, rather than ill health, as in my case, brings them in.

I first began to drink in high school, when I felt on the edge of things. I always felt that I was a wallflower. As I look back on it now, I wasn't. I just felt that way. When I drank just a couple of drinks, I felt terrific. I felt popular. I felt charismatic. I felt dynamic. I drank because it made me feel loaded with personality, charged up, personality-plus. It made me feel on top of the world.

I was in a serious automobile accident in my senior year of high school; it was not from drinking, but it postponed my going to college for a year. So I went to Pierce Business College in Philadelphia, and I am not a Pierce Business College type. To compound the disappointment of not going away to a regular college, I had to settle for a college I considered second-rate. I started drinking seriously during that year. As I look back on it now, I was an out-and-out

185

alcoholic by the time I was seventeen. When I was eighteen, I enrolled in Pierce, but I didn't go to classes. The boys would get liquor for me. Can you imagine? At eighteen I'd give them money, and they would go out and buy me a pint of whiskey. I didn't feel much ill effect from it, physically. They thought my requests were unusual, of course, but it wasn't considered ladylike to go to a bar or buy a bottle myself, so I did it that way.

I finally went away to college, but I was thrown out of several of them for drinking. I didn't go to class; I just drank. To think that I kept at it until I was way up into my forties is incredible. Incredible. The suffering that I put so many other people through, the suffering I put myself through. I just couldn't quit drinking.

I have kept a diary since 1954, and I got out the diary the other night. I couldn't believe what I was reading. I could not believe how many years —not days, years of my life—were spent in drunkenness. I have written across page after page—Drunk. The next day—Recovery. Drunk— Recovery. Drunk Drunk Drunk. Years and years and years of my life went right down the drain. I could not quit drinking. I worked out how many years of my life I really worked. It was actually a total of only nine years before I quit drinking.

One time I was in a mental hospital for a year, for drinking and drugs. Three times in hospitals, total. I got so sick. I tried so many times to quit. I would start, quit, start. Finally, everybody who had stuck by me left me—and they had stuck by me a long time. I don't believe I have ever been quite as frightened as when I realized how really sick I was, how dependent on the bottle I was, and how everybody had gone. I was really alone. I think that made me straighten up faster than anything. I was so sick. Nothing was functioning anymore. When I took a drink, I'd never know what was going to happen. I'd regurgitate or I'd get the hiccups or I'd start sneezing. My body just said, "I've had it," and it quit. I was lucky.

Until the day I actually quit, I couldn't conceive of life without alcohol. At first, even after I'd quit, I didn't permit myself to think that I would never be able to drink again. For the first three to five years, I always kept an open door. Maybe a cure would be found or a magic pill would come along. Now I'm happy to be free of it. If anybody asked me to drink now, I wouldn't. It just seems dumb to me.

I don't think there should be just one self-help program for alcoholics. I don't think there should be just two. I think there should be three, four, five, six, seven, eight, nine, ten. There should be different choices among self-help groups. So far, the program that has shown the greatest success rate is AA.

AA is a marvelous program. The fact that it has worked and lasted for so long speaks to its greatness. I only hope that Women for Sobriety lasts as long and can be so self-contained. Then we'll have something to crow about. It's going to take time to see if it will. My belief was that women needed something that spoke specifically to their needs, which are gender oriented. That's how Women for Sobriety came into being. Many of our members use both AA and our program. Others just use the Women for Sobriety program.

Our program is based on a concept: that the things which we think become our reality. That is the whole philosophical basis of the program. We begin by realizing that our images become the reality of life. I cannot have a reality unless I first have the idea; idea and image precede action.

Before, I used to think, I'm nobody, I'm no good, I'm nothing and nobody loves me. I acted out those negative thoughts, and that is exactly the way society dealt with me. Society turned me off and rejected me. Then I could say, "See, they rejected me, poor little me," and I could crawl into my shell, take my bottle and cry, isolate myself and get drunk.

In Women for Sobriety we reverse that process by saying, "I am a competent person. I know I am a competent person. I am capable and caring. I am compassionate. I am a loving person." The idea is to know these things in idea, to know them and see them clearly; then, even without our doing it consciously, we act them out. In acting this out we change our whole lives. It changes our entire attitude about how we will be as people. We become competent people and that is how we recover.

All Women for Sobriety "statements" promote

developing a positive person. We begin with, "I have a drinking problem that once had me." We accept our disease and the responsibility to take care of it. We are in charge of that disease, and we pick up a drink or we don't. "I am what I think," shows that we can control our lives. We learn that problems bother us only to the degree that we permit them to. We can control those things that bother us. We are in control of our reactions, and we are in control of our actions. That is very important. A key in our program is, "The past is gone forever." This is an especially important concept for women. We have gone through so much humiliation and, unfortunately, families and society tend to remind us of it.

We also have two statements which deal with learning how to accept love and how to give love, because alcoholic women—and alcoholic men, too—have a lot of trouble loving. We have statements dealing with negativity and statements dealing with encouraging acceptance of life and enthusiasm for life. The fundamental object of life, we say, is emotional and spiritual growth. In regard to acceptance we say, "I am a competent woman," and we accept the responsibility to help others. Those are, in a few words, some of the principles and philosophies of Women for Sobriety. Recovery is really dependent on coming to grips with one's inner self and then growing.

I believe that many things can't be talked about in mixed male-female groups. Not because they are so secret but because men and women often don't share interests and frustrations. I've heard men say, "She's always talking about the baby diapers and the wash." But these are her frustrations. She might say of him, "All he ever talks about is business, business, business." Those things which frustrate a man or a woman might in some cases be boring to someone of the opposite sex. Separate groups help greatly in the beginning. I'm certainly not opposed to mixed groups, by any means, but there is a great advantage to all-male or all-female groups within the self-help movement.

Considering the fact that AA has been in existence since 1935 and that we started in 1975, our acceptance has been very swift. But not enough women are in the recovery process. I don't know exactly why, but I have an idea. My feeling is that most programs over the years have unconsciously been male oriented, male directed. They've assumed that an alcoholic is an alcoholic, period. As far as the disease is concerned, of course an alcoholic is an alcoholic, but these alcoholics we're talking about are also men and women. We have overlooked that all these years.

It appears that recovery rates for men are very high and recovery rates for women low. Therapists and counselors have said for years that we're uncooperative, too hard to deal with, too neurotic, too emotional. No one has ever said, "Maybe we're not reaching women." But it's beginning to change. Treatment facilities are beginning to advertise programs for women. And that's the way it should be. It's changing, but we've got to do a lot more. We have put too much emphasis on talking just about alcoholism, not male alcoholics and female alcoholics.

Gale Storm had a proper upbringing in Texas and knew all about being a lady. She never took a drink until after she was married and was never a loud-mouthed or falling-down alcoholic. Like so many women alcoholics Gale was a controlled drinker and she drank out of view of the public. She never wanted anyone to suspect. As Gale puts it, "To say alcoholism snuck up on me is the understatement of the year."

After several doctors and three hospitals, Gale ended up at Raleigh Hills, a treatment center for alcoholism, where she finally understood the disease concept of alcoholism and quit drinking through counterconditioning therapy.

Gale Storm is an alcoholic. A former film star, she played the lead in the television series "My Little Margie" and "Oh! Susanna." Gale and her husband, Lee Bonnell, live in California.

Gale Storm

I never saw other people as bad. I only saw myself as bad. When I went through Raleigh Hills Hospital, I felt terrible. I just wanted to bury my head under the bed and stay there. When your face is so recognizable, people talk about you. I was afraid, but I was also bent on getting help. I'd tried three hospitals before that, and there had been a consistent pattern of failure. I was desperate. I went in there hoping and praying, "Oh, God, if this can just stop me from drinking. Why can't I stop this? What's the matter with me? Why can't I use my will power? I'm hurting myself, I'm hurting my family." This hammering at myself was constant; and I couldn't control my drinking. It was the most frightening thing in the world. I never thought I'd fall in love with a hospital, but I love that hospital.

By the time I went to Raleigh Hills I was getting up at night to go to the bathroom at fairly regular intervals because I could also go to the kitchen. Nobody else was awake. I could go to the kitchen and I could have a drink. My body was demanding it. I hated myself. I would never treat another person the way I was treating myself then. I shudder to think of the horrible things that I told myself. I degraded myself constantly. My sense of self-worth was down the drain. I loathed myself. I didn't need anybody to say one unkind word to me because I had said them all.

I could not quit drinking; I couldn't. I tried, but it was always with me. I thought, Well I can stop if I want to. Tonight I won't have anything to drink. The few times I tried it, I would sit there with people I knew, and in a very short time feel as if I was in the fringe area. I would hate that 7-Up I was holding. I'd find myself getting angrier and angrier. Not angry at anybody else because they could drink, but angry at myself. I turned it all inward, frustrated that they could all enjoy themselves and I had to sit there like a stone. All I wanted to do was go home. I was miserable.

I was such a lady. I paced my time drinking so that I would never be drunk and reeling around, a loud-mouthed woman. There is no such thing as an attractive, cute, funny, drunken woman, and I was walking on eggs because I didn't want anybody ever to suspect. I'd ask Lee when he'd come home from the office if he had talked to anybody about me or my drinking. I couldn't stand that. It hurt me terribly to have that kind of image.

When I was growing up in Texas, I was taught that liquor was bad. I was always the nice girl. But when you start to really drink, it's compulsive. It was terribly frightening. Hiding bottles, sneaking drinks, adding to drinks—these things were completely foreign to the way I had been raised. When Lee and I were first married I didn't drink. I had never tasted liquor. If Lee even accepted a drink when somebody offered it, he'd get a glare from me. But we'd go out to social functions, and I got so I'd have drinks, too. I cultivated a taste for it. I liked the feeling it gave me. My drinking didn't seem to increase, so I had no warning that I could have an alcohol problem. I very seldom had hang-overs, because I didn't drink that much. I can't even visualize when I started heavy drinking. Many people can find some traumatic experience to blame it on. Well, I didn't have one single thing to blame. To say alcoholism snuck up on me is the understatement of the year.

Eventually I began to hide bottles because Lee gave me a bad time. He'd start by saying, "Honey, we've got to talk about your drinking." And I'd say, "Look it just so happens that I can drink more than other people. I just drink. Some people can." I would use all those excuses on him. I'd be indignant or I'd be angry. The tension between us was terrible. And my drinking got worse and worse.

I looked terrible. I was used to having a nice trim figure. I never had to diet or anything and here I was wearing A-frame dresses. I could not wear one thing. My liver was four times its normal size. I looked six months pregnant. The first hospital I went to was UCLA, for a biopsy. They did a whole bunch of other tests, too. The doctor told both of us, "You have four choices: you can go to AA, stop cold turkey, go for psychiatric help, or die." Those were my four choices. I tried AA and I can't say AA didn't work for me. I just didn't let AA work for me, and if you don't let it, it won't.

I went to see an endocrinologist before I saw the psychiatrist. He talked to me plain and simple about the alternatives you have if you're an alcoholic. Lee and I were going away for a long weekend, and I said, "I'm not going to have a drink all the time we're there. I will not take a bottle." And I meant it. That was a long weekend and I didn't have a drink. I was proud of myself for that. I couldn't wait to tell the doctor because I thought he would be so pleased. I said to him, "Guess what? Lee and I went away for a long weekend and I didn't have one drink the whole time. How about that? That's the first time I've ever been able to do that for three to four days." He looked at me and he said, "Are you kidding?" I said, "No, I'm not kidding. I wanted you to know that because that would be a little bit of a step forward." Then he said, "You know that's not true." I said, "Why would I tell you if it's not?" He said, "I don't care what you say, all drunks are liars, they are cheats, they are sneaks, they are never to be trusted." I got so mad that I yelled at him. I really told him off. I said, "That is the most awful thing to say to a person. Do you know what you are saying to me? You are telling me that you will not accept anything I say as truth." He said, "Alcoholics will never tell the truth." He didn't add, "as long as you're drinking or unless you get help." That hurt me so badly. I got so mad at him, I was ready to kill him.

Now, the stigma of going to a psychiatrist was as bad as alcoholism, as far as I was concerned. But Lee found a psychiatrist who was recommended by our church. I don't think I went more than a week. Every time I went I would just rack my brain all the way over there, trying to think of things I could tell him. I felt he was looking at his watch most of the time. Did I hate my mother? Did they beat me as a child? I thought to myself, Even if we decided what caused my drinking, then what would that do? How would that stop me from drinking? He said he felt that the right thing to do, what would help me the most, would be to put me in Cedars-Sinai psychiatric ward. I didn't like the idea but I said, "If you say that's going to help me, that's what I'll do," and that's what I did.

There was an experience. I went in for seven days. I hurt so for the other people but I kept thinking, Maybe they're going to help me. They had group therapy. I had never experienced group therapy and I thought, Maybe this will do it. I got so I said, "I'm an alcoholic" to the group and I'd burst into tears. I admitted it and I thought maybe that was the key, to be able to say it. I left because I had been booked for a theater in Arizona, but I promised I would come back in.

When Lee left me there the second time I was hanging on to his coattail. I was screaming and crying when those doors shut. They put me in with a roommate who was manic-depressive. They let me go home some weekends, and Lee said he couldn't believe it. I would sit like a vegetable, I was taking so much medication. Lee took me out of there and right over to Las Encinas, which was like heaven because the other had been so bad. I stayed there for several months. I came home on the weekends and drank. Lee didn't know about it, except for one time when I was on Antabuse and had a drink. My Lord, I turned beet red. Your respiration can stop with that; it scared the living daylights out of both of us. I never did admit what caused it. I started drinking again when I left Las Encinas for good. Immediately, as soon as I got home. Just as I had before.

Finally I went to Raleigh Hills. When Lee took me, I said, "Honey, I cannot answer all those questions. I can't. You know all the answers better than I do." He said, "Don't worry, I'll answer them for you." So the only thing that the counselor asked me was what did I drink. I told him, vodka. In about two minutes, a nurse appeared at the door with a tray and two glasses on it, one with water and one with vodka. I thought I'd died and gone to heaven. They were bringing me vodka. That's how they detox you, on the poison you've been putting into your own body. They don't have television. They don't have radio. They want you focused in on liquor all the time. They want you to have complete concentration on the bottle. They bring you a drink every two hours for a certain length of time, night or day. They wake you up and give you that vodka or whatever you drink. Then you dwindle down to every three hours. Then it stops. This is all within four to five days. Your body becomes stabilized. If they had been giving me pills, I wouldn't have made any connection with what they were doing to detox me. It kept my mind right on the bottle.

After you have had the detox, you have a complete physical, and then you start your first "treatment." I prefer to call it counter-conditioning rather than aversion. The principle is that you have to condition yourself to learn to drink, as I know I had. Gradually I had gotten used to the taste of it and to enjoying the way it made me feel. This is conditioning your body and your mind. What Raleigh Hills does is reverse that process and use psychological counter-conditioning; they build you up again so you think you're worth something. The aversion therapy, or counterconditioning, takes place every other day for five days—about fourteen days in all. Every other day you have a "treatment." The treatment nurse is very important. She has to be a well-trained, skilled person because each patient is different. You get up at 5:30 and you've had nothing to eat from before 12:00 the night before. There's nothing in your stomach except liquid. You've just had tea or coffee or water. You go into a small room where there are shelves all around with every kind of booze you've ever seen in your life. Many I had never heard of. She has these glasses lined up. They give you an injection of Emetine. They have in front of you a full-length mirror. You watch yourself. The nurse talks to you the whole time. She's talking about alcoholism and the good things about not drinking—it's very positive. You're in there only about twenty minutes. They'll start you out with vodka; it would vary every treatment—vodka, gin, bourbon, beer, wine. Of course, you start to upchuck after you have had a drink. Emetine adds to your nausea, and you start getting very nauseated. You get so sick that you upchuck again and again. It's just liquid so it's not quite as revolting as it sounds, but, of course, it's not pleasant, either.

There are five treatment days, one every other day. Every morning, the doctor makes his rounds and checks on you. They also have round-table discussions and they are marvelous. I found out from the doctor at the first round table I went to that alcohol affects every cell in your body. He made me understand that your brain cells are affected, too—that's a real grabber. They also focused on things like self-assertiveness. I had no idea I had given up so much, such as the right to an opinion. I didn't know I'd given that up, but I had. I didn't feel worthy.

After the stay there, you go back for what are called recaps for one year. The first recap is two weeks after you leave. The second one is four weeks after you've been out. The third one is six weeks. In other words, the time since you left gets wider and wider, but you are still cementing. They find that if a person doesn't go back, it's very easy for him or her to start drinking again.

When I was released from Raleigh Hills, I was really afraid to leave. I thought, Oh, my God, what if I react like I did every other time? The minute I plunk down in my regular surroundings, will I head right for the vodka? I didn't know for sure, but I felt I wouldn't because I had learned so much and I understood so much. That was the first hospital where they told me it was a disease. If they had said that to me in any other hospital I went to, I would have gotten off my back sooner. I wouldn't have been so hard on myself, because I would have known that it was a disease. It isn't a case of using will power, doing it yourself. Those other hospitals didn't know what to do with an alcoholic, because they were not hospitals for alcoholism. If they don't know about it, how are they going to help a patient?

When I came home from Raleigh Hills, I didn't want to drink. Not one bit. And I knew that for sure. Not too long after I had gotten out, I was sitting by myself at the dining table, reading a book. All of a sudden I started to laugh out loud, which is strange when you are alone. I just laughed and laughed because it was so wonderful. I felt so good. I had absolutely no temptation. I expected to have circumstances or situations that mght lead to drinking, that I would have to fight temptation at times. I fully expected that. I just assumed that was part of it. But what I was feeling was freedom. What a beautiful word, I thought, *freedom*. How marvelous. I hadn't had a word for it before. The feeling was freedom. When I considered what Raleigh Hills had done for me I thought that it had to be something God had planned for me. At first I had thought, What a waste those three other hospitals were—the pain, the suffering. What a waste, when all the time, here it was. Then I realized it wasn't a waste at all. If I had not had those prior experiences, those failures, the three hospitals where I failed completely, I would not have had nearly as firm a foundation for stopping. I feel that God planned the whole thing. I was never ready until I went to Raleigh Hills. And in all the time since then I have not had one split second of temptation. Nothing. That's the metamorphosis. I'm born again. I came out of the cocoon. I changed.

"I am the exception," says Grace Slick and cautions you not to compare your drinking with hers. However, like so many alcoholics, Grace did compare herself, when she was drinking and drugging, to those around her and didn't see herself as different. Just the opposite of Gale Storm, Grace's drinking and drug use was very public. In the rock world, the more bizarre the behavior, the better. One of the most common characteristics of the alcoholic personality is a change in behavior after drinking. It was always after alcohol and/or drug use that Grace's Jekyll-and-Hyde personality changed.

Grace Slick is an alcoholic. She is a writer and the female lead singer with the highly successful rock group Jefferson Starship.

Grace Slick

I didn't see myself as being different. Everybody around me had a drug of choice that they were using to the fullest extent. I would see people around me whom I considered to be straight and I'd think, How sad for them. How very boring their lives must be. I didn't have a particularly ugly time with drinking. I enjoyed it most of the time. It gives up when it's going to give up on an individual, and it gave up on me when I was somewhere around thirty-four or thirty-five. It started losing its fun value.

It wasn't as awful as it could have been, and I thought I'd never say this in my life, but one of the reasons I quit drinking is that I was caught by the highway patrol before I was ready to stop. If I were still going now, I would be miserable. I'm very stubborn and real stupid as far as continuing anything that I like. I'd still be going at it and wondering why my life was just awful. Fortunately, the highway patrol in California is very strict, and they caught up with me before I caught up with myself. The highway patrol was definitely ready for me to stop. My behavior helped in that. I was not a closet kind of pass-out drunk. I was real obvious. I mean, I'd be numb and telling everybody where to get off or driving 125 miles an hour. That made it easier for other people to make me aware of it. But I thought I was having a great time and everybody was spoiling my fun. The denial system that I had, that most alcoholics have, was very strong.

I'd say to myself, "The odds of having an automobile accident if you have driven for twenty years are very high, drunk or sober. So what if I have an automobile accident?" It's that kind of denial. The fact that alcohol may have precipitated my fighting with the band, was not something I was going to look at. The same attitude applied with people calling me an alcoholic. I'd think, yeah, probably, so what? The business of taking drugs to an extreme was hardly unusual in my circle.

Is your nose stuffed up? Snort a little coke. Tired from jet lag? Snort a little coke. Want to calm down a bit? Have a little alcohol. You want to do this? Have a little of that. There was always something for everything. It is hard to figure out that something that has been your friend, basically, and has given you joy for a long period of time has turned on you. Nobody wants to admit it, believe it, or acknowledge it.

I'm an old person in a young person's business. I was old when I got started. I was twenty-six when I got started in rock 'n' roll. So the first thing was alcohol. The second was definitely marijuana. Then, I think, cocaine. A lot of people had pills, but for some reason I didn't like the way they looked. I guess most of the pills were speed, and I'm pretty wired already, so I didn't think I needed that. Later on I did Quaaludes and acid. But my drugs of choice were cocaine and alcohol, because they feed each other, or Quaaludes and cocaine.

There is an old saying, "Let's go get para-lyzed," and it refers to alcohol. It's from my parents' generation. Well, one night I was in a recording studio, sitting cross-legged on the floor and reading some lyrics. I had a bottle of wine. I was leaning against the wall and all of a sudden I couldn't move anything but my eyes and my mouth. I could speak, but the rest of my body couldn't move. I was scared shit. I did not know what was happening. I thought it was some hor-rible disease. I had them call the doctor. He was sort of a rock-'n'-roll doctor, who said, "How much have you had?" I said, "Oh, hell, I don't know." He said, "You're paralyzed." I said, "Yes, I know I'm paralyzed. What is it? I'm scared." He said, "You just drank too much." I said, "No shit?" And he said, "Yes, just sit there and wait awhile." And, sure enough, pretty soon I was able to move. I had actually paralyzed myself. The odd thing was that I wasn't drunk enough to pass out. Apparently it was my body chemistry at that time.

I had a good childhood. I liked my parents. I can't remember feeling different as a child, or unusual. In high school I was a cheerleader. That's what I wanted to do. I hung out with the crowd I wanted to hang out with. College the same thing. But I did something I guess I should have noticed at the time, back in high school. On Fridays everybody would decide who they were going out with. But my girlfriend and I would

204

say, "We're going out with Gordon Gilbey. We're both going out with Gordon Gilbey." Gordon's and Gilbey's are brands of gin, of course. Her parents drank Gilbey's, mine drank Gordon's. We'd get one of each. That's who we went out with. She and I would go out and get paper cups, about five of them, because gin eats its way through the cups. That alone should tell you about drinking the stuff. Anyway, we'd just sit around and drink gin.

I got a good job early, made a lot of money. I've enjoyed the people I've been with. There is absolutely no excuse for my abuse of alcohol. People say, "Well, you were always drinking a lot because, because, because, because . . ." I think it's a genetic disorder, myself, and it slips right by you. You can become an alcoholic/addict simply by continued overuse.

In all the times I've had run-ins with the police in the car, it was never moving. I've never been stopped. There is no number for my offense in the vehicle code, I don't think. Drunk Mouth is what I call it.

Once I was sitting with a book, a bottle of wine, and some cheese, being arty. I think I was reading poetry—in a pickup truck in the hills of Marin County—and a cop came by. I was having a loaf of bread and wine and cheese. He came by and said, "I'm going to arrest you for sitting half in and half out of your truck, drunk in public." If I'd had my wits about me, like most women when they get arrested, I would have said, "Oh, officer . . ." Women pull that, and a lot of times it works. Not I. What do I do? "Drunk in what public?" I say. "What do you mean? What are we talking about, the trees, these deer here, these leaves on the ground? What public? You're the only public here, and if you hadn't stopped you wouldn't et cetera, et cetera." I'm doing that to a cop. So of course, I go down for Drunk Mouth.

Another time I was driving my Aston Martin about 125 miles an hour over Waldo Grade. I didn't bother to check the oil gauge. So, down at the bottom of a hill, on the Richardson Bridge, smoke and flames started coming out of the engine. I pulled the car over. Someone in a Volkswagen pulled over and said, "Do you want me to get the highway patrol for you?" I said, "Yes, please." So he went and got the highway patrol. This cop weighs 205 pounds and has his thumbs hooked in his belt, which has a potbelly over it. I just didn't like the looks of him. He said, "O.K., what's going on here?" Remember, there are flames coming out of my car. I said, "What the fuck does it look like is going on? I'm having a goddamn party at four A.M. with fucking flames coming out of my car." That's the way I'm talking to him. "Down to the Civic Center, you drunk," he says. Drunk Mouth, again.

The other time I was fighting with Paul Kantner; that's when I was living with Paul. I was driving. We were mad at each other for something. We were going slow, and he pulled the keys out of the Aston Martin, threw them out the window, opened the door, and walked home. The reason he did that is because he didn't want me to be able to follow him and badger him, in case I wanted to keep fighting. He wanted me to have to look for the keys so he could run down the block and get out. So the Aston Martin is in the middle of the street—can't move without the keys. I'm over on this woman's lawn on my hands and knees, looking for the keys to my car. I had had two drinks, which smelled. The cops came by. "What are you doing on your hands and knees? What about this car in the middle of the street?" I said, "Oh, I do this all the time on purpose. I throw my keys." I'd just start in on the cops when I was drunk. Down to the city again. It was always my reaction to them that got me into trouble. It was violent, offensive.

We're talking about Jekyll and Hyde. Yes, real pleasant. There's a little hole in the rafter in my home. It's a bullet hole. One night I couldn't remember if I'd ever fired a gun, so I just fired it straight up at the ceiling. I liked weapons. Another night I heard some kids outside my house, so I chased them with a samurai sword. I was home alone and I was scared. Instead of waiting or listening the way I would sober, to see if it was just kids, I decided some people were coming to get me, and I got the samurai sword and ran out there like a madman.

The California Highway Patrol sent me to my first AA meeting. One of the people down there at the Civic Center said, "Take a card and go to AA and get the card signed." It was kind of like parole. "No," I said, "you don't understand, I can pay for my own dinner." I thought AA was like St. Vincent de Paul's, where they give drunks free meals. I couldn't figure out what she was telling me. Anyway, I took this little card and had it signed so they'd know I had been to the meeting. And I liked it. I didn't resent it or anything. It was very interesting. I loved hearing the stories. These were real people. These God-awful horror stories. I was just amazed.

AA basically ruined my drinking. They did a real good job, which I'm glad about now. When you go back to drinking, the alcohol still works, but it isn't quite as much fun after being at those meetings and discovering you're an alcoholic. You think, What the hell are you doing, killing yourself, you jerk?

I'm very comfortable around AA because it's a part of my life now. It was not then, it was sort of an excursion. It was like going to study voice lessons for six months. I was interested, I paid attention, but it was not part of my life. It was like going to a movie. Six months into it, I thought, That's enough of that. Now I'll get drunk. And I did. I went out and tried drinking again. My husband was right on top of it. The next morning he took me to Duffy's, which is sort of an Olympic swimming pool retreat. It's a good place. Once again I went back to AA. I'd go to the meetings for another six months, liking it, saying, "I'm an alcoholic," but not buying the progression. I'm still thinking my problem is the car and my sarcastic mouth.

The last time I drank was in New York City. I was going on national television. From singing, I'm used to using my mouth and I don't worry about slurring my words, so I was going to try controlled drinking. It didn't work. I hated it. Within half an hour I thought, Oh, God, and went out and kept having more. So I kept drinking all day. I woke up the next morning. I knew that I had been on television. I knew that much, and that was all. I had been in a blackout the whole time.

My heart just sank. All my friends, my parents, my daughter, the band—everybody knew I had stopped drinking. I've blown it, I thought, on national television. It was the only time in my life I've ever felt close to being suicidal, thinking, You're the biggest asshole in the world. Nobody would be in AA and go out and drink on national television. Nobody's that stupid.

I called the record company to find out what had happened. I was scared to ask because I had a real flamboyant mouth, and I didn't know what the hell I had said on television. "What did I do last night, Barbara?" I asked. "Oh, nothing," she said. "You were fairly lucid most of the time." She was real casual. She said, "What's the matter?" Finally I got out of her that it was a pilot and on tape, not a live show. The pilot never sold, so in the end it didn't matter. But I had scared myself. That's when I started taking the AA program real seriously. If you're that out of control, you need a lot of help.

Today I don't like to fight with people, but when I was drinking there was usually somebody whom I had offended either the night before, or the week before. There was always something abrasive in the air because I hadn't quite cleaned up something I had done while drunk. There was always something going on that had to do with my drinking. It could either be direct, like mouthing off at somebody, or it could be indirect, something I was not doing because of drug use or alcohol, like not taking my daughter China to the beach. I know several people today who are having trouble recognizing the effects of their drug use because the offense is what they are not doing. It is easy for these people to deny their own problem when they compare themselves with me. I'm real flamboyant. It was perfectly obvious: cars, police, badmouthing people, staging stuff. That is not the rule. I'm the exception, and I want to keep reminding people of that. That is not the rule of alcoholism. It is usually a slower, grimmer process, and it's usually sins of omission rather than commission. I was really obvious. I got paid to be that way. The more flamboyant you are, the more they come to see you. It was the same with Keith Moon, Joe Cocker, and Alice Cooper. The weirder you get, the more people love it. It feeds your addiction. I feel bad about that because it is such a convenient thing for a lot of people I know to say, "I've never done anything like that." What is happening to them is the more common problem, which is not taking care of business. I always showed up, and people were sorry I showed up. For most people, it's not showing up for work, not talking to the kid because you have a headache, not doing what you're supposed to do. I wish they didn't have my example to hang on to.

God, I wish I could say something that would make everybody believe that it's O.K., that it's wonderful to stop drinking. People who are the type of alcoholic I am, whatever that is, are afraid of a boring life. "I guess this is the end of my life, because I've got to stop drinking. I guess now it's all downhill." Well, it isn't. You find that you are perfectly capable of having a great time—and you can get so much more done. I know that any positive thought that comes into my head about me and alcohol is nuts. Alcohol is not an option for me.

7 *Alcoholism and Homosexuality*

It is estimated by the professionals in the field of alcoholism that as many as one in four homosexuals is an alcoholic. Alcohol plays a pivotal role in the gay lifestyle, whether the homosexual is "out of the closet" or a member of "the invisible society," whether the homosexual is comfortable with his or her sexual identity or not.

Because of the hostile reaction of the general population toward homosexuality, gays tend to feel more comfortable in their own bars or at private home parties. Alcohol is very much a part of both scenes.

Some homosexuals are so tortured by their homosexuality that they isolate themselves totally from everyone. In this case alcohol eases the negative feelings about self and passes the time. Many of these alcoholics only place themselves in a position "to be discovered" after drinking.

The homosexual alcoholic must deal with the twin stigmas of alcoholism and homosexuality, and the alcoholic homosexual is faced with a need for accepting both.

As Robert Bauman points out, "God loves all

His children. No matter what they're like, He made them in his image."

Robert Bauman is an alcoholic. He is a former three-term U.S. congressman from Maryland and is now in the private practice of law.

Robert Bauman

The last time I had a drink was on May 1, 1980.

I think my alcoholism definitely had to do with my inability to cope with my personal circumstances. Perhaps the central problem I faced was that I was a man who had been married, at that point, for seventeen or eighteen years, had four children, was Catholic, and was incapable of dealing with my sexuality. One of the driving forces behind my drinking was a desire to escape from all of this. I did not drink to inspire myself to do things in a grandiose way. I didn't need a drink to go out and make a speech. I'd made speeches all my life. I didn't need a drink to get through the day. I drank to escape. I drank for relief from the realities of my life. I drank, in one sense, to muster up courage. My pattern was to drink and then go out and embroil myself in some kind of sexual escapade. Drinking was not facing reality. I wanted to be unconscious of what was happening to my life. The bottle was the easiest way out.

The incidence of alcoholism in gay people is much, much higher than in the general populace.

Often the two go hand in hand. My guess is that if you are gay, with all the problems that presents, many times it leads into drinking as a way out. This is the Catch-22 for gays because the major social forum for gays in this country, at least in the last ten to fifteen years, has been the bars and other places to drink. At the bar you immediately order a drink, two drinks, three drinks. The principal meeting places enhance the possibility of alcoholism. If you have the tendency toward alcoholism, whatever the source of that tendency—genetic, environmental, behavioral—and you can argue over that—if you have the tendency and you are into cruising and bars in the gay community, you're set up. You are an accident waiting to happen.

On the other hand, if you're home isolated and unable to express your feelings toward other people and you're all bottled up, that's a good reason to uncork the bottle. And a lot of people do that too.

My father was an alcoholic. I cannot argue in favor of any genetic connection in my case, though, because I was an adopted child. He was alcoholic enough that he eventually associated himself with organizations that sobered him up, and the last three to four years of his life he was dry. He had to be because his alcoholism affected his work and his family situation.

When I was a small child, I recall, particularly at holiday times, my father would get smashed. He was then an accomplished musician, well placed in dance orchestras in the East. Inevitably, he would have to have a series of Christmas parties for the band. He was a home movie buff in the thirties and forties and fifties, so I can watch myself grow up on 16-millimeter film. A lot of these films were taken at his parties, and Dad was always smashed. There he is on film, crocked. And there I am, little Bobby, two, three, four, five years old, being handed a little shot glass of beer. That was my reward for coming down in the middle of the night when these parties got loud and I woke up.

At some point in my childhood I purposely and consciously formed a decision not to drink, because of my father's problem. He wasn't violent. He didn't beat me. He got angry sometimes and he'd hit me when he was drunk, but he wasn't a father who constantly beat me when he was drunk. He only did that if he was really angry. He would more likely fall asleep. When he was sober, he didn't seem interested in me. When he was drunk, he was only interested up to the point where he was angry, and then he'd sort of drift out of it and go to sleep, so I can't complain of child abuse.

I came to the opinion that I wasn't going to drink at an early age. And I did not drink until I was nineteen or twenty years old and in college. I scrupulously avoided it, even when all of my peers in high school were drinking beer. I just didn't. Anytime the occasion would arise, I would say to myself, I don't want to start now.

I started drinking beer in college simply because it was the thing to do. At some point, I convinced myself that drinking beer as a small child never really affected me that much. Dad always drank hard stuff, so I thought maybe beer could be all right. So beer was my only drink. I would tell myself that the other stuff was dangerous, but beer wasn't.

From 1960, when I was married, I started drinking wine—I guess I was about twenty-two or twenty-three. My wife liked wine. In fact, our first date was the first time I'd ever had a glass of wine, white wine. I developed a taste for that. And now and then I'd get drunk. It really didn't become a problem until the early 1970s, after I had been elected to public office. My pattern was not to drink in public unless it was an obligatory glass or two at meals or at a social function.

When all my difficulties happened in 1980, most people didn't believe I was an alcoholic because almost nobody had ever seen me publicly drunk. In those last years, I started having one or two bourbons before going to a party so I'd be ahead of everybody before I got there. That's a sure sign of alcoholism. In that same period, I would usually drink at home on weekends, when I was away from the public, particularly if I had no functions to go to. The pattern was there. Eventually I started drinking midday, though on week nights I'd always wait until after five. I'd get home and have a drink immediately.

Toward the end, I remember once waking up

lying on my back, looking up at the library ceiling in my house and not knowing why I was there. Dawn was coming up. I vaguely remembered we'd had a dinner party the night before. We'd had guests, and the last thing I remembered was pouring another round. It was a partial blackout because I didn't remember the rest of the evening. I went upstairs to bed with the worst headache that morning and I didn't get up until two in the afternoon. Our guests had stayed overnight, and I was barely able to get up to say good-bye to them.

My wife would often say to me, "Bob, don't you think you've had enough? Aren't you drinking too much?" or "Let me drive." One night I fought with her. I decided I was going to drive an hour and a half back home from a function. I insisted. I had the kind of personality, particularly when drinking, that would get sort of nasty. "I'll do it," I insisted. "I'm going to drive."

At the end, in the winter of 1979-80, it was not unusual for me to leave the House floor, go to my office to sign mail, answer phone calls, and call people back for an hour. It might be eight o'clock or eight-thirty at night when I was through. Then I would have a drink in the office, maybe two. Not big ones, but drinks. After that I'd go to a restaurant with some staff members from the Rules Committee, on which I served, or my own staff. We'd go to a restaurant on Capitol Hill, the Monocle, a watering hole. I would have had two drinks in the office, a couple of double vodka martinis, maybe three, before dinner. I'd help two or three people polish off a bottle of wine during the meal. After the meal, I'd have two or three Irish coffees, then three or four stingers. In the space of two hours I would have consumed all of this alcohol. Then I would get into my own car, sometimes shucking my staff aide who wanted to drive me, and go to a bar and continue drinking. I was doing that one night a week, but it got to be two nights a week, and sometimes three.

Many of the difficulties that came out in the press in 1980 happened when I'd had a full head of booze. I was driving through red lights. I couldn't get out of parking lots. One night, driving home by myself, I ran up on the guardrail. The police officer who responded was someone who knew me and "helped" me by not exposing me. I hadn't injured anybody, though the guardrail was sort of smashed up, and the car had two thousand dollars' worth of damage. It was towed away, and I was taken home in a police car. Now if someone had had me charged with what I should have been charged with, I might have avoided a lot of things that happened later. But that's a might-have-been.

There were a number of times when, having gotten totally boozed up, I would go out to gay bars. I didn't go there very often, but a known member of Congress with congressional license plates doesn't have to go drunk to a gay bar very often—just a few times will be noticed.

I didn't live in Washington. My home was eighty-five miles away from there. Too often, I was getting home at three or four A.M. and getting up at seven A.M. to be back in Washington at nine. Like a lot of other alcoholics, I seemed to have developed an amazing capacity to drink and the stamina to carry this off. I could get up the next morning with a hell of a headache and, by the time I had to be on the floor of the House, I would have shaken it enough to negotiate the rest of the day.

As I've said, I didn't do this every night. And there were periods during those last few years when I would stop drinking for two or three weeks. Another indication of being an alcoholic is that you can stop any time you want to. I went thirty days one time. Then I'd go right back. I couldn't stay stopped.

There was no specific incident that sparked the investigation, but the authorities became interested in me for some reason. I personally feel that there was some political connotation, because the investigation was going on for eight months to a year before I knew it was happening. And it was not revealed until four to five weeks before my 1980 election. There were all kinds of reasons given to justify the investigation. They thought I was a security risk, although there was never any indication that I was revealing information. Once, years ago, a KGB agent from the Russian embassy staff approached me. He wanted to talk conservative politics. I immediately called the FBI. They said, "Talk to him," and afterward they debriefed me. So security wasn't it.

But I had been to a particular gay bar enough times that my name came up in the course of some other police investigation, and a young man who was involved—apparently in an attempt to ameliorate his own circumstance—said, "Hey, I know a congressman," or "My roommate knows a congressman and in exchange for that information could you go light on me?" This was in the press, so I assume there was some validity to it. The FBI approached me in September, six weeks before the election, and said, "Here is what we have." I told them that those events never happened. The U.S. attorney gave my lawyer to understand that they would convene a grand jury and indict me for all of these things, which is the standard practice, whether they could prove them or not; but if I would plead not guilty as a first offender to a charge of solicitation, which is a misdemeanor, then trial and these charges, I stupidly thought, would all be forgotten.

I thought I wouldn't get nearly the publicity by simply pleading not guilty, so that's the course I chose. I was foolish because I was thinking in terms of holding down the political damage. I should have known that because of my position in Congress and the conservative movement, my outspokenness—all those things—it didn't matter what I got into court for, it was going to be notorious. As it turned out, the memos that the U.S. attorney's office processed and the FBI investigative report were both handed to the press. When I went into court, the *Washington Post* had the FBI investigative report. I've never seen it. I tried to get it afterward, but they wouldn't give it to me. So there was no specific incident. It was just my showing up in these gay bars, drinking, making contacts with young men —who, by the way, were adults in the District of Columbia. I was never arrested. I was never dragged into a police station. Nothing like that.

What did happen was that there were situations in which I was involved, always while drinking. I had to get a full head of steam to do these crazy, asinine things. No one in his right mind —and alcoholics are insane in their conduct sometimes —would have done as blatantly and openly what I did as a prominent political figure in Washington.

Of course, a lot of armchair psychiatrists said afterward, "He wanted to be caught." And in a strange way, I think I did. Life had become too much for me. I was overpowered by a lot of things in my life and this was my way of crying for help, of saying, "Do something. I can't. I can't stop drinking. I can't stop doing what I'm doing. Help!" I chose a very dramatic way, a very destructive way to do it.

I wound up with 48.2 percent of the vote in 1980, in a very conservative district, four weeks from the day all this became public. In losing, I also got ninety-one thousand votes, which was nine thousand more than I'd ever gotten when I won. There was a lot of tolerance, a lot of broadmindedness, a lot of support in my district, and I'll always appreciate that.

I had been confronted by my wife in January of 1980, nine months before the election. I took my last drink on May 1. Between January and May, well before the public knew anything, and before I knew about the investigation, I went to my family priest, Father John Harvey, who had been a friend of my wife. I had known him for twenty years. Coincidentally, he is one of the foremost Catholic experts on the subject of homosexuality in the United States.

Carol said she found some gay literature on the seat of my car. It wasn't the first time, and she said, "This can't go on. You must do something. I want you to go see Father Harvey." I called him. I knew Carol well enough, after all of our years together, to know that she meant what she said. I went to see Father Harvey. We met in the House restaurant. Just think of the other people sitting there who could have overheard this conversation. It would have been a lulu for the gossip columnists the next day. This little Irish priest and the Watchdog of the House, as they called me. He just pried the gay aspects out of me, and I also described my drinking. He said, "It seems to me that what's happening there always starts with your drinking. You start out by getting drunk, and then the other things flow from that." Then he said, "I want you to go to see a friend of mine." He recommended a clinical psychologist in the D.C. area, Dr. John Kinnane, who specializes in alcoholism and also in homosexuality problems.

I saw Dr. Kinnane in February, March, and April, and it took him the better part of ninety days to convince me that I was an alcoholic. We didn't get to the gay business. We skirted around that. We talked about it, but I was convinced I wasn't gay, that it was a tendency that had to be dealt with but it wasn't major. I just couldn't face being gay. It was too horrible to talk about. He strongly recommended that I go to organizations that help alcoholics, and he recommended some in the Washington area. I didn't want to go. I didn't want to be seen at a group where alcoholics gathered because I wasn't an alcoholic. It was a terrible blow to my pride to think that I couldn't control myself, that there was anything in my life that I couldn't deal with reasonably and logically and overcome. I could save the world on the floor of Congress. I could save the United States. I had policies for everything. My ego was enormous. I walked all over people who got in my way. To be told that I couldn't pick up a glass of wine and drink it, that was the thing that hit me. One day I said to Dr. Kinnane, "You mean I can never have another glass of white wine over a good piece of fish with my wife at dinner?" And he said, "Never. You can never have another drink. You're an alcoholic. That's my opinion. You are going to have to decide for yourself. No more white wine. No more nothing."

I tried to taper off. I drank only white wine or beer for a while. I did away with the vodka. Then, one last time, on May 1, 1980, I really did it up raw. I drank and drank and wound up in a D.C. hotel. I blacked out. I had lost my car and I woke up the next morning in a place I didn't even know. Fortunately, I did remember that I had an appointment with Dr. Kinnane at eleven. I had the card in my pocket. I found it.

I went to Dr. Kinnane's office; he took one look at me and said, "My God, what's happened to you?" I looked like death warmed over. He picked up the phone and called Wilbur Mills. He took me to a meeting of an organization that helps in these situations. I was deathly afraid that someone was going to recognize me. As soon as I walked in the door, someone, a former member of Congress, did recognize me. I said, "Gee, I didn't know you had this problem." He said, "Yeah, it cost me the U.S. Senate seat. It's good to see you here. If you need help, this is the place to come." Wilbur squired me to a number of meetings until he felt that I was strong enough to keep going on my own. I went about four, five days a week in Washington for the six months I was still in the House.

So before the world knew I had a problem, I had faced the problem to the extent that I could. I had stopped drinking cold turkey in May, and I really felt much better. It took thirty days to clear the system and the brain a little, and I was still going to Dr. Kinnane on a weekly or twice-weekly basis.

I think the thing that finally convinced me that I was an alcoholic was the fact that my life had become unmanageable. Dr. Kinnane kept pointing out to me, "Well, if you're not an alcoholic, why is your wife so upset about it? If you're not an alcoholic, why is your financial situation so terrible? You're a lawyer, you're a congressman, yet you're broke. Why are all these things happening to you, Bob, if you're not an alcoholic? What do you do when you get uptight about all these things that I have been mentioning? You take a drink, don't you? And then, what after? You take another and another." I couldn't hear that twice a week for an hour and not finally recognize that it was me he was talking about. That was what was happening to me. That had happened to me. It had already happened. It keeps going on. Every day it happens. I finally said to myself, "My God, I may well *be* an alcoholic. Look at the mess I've made. Look at the wreck I've made."

Once I stopped drinking and he dried me out, or I dried myself out, we started dealing with other things, I started to think in terms of the inner relations between my personal problems— my sexuality, the pressures of public life, my marriage, my children, and my alcoholism.

I thought things had improved at home. I think

they had. For the first time, I was having to face things like, "How do we pay the mortgage next month?" Or, "What am I going to do about politics?" I found that for the first time in twenty years of marriage, I was talking to my wife. I couldn't avoid arguments by taking a few drinks, so we started talking more. I feel that up to a certain point, our relationship improved. I stopped going to gay bars. I stopped cruising. I was no longer doing the nightly drinking and dining that I described. I was coming home nights. After I'd leave the office, I'd be home in an hour and fifteen minutes. Things changed appreciably. But in early September, when I was confronted by the FBI privately, and then three weeks later in court, that placed a strain on things. The funny thing about it is, as relates to my alcoholism, I thought of taking a drink when all this hit. I also thought of suicide. But I said to myself, "I'm not going to do it." I had heard enough at meetings and in my psychological counseling that I just knew the worst crisis in your life wasn't the place where you needed a drink. It was a place where you needed not to drink. Besides, I wasn't going to give them the satisfaction of jumping off a bridge or starting to drink again. I had just enough ego left, even though it was really getting battered around, that I said to myself, "I'm not going to do it. I'm not going to drink again." Afterward, my doctor said to me, "Boy, if you got through this without a drink, that ought to be damn good proof to you that you're not going to drink again." But alcoholics know that the possibility always exists.

I had been in counseling for about five months and I was two months dry. I was coming back from some social function, and I said to myself, "What would be my reaction now, two months after my drinking has ended, if I went to a gay bar?" I parked the car blocks away from the only gay bar I had been going to, and I went into the bar, just into the vestibule. I didn't stand there more than a minute or two, and I was terrified. I looked around and said, "What am I doing here? I'll be recognized. They'll know who I am." I wanted to see what my reaction would be. I was just curious, "What would it be like if I went back in here sober? I've never been in here sober." I couldn't stay there. I turned and left. Got the hell out. Do you know, someone saw me there that night? Subsequently, when all the stories hit the press, they said, "Why, he was still going to gay bars in July this year." It's true; I went back one time for a matter of seconds and saw the squalor of the place, the dirty floor, the black painted walls, the people, what they looked like —though I'm not trying to put them down—and I said, "What am I doing here now? What was I ever doing here?"

Despite the fact that I have now accepted my homosexuality, rarely have I gone into a gay bar in D.C., and then usually with friends. I think I've been in such a bar twice within the last three years. (I have run into some interesting conservatives, liberals and congressmen there, too.) But that's twice I've done it, in all this time. It doesn't appeal to me.

By the summer of 1981, I was tending to the position that I had to face the sexuality issue as I had the alcoholism. The last straw was when Carol initiated proceedings in the Diocesan Tribunal to have our marriage annulled. That annulment came through in August. The Diocesan Tribunal, which deals with marriage, divorce, and annulment, judged that I'd had no capacity to contract the marriage originally because I had been a homosexual. So the marriage was annulled. It did not exist in the eyes of the church and never had. At that point, I said to myself, "Look, here I am going to a psychiatrist, trying to cure myself from being what the church decided I am and have been for twenty years. What am I trying to fight?" In many ways, it was a convenient, final capping off of things I had been thinking for an awfully long time. I just didn't want to accept it.

The horror of being gay is indeed worse than that of being an alcoholic. Alcoholism, not to take it lightly, has achieved a certain acceptance in this country in the sense that people now understand it better. It is known, although some people will never accept it. They'll always say that it is a moral weakness, or that you can stop if you want to. But being gay has never reached even that degree of acceptance or tolerance, and may not for many, many years, until people

231

understand what being gay means, as they are now learning what being alcoholic means.

In a way Carol did me a favor because she forced me to face the realities of what was happening in my life. No psychiatrist ever tells you you are gay. They say, "Here are all the indicators. Here are all the facts as we have known them over the years, and this seems to be your pattern." Sooner or later, you have to draw some conclusions.

Until I stopped drinking my mind wasn't clear enough to deal with anything else. There is no way that I could have continued to drink and address my homosexuality in therapy. Drinking was a way to escape from all of that, not face it, not deal with it. It was a double denial because I was denying them both. Then I accepted my alcoholism. My mind cleared up, and then I accepted my being gay.

Gay alcoholics have an even more acute and deeper need for help. Seek help for your alcoholism immediately so that you can recognize the dimensions of your sexuality for what it is. If indeed you are gay, accept that for what it is and deal with it. I don't advocate immoral acts. I don't advocate any particular lifestyle. I don't advocate that you leave your church or denounce morality. Chances are that if you are a homosexual it's not a matter of choice, it is something innate in your nature. It's formed in your earliest years, perhaps by birth. You should deal with it.

In our society, instead of dealing with it we are

taught to hide it, to be ashamed of it, to consider ourselves to be less than human beings, to be some sort of monster. Your entire life is colored in millions of subtle and not so subtle ways to think that you're not human, that you're less than human because you're gay. It could be that you find that you're not gay. If you display the pattern of conduct that I did, you may be gay. But that's not so terrible. God loves all His children. No matter what they're like, He made them in His image.

Don't run away from the homosexual feelings by drinking. That is the classic avenue for many gays. I'm active in organizations where a lot of people who are both alcoholic and gay seek help. When you listen to the stories, the repetition of themes is there: denial, poor self-image, very little self-esteem, family members who beat them down, parents who are alcoholic. The whole thing is repeated over and over almost as many times as you run into people who are gay and alcoholic. You hear of so many people in gay circles who die in auto accidents, drink themselves to death —cirrhosis of the liver, hepatitis, physically run down by drinking or using other drugs. You'll find an awful lot of other drugs, too. I don't think this happens because gays are involved in the drug culture more than the general public. It's because they can't deal with themselves as they are. They are taught not to. They're taught to deny themselves. If you go through your entire life denying who you are and what you are, it colors every waking moment of your life. You are trying to be something that you aren't. My God, it's an awful burden to carry.

What I am advocating is *don't drink*. The last place you should go for help if you think you're gay is a bar. The first place you should go, particularly if you're having a drinking problem, is to an organization like Gay AA or a counseling service that some gay groups offer. There are a lot of those listed now. Deal with what I called in my public statement the twin compulsions of alcoholism and homosexuality. They were indeed compulsions in my life. They're not compulsions anymore. I'm an alcoholic and I don't drink. So at least I'm recovering. As far as being gay, that's the way I am. If I had to do it over and had some control over it, I think I'd choose not to be gay, simply because of the way our society treats gays. It's not the easiest thing in the world. I wouldn't want my children to suffer through what I did. But, on the other hand, if you are gay, accept it. Deal with it and live out your life.

8 Wives and Alcoholic Husbands

Wives of alcoholics worry about their husbands' drinking and often blame themselves and their children for being the cause. Alcoholic husbands very often say that their wives are responsible for their drinking and that they are misunderstood at home. At home the alcoholic husband is very quick to point out that he is the breadwinner and complains of the great pressures he is under at work.

Life in the alcoholic household revolves around the whims of the alcoholic husband. Meals are delayed, social invitations are refused, holidays are ruined, and financial problems arise.

The wife of the drinking alcoholic threatens, and the alcoholic promises to mend his ways. He quits drinking and she hopes and prays—only to be heartbroken once again when he drinks. The wife and children are often subjected to abuse and ridicule, but she endures and tries to hold the family together as it falls apart. The wife of the drinking alcoholic loves her husband and often puts up with his alcoholic behavior for "the sake of the children," as her duty. Often the wife finds herself covering up for the alcoholic's drinking even though the alcohol appears to her to be more important to the alcoholic than she or the children. As the years go on, the alcoholic's drinking must become worse and the alcoholic's wife accepts the alcoholic's world. She, too, loses hope and accepts that this is the way it is and this is the way it is supposed to be.

It doesn't have to be that way.

According to Sybil Carter, "I went to the bitter end and did everything I thought I was supposed to do. I was the best wife anybody could ask for."

Sybil Carter cleaned Billy up if he got sick, picked him up if he fell down, and covered up for him by lying. All along, she thought he didn't care about her or the children. Until she went to Long Beach Naval Hospital for treatment herself, she didn't understand alcoholism as a disease and thought Billy could quit if he wanted to.

In her brutally honest story Sybil Carter relates how her world was turned upside down while she was in treatment and learned what she had been doing wrong.

Billy Carter is an alcoholic. The brother of former United States President Jimmy Carter, he is vice president of marketing for Scott Housing Systems, Inc. He and his wife, Sybil, and their two youngest children live in Georgia.

Sybil Carter

We got married when we were very young. I was sixteen years old. Just a baby, really. Billy was seventeen, right out of boot camp. When he was in high school and he went out with me, he did not drink. If he did, I didn't know it. He went into the service, and after we got married his buddies would come over on weekends and they would drink beer. At that point, I didn't feel it was a problem. We were busy raising a family. I think Billy knew that he had a problem a long time before I did.

When Billy first decided to go to AA I was astounded. Billy would work hard all week and he might come home and have a beer or two, but to me that was not an alcoholic. On weekends we would go out with couples and we'd go to dances, to parties, and Billy would get drunk sometimes, but not all the time. Things would happen to us the way they did to other couples if one of them drank too much. I might get angry with him because of something he said or something he did.

It did not happen every weekend or every time we went out, just occasionally. I was not aware that Billy was drinking as much as he was. It didn't show in his appearance. Whether he was just in better control of it at that time, I don't know.

Probably after we had been married ten, eleven, twelve years, when we were at home in the peanut business, I realized that his drinking had become heavier. It really bothered me the most when the children began to grow up. The older children were teenagers or almost teenagers, and I was the go-between with their father and them. He was always very strict with the children. There were so many times when I knew he was drinking, and he would make a decision about something that concerned them. He would not give any reason for his decision. We always tried to back each other up with the kids. If he said no to something, I would try to find out why he said no because he would never explain his reasons to the children. He would just say no, or "Because I'm your father and I said no." I felt that was unfair to the children.

If they wanted to stay over at a friend's house or to go to a ball game, he'd just say, "I want you to stay home tonight." It was really a problem because the children couldn't understand why. Here I was saying, "Your daddy doesn't feel well," and all the time, of course, they knew he was drinking. I was trying to say to them on the one hand, "Respect your daddy," and they're standing there saying, "Why?" I wasn't really giving them a reason, either.

Billy was never, never violent to any of us. He never raised a hand to any of us. But he could really be nasty verbally. To keep the children from going through that, it was easier to do what he wanted. He was boss and what he said was the way it was going to be. It was easier to go along with it than to argue with it.

Whatever Billy watched on television was what

we watched. Whatever Billy wanted for a meal was what we had. If the meal was not on the table when he got home, he was very angry. Everything had to be done just the way he wanted it or he would get angry. The children went to their rooms a lot of times when their dad came home, just to get out of the way. We all tiptoed around the house, around Billy and his moods and his drinking. It was hell, literally hell.

Schedules were not met and lies were told over the phone to protect him. "We are not coming to the meeting" or "We can't come to the party because Billy doesn't feel well" or "One of the children doesn't feel well." Never "Billy is drunk" or "Billy just flatly refuses to come." He would say, "Tell them I'm sick" or "Tell them we can't come" or "Give some excuse." I didn't have to do it, but I did. I took the responsibility for what he did and I should not have done that. He didn't use force to make me do it. I did it. I did it to keep the children from hearing an argument.

It wasn't all bad. There were a lot of happy times, too. Billy was a good father. He loved his children. But he got up at five or six A.M. and went to work before they were up. At night, when he came in, they were already in bed. It was a demanding job, and he worked all day and he worked hard. On weekends, though, instead of spending time with his children, he played with his friends and drank. So he missed a lot of the growing-up years of the first four children.

We used to have high school basketball games. In a small town, almost everybody goes. Billy would go, and he would be drinking. The children saw him fall down the stairs. They were so embarrassed. They would come home and say, "Please don't let Daddy come to the ball games." They would never say it to his face. They would always tell him how much they loved him.

We have six children and I can remember wondering to myself a lot of times, when he was drinking, if the children and I were to blame. You blame your situation and wonder, Could it be because he works as hard as he does? We lost three children, so we had a lot of things along the way that added to it. Could we be that big a burden on him?, I wondered. Could it be stress? Could it be his job? He was constantly working. It takes a lot to feed and clothe a large family. In the back of your mind, you're thinking, Well, it could be us. It could be us that's making him drink. You are constantly looking for reasons and wondering if you are it. Not until I was in treatment and he was in treatment did I realize that I was always taking the responsibility for what he did. He never asked me to do it. I just did it because I thought that was what I was supposed to do. I loved him and thought I was protecting him.

With Billy's family being who they were, in politics and in the limelight, I think a lot of the way I handled things had to do with not saying anything that was going to cause a furor or bring embarrassment to the family. You play everything down and keep it quiet; you don't let it out. The funny part about it was that all the time I was thinking this, he was out there doing his own thing, getting drunk. I don't know why I didn't think everybody else knew. I took a lot. Had I been somebody else or had the family not been in the public eye, I would not have stood it as long as I did. I know I would have thrown up my hands much earlier and said, "Go to hell."

One time I went to Jimmy and talked to him about Billy's drinking. Jimmy agreed with me that Billy needed help. Jimmy's way was, "I'll do anything I can for you." But Jimmy would not go to Billy and say, "You need to quit drinking" or "You had better quit drinking," or "You have to quit drinking." I don't know if Jimmy ever really talked to Billy about it or not at that time. I know he didn't in the later years. Jimmy seemed to be of the opinion that Billy could quit on his own. I think I decided then that this was my cross to bear, and I was going to bear it the best way I knew how.

When Billy was running the peanut business he did a wonderful job. I kept the books at the office and we worked together. I don't think you could find anybody who knows anything about the peanut business who won't tell you that Billy did a fantastic job. He loved the work. He grew up in the business working with his dad, so he knew it. He loved the farmers and they loved him. He never asked anybody who worked with us to do anything that he wouldn't do himself.

In the earlier years, when Jimmy was governor, I never saw Billy take a drink during the day when he was working. When he would get through in the afternoon, he would drink beer. But when the business was taken away from him, I could see a decided change in Billy.

When Jimmy was elected President it was unreal. It was like you went to bed one night and everything was normal and quiet in this little old sleepy Plains, and you woke up the next morning and found yourself in the middle of a world's fair. You went out your back door to get into your car to go to work and people were standing in your yard taking your picture. People were walking into your house without knocking. Your children couldn't go outside and ride their bikes without people taking their pictures or going up and touching them. You've got a little baby and you're afraid for the lady who takes care of him to take him for a ride in his stroller. You've got the telephone ringing and your children answering and some idiot saying, "There's a bomb under your house. We're going to blow up your house. We're going to kill your daddy before the day is over." You've got all these things going on. You've got your children screaming and crying. You're just trying to be a normal person during all this and keep your children normal and happy and well adjusted, and it's a nightmare.

People said, "Well, it must be wonderful to have Jimmy be President and you live in the

White House and go to all these parties." I went to the White House twice in the four years that Jimmy was President. We didn't live at the White House. We didn't go to every party that was held in the White House. We didn't know what decisions Jimmy made about policies or political things. We didn't run for President. We just happened to be his family. And we had people saying, "You can't do this because Jimmy is President." Or "You mustn't talk that way or you mustn't dress that way." We had to act in a certain way because Jimmy was President. The bad part about it was that we didn't change but people around us did. They expected us to act differently because Jimmy was President of the United States. I think that's one reason Billy started drinking heavier than he had before, to prove a point, to prove that he had not changed and he would not change. He would not conform to what everybody else thought he should be because he was the President's brother.

My resentment grew because Billy started traveling. It was not a resentment so much toward him as toward the press and people in general. I became tired of being pushed around. When you get in a place where there's a lot of people and Billy is there and everybody wants to meet him and everybody wants to shake his hand and everybody wants his autograph and you have a reporter turn around and say, "Who are you?"—I finally got to the point where I would say, "I'm his maid."

I was happier at home with my kids, anyway. During that time there were a lot of stories in the papers and everybody would send me a copy of any story Billy was in. I knew that he was drinking more. I could tell by the way he talked and the things that he said and the way he acted. I felt I was lucky not to be with him, because I would have been angry all the time. I worried about what he was going to say that would be in the paper or what he didn't say that was going to be in the paper. It was just easier to stay home with the children and not be involved.

I threatened Billy a number of times. I said, "If you don't quit drinking, I'm going to leave and I'm going to take the children." Billy would say, "I promise you I will. I know I drink too much." If I had a nickel for every time he promised me not to drink again, I would never have to work again. I'd be rich, independently wealthy. And every time I would believe him, because I wanted to. I loved him. I don't think during all that time I ever seriously thought about divorcing him, because I felt if I did that, it would be the end of him. He wouldn't have anybody to take care of him. He wouldn't have anybody to love him. And that would be wrong. That would be a sin on my part. I married Billy and I promised to love him and take care of him, and that was what I was there for.

When Paul Braun, our friend and doctor, came to me and said, "Sybil, Billy is sick; he is going to die if he doesn't quit drinking," I said,

"Well, Paul, I have done everything I know to do." I had talked to Billy a number of times. I knew he drank too much. He would be gone a week or a week and a half at a time, not seeing his children, not seeing me, maybe calling once or twice. He would come home drunk. By that time it had gotten to the point where I didn't care anymore. I just did not care. I didn't care whether he came home or not. In fact, we got along a lot better when he wasn't home. There was no bickering. The kids were happier when he wasn't there. They didn't have to worry about being quiet. They could live their lives and do what they wanted to without having to worry about what he was going to say or do. I didn't care, and that was bad. But still, when he came home, I was right here. I was a glutton for punishment. I still took responsibility for what he did, lied for him, made excuses for him. I was like a zombie. It was as if I was programmed to do that and felt I would be wrong if I didn't do it.

I had mentioned to Paul that Billy could not keep anything on his stomach. I knew he was getting sick. It was early 1979. Paul said, "If we can get him into the hospital to take some tests, let's do it." I said, "O.K., but he's not going to do it for me." I had tried and tried and tried. I said, "Maybe you can get through to him." So Paul talked to him and said, "You know, Billy, I think you might have pneumonia. That cough is really bad." Billy was smoking an awful lot. Paul said, "Please come in and just let me check you over good." So Billy finally agreed. I knew he must feel bad if he agreed to go in.

Paul said, "I'm going to get him so that I can take some x-rays and tests." Paul really shot him a line about what some of the tests were about. After the tests, Paul told Billy about his liver. Paul came out to the house and said, "Sybil, I talked to Billy about drinking and the fact that he needs to quit or he will kill himself, and he said for me to come and talk to you and see what you thought about him going into treatment."

I said, "Paul, God knows I want him to, but I can't make Billy do anything. I don't want the decision to be my decision. It can't be mine. It has to be his. Because I've said it a hundred times, 'Billy, you have got to stop drinking.' " I realized that Billy could not quit drinking because of me or the kids or anybody else.

Paul said to me, "Billy thinks if he goes for treatment that you will leave him."

I said, "Now, that really does not make sense. Why does he feel that way?" He said, "Well I don't know, but I think that's what he feels. I get the feeling from his conversation that he thinks you will leave him if he decides to go somewhere for treatment."

I said, "My God, Paul, I've been with Billy all these years and I've put up with all the shit and I've stayed here and I've raised his kids. Why does he think that when the time comes for him to get help that I would leave him? Doesn't he have any sense at all?"

And Paul said, "I don't know, but will you just talk to him?"

So I went to the hospital and I talked to him. I said, "Billy, I don't understand. You know what the problem is." He said, "Well, everybody in the world is going to know if I go for treatment. Every newspaper in the world. The children are going to know. Everybody is going to know. All of my friends are going to know." I said, "Billy, they know already that you are an alcoholic." He just lay there and said, "You wouldn't leave?" I said I wouldn't have any reason to leave. "It would be the happiest day in my life if you went. Not just for me but for you. You are just existing; you're not living." He said he was worried about the kids. So I went home and told the children. The four oldest could drive and they all went over to the hospital at separate times to talk to him, to tell him how proud they were that he had decided to do something about his problem. I think that's what really made him decide that he would go for treatment.

We got him through those days in the hospital in Americus. He went to see the children at home, and we left immediately. I was the delivery lady. I got out to Long Beach, dropped him off, and said I was going home. Dr. Joe Pursch said, "No, you're not." And I said, "Oh, yes I am. Here's the drunk; now make him well. I'm going home to see about my kids. I've got things to do." He said, "No, I don't think so." And I said, "Why do I have to stay?" He said, "Because you're sick." And I told him, "No, I'm not sick, I'm going home. You don't understand. I've got six children who need me at home. I didn't come prepared to stay. Billy is the one who needs treatment, not me."

He said, "But you are sadly mistaken. You need treatment as badly as Billy does." I said, "I'm not an alcoholic." He said, "No, but you are an alcoholic's wife." I started to cry. I had never met this man before. I stood there and cried, and he told me if I went home I was copping out. Why should I expect Billy to go through treatment if I was not willing to? After everything I had been through, I thought, You pompous son of a bitch, you don't know anything about what an alcoholic's spouse goes through and here you are trying to tell me. I finally told him, "I'm going home."

And he said, "Well, if you are not willing to get well, too, then Billy is probably not going to stick." I said, "O.K., I'll give you this much. I'm going home. I'll see about my children. I'm going to tell them that their daddy is not strapped in a hospital bed and he's not in a loony bin with crazy people, because they don't know what is happening to him. I didn't come prepared to stay. I didn't know I was expected to stay. You can believe me or not, but I've got six children at home and I have to make arrangements for somebody to stay with them, to my satisfaction, to know that they are taken care of. Right now, they are my first consideration. I have to be satisfied about their well-being or I can't stay up here."

He said O.K., but he didn't think I was coming back. Later I found out that he was goading me all the time. He thought I was copping out. I told him, "If I tell you I'll be back, I'll be back." So I left, and I came back.

Those three weeks were the worst three weeks of my life, without a shadow of doubt. My whole life was brought before my eyes and torn apart. Every statement I had ever made, everything I had done was ridiculed and belittled and torn apart. I was told that I was a do-gooder and holier-than-thou and that I was as much to blame for Billy's drinking as he was because I took responsibility for what he did, and that I really helped him be an alcoholic. Every day was like going to hell and climbing back out again.

I wasn't allowed to see Billy. He was in one group, I was in another. I couldn't figure out what I was doing there. It was as if everybody was against me, and if I cried they belittled me. If I didn't they belittled me. I was criticized because I had compassion or what I thought was compassion. I was called a do-gooder because I'd done the normal things that I did in taking care of Billy and my family.

I finally realized that what they were trying to do was make me see that I was a human being who had rights, that I was not put on this earth to be Billy's doormat. In essence, that's what I was. So I learned the hard way that I could be

251

happy, that I didn't have to be responsible for what Billy did, that I could have interests of my own, that my life was not completely entwined with his, that I didn't have to agree with everything he said.

What they try to make you understand is that you have to get rid of all the anger and resentment that you hold toward the alcoholic, because if he begins to recover and you still have all the resentment and anger, then your relationship is not going to work. The family situation is not going to work, because he's getting well and you're staying the same. You're still angry with him because of what he said last November at a party, and it's there and it grows and grows and grows. In essence, your whole life has to be turned around and changed.

I had to be made to realize that I could live my life without Billy. I had never said that before, because I didn't think I could. I finally realized that I could. I didn't need him to live. I loved him and I wanted the marriage to work, but if Billy were not there, I wouldn't die. I could get along without him. And the day I admitted that I could live without Billy was the day I began to be a whole person, on my own. I realized that all the things I had been doing all those years were wrong. It was as though my whole life had been for nothing. That's a hard pill to swallow. I was really not helping him. I was harming him all the time by agreeing with him and helping him to drink, being a crutch for him. I felt as if I wanted to die.

When we first got home, Billy decided the treatment was the worst thing that had ever happened to me because it had really changed me. I'd turned into a bitch, he said, whereas before I had been nice and sweet and docile. I guess in his eyes I was a bitch. If I disagreed with him, I said so. Before, I would never have said it. I would have been afraid that he would get angry, and I didn't want that disapproval or the verbal abuse that it brought. But there is an awful lot of love between us now, and a lot more respect. There has always been a lot of love, but it was misguided love. I guess it was family-rooted love because we have been married twenty-eight years. It was a childhood-sweetheart-type thing that has just gone on through the years. As I have said, in recent years I always loved Billy but didn't like him a lot of times, and I am sure he feels the same way about me. In fact there have been times I have loved him but hated him at the same time. There have been a lot of times I wished he was dead. Lots of times I said it jokingly, but a lot of times it was no joke.

I still have problems. I think since Billy has been sober the adjustment period has been harder than the drinking was in some ways, because he has become a different person and I have, too. It's exciting because we're learning to know each other all over again. There are areas that we get into now and talk about that he never would have talked about before. We share a lot of things that we didn't share, especially feelings about things. That was one of the points they kept bringing out in treatment. "I don't want to know what you think, I want to know what you feel," they'd say. To me that was the same thing. I kept on saying, "Well, I think so." And they'd say, "I don't want to know what you think; I want to know what you feel." They kept throwing it back in my face. "You don't want to say this because you are afraid of what he'll say. You don't want to be criticized. You can't take criticism."

Life is a whole lot better, as they say, a bunch better. We are closer today than we have ever been in our lives. And happier. And we don't have any big problems hanging over our heads. He likes his job and we enjoy being where we are and our kids are all healthy and happy. What else could we ask? I think we're richer for the experience that we went through.

I am happy with myself. There are a lot of things I would like to change and need to change, but I have no qualms whatsoever about doing what I want to do.

Up to the time I went for treatment, I felt as though I existed for Billy and the children, and I put myself last. After treatment, I put myself first. I do the things I do now because I want to. If I do something for Billy it's not because he demands it; it's because I want to do it, not because it's expected of me. The same thing with the children. I have spent all my married life, in a sense, protecting my children, not from violence, but from hurt and anger. I've been in the role of a protector. Now I want to be the one who's protected. I want to be the one who's petted and looked after and loved and spoiled a little bit, and I am. They do that for me.

Being married to Billy has been interesting for me. I've been angry a lot of times, mad as hell part of the time, sad a lot, and happy a lot. But I have never been bored, and I want to stick around because I want to see what Billy is going to come up with next. I want to be there. Whatever it is, I want to be there.

Physical sickness and fear caused Billy Carter to go into the hospital. It was just for tests and, like most alcoholics, he had no intention of quitting. Confronted with the information about his health, he feared that Sybil would leave him and it would be played out in the press, which Billy feels has not always been fair with him both before and after his drinking.

In looking back, Billy Carter regrets more than anything else the hurt he caused Sybil and his children.

Billy Carter

I drank like everybody else did, in high school and earlier. Not too much, not too little; I just followed the crowd. Later on, in the service, I probably drank too much. My first inkling I had a problem was in the early sixties, when I tried AA for the first time. The first AA meeting I ever went to was probably in 1962. It was an old-line group. I drove an automobile and I hadn't lost my job, so I figured there was no way I could be an alcoholic that young. So I started back, and I drank again for four or five years. I tried AA again, around four or five years later, but it didn't stick. I went maybe three months and then stopped going. One time I quit drinking for eighteen months, then started back. I drank steadily from then on. I drank every day.

I didn't drink any heavier than any of the people I saw socially, so I'd found my own level. I first started getting into the papers because I was a beer drinker. I had a beer joint. I didn't drink any more than most of the press people who were writing about my drinking. We were drinking buddies even when Jimmy was governor, and even after he started running for President. It was the only thing to do in town. I got a reputation as a beer drinker. I always drank beer, but I guess you might say I drank beer for show, more than anything else. During that time, I was drinking hard stuff a lot more than I was beer. I drank beer in public, lots of bourbon, otherwise.

I drank with the press and had a good time with them. I talked a lot then. One of the first things I found out was that they believed almost anything you told them. They printed it. It got to be kind of an ongoing game. I had a usually friendly, but sometimes unfriendly, war going on with them. My drinking caused some of it, I guess. I would have been a lot more quiet and in the background if it had not been for my drinking.

Nobody knew who I was when Jimmy was governor and I was drinking. Nobody knew who I was when he was first running for President and I was drinking. Then the press got so hot on his born-again Christianity because the Yankee Catholics were scared to death of it. They had to have something to offset it. I was there. I don't regret it. Lots of people say I lost Jimmy the presidency the second time. I didn't lose forty-four states. I think I had a lot to do with him winning the first time.

My hard-drinking years were after Jimmy became President and I quit the peanut business. My lifestyle changed completely. If Jimmy hadn't been President I probably would have drunk myself to death, like 99 percent of the alcoholics do. They told me that at Long Beach.

I don't think my drinking progressed any more the last three or four years I drank, except that I had more time to drink. I traveled full time. I very seldom worked during the daytime. Most of my work was at night. My reputation was such that I was expected to drink. It was Billy Beer time.

When I was on the road, speaking or doing whatever I was doing, my son-in-law, Mark, and Ty Coppinger, who now coaches football at the University of South Carolina, traveled with me. I drank until four or five hours before I was supposed to make an appearance. I'd take chlorohydrate to knock me out for six hours, then get up and do what I had to do. If I had to give a talk, I wouldn't take a drink until I went on. After I went on, Mark would give me vodka in a glass. I would drink it down. If I stayed on over thirty minutes, he would bring me a glass of water with vodka or gin. I would function that way and go back to the room and drink all night. I didn't like to be by myself. Someone would stay with me all the time. They'd rotate nights sleeping. I think that during that time, probably Mark, Ty, and Sybil were the only ones who had any idea how much I was drinking.

Eventually, when I got up in the morning, I had two drinks and puked blood for thirty minutes. I needed a drink to function for the day. I knew something wasn't quite normal. I couldn't hold any food at all on my stomach. I would go home and my daughter would cook what I wanted. I'd eat half a meal and throw it up. So I wouldn't hurt her feelings, I'd come back and eat the rest of it; but I'd throw that up. I couldn't hold anything down. All this time I was still functioning fairly well. There were still a lot of people who didn't think I drank anything but beer. I was drinking, I think, close to half a gallon of booze a day then, plus beer. I was getting paid to drink beer, so I drank some. I would keep a beer can in my hand most of the time, and I drank a lot of vodka and bourbon all day long, too. Like most alcoholics, I never missed anything I had to do. I was a functioning alcoholic. My tolerance, instead of getting lower and lower, was getting higher and higher. I was functionally sober with a 2.5 alcohol level. That's what it took to keep me operating. They told me that at Long Beach.

Then I got afraid. I got afraid I was going to die. It was getting so bad I couldn't handle it. I had been under the impression that every alcoholic is under, that I could quit any time I wanted to. I couldn't. I thought, When I want to quit, I'll quit by myself. I couldn't.

I tried. Sometimes I said, "Hell, there's no need to quit." I would always have the same story in my mind, "I *can* quit, so what's the need to quit." Finally, I just gave up. When I went into the hospital, I had no desire to quit drinking, and I didn't go in to quit drinking.

I had no thought of quitting. I just wanted to slow down. And even after I went into Long Beach for treatment, I had no thought of quitting for the first three to four weeks I was there.

I went to the hospital because I was killing myself drinking. I'd quit eating. I'd gone on a complete alcohol diet, nothing else. It was full time. I don't think I had eaten any solid food in over fifty days—I couldn't hold it on my stomach. I went to the hot-vodka route. It would have to be room temperature for me to drink it, particularly when I started in the morning. Anything colder wouldn't stay on my stomach.

This was February of 1979. I agreed to go into the hospital—for acute bronchitis. That's when the press got on it so hot. They didn't know why I had bronchitis. I went in to sober up. I agreed that I wouldn't drink while I was in the hospital. But I went in with four pints of vodka in my briefcase. When I got everybody out of the damn room and got ready to settle down for a good night, I opened my briefcase, which was still locked, and my vodka was gone. I never did figure out what happened to it.

In treatment I resented everybody. Why the hell was I there? Why was I there when everybody else was out having a good time? Why was it me? I finally realized that it didn't make a difference to anybody else whether I quit or not. The only one it made any difference to was me. I could go ahead and drink myself to death. I could go ahead and stay drunk full time. I think after three, four, five weeks I realized that if I was going to quit, I couldn't quit for Sybil. I couldn't quit for the doctor. I couldn't quit for my kids. I had to quit for myself. It finally clicked. I could quit for myself. It was worthwhile, too.

I can truthfully say I have no desire for a drink, and I think if I were to drink today I would immediately drink myself to death. I would feel that I had given up completely on myself. I don't stay sober for Sybil Carter or Jimmy Carter. It sounds egotistical as hell, but, as far as I'm concerned, I don't drink for myself, and that's it.

If I hadn't started to drink, I never would have had to stop. Now it makes me feel good when somebody comes up to me and says, "Well, I quit drinking six months ago. I thought if you could do it, with all you went through, I could do it." People respect me for it and I don't catch any static from anybody about not drinking. I know it's all right with me if I don't drink. It doesn't bother me anymore. The only people who resent my not drinking are people who have tried to quit themselves and haven't been able to.

I don't think I did anything spectacular. I don't think I did anything anybody else couldn't do. I'm definitely not a hero about it.

I regret that my drinking hurt Sybil and my kids. If I hurt some of my friends, too, I regret that. I've become real close to my four oldest kids since I quit drinking. I hardly knew them when they were coming up. I regret that more than anything else. I regret the way it hurt Sybil, but I think Sybil and I are both stronger since we came through all this. Heck, we've been married twenty-nine years and still love each other. I think we're as happy as anybody now.

I enjoy life more. I enjoy every day. I think I'm happier now than I have ever been. It's different. I enjoy the job I've got. I look forward to every day. I feel basically good every day, but I don't think I have changed much. I'm a little quieter. I'm not the life of the party anymore. I can't dance anymore, but we do basically what we want to.

I live a normal life. I enjoy not drinking. As I said, it's all right for me not to drink.

Florence Caesar could tell, just by looking at Sid Caesar, that he had been drinking. Things had to be "perfect and smooth" around the house, and she sometimes wondered if it was something she had said that set off Sid's drinking. On the other hand, Florence did realize "it was his problem." As his alcoholism progressed, it was a relief to have Sid fall asleep, drinking.

The kids were critical of Sid's alcoholic behavior. According to Florence, "The youngest one said one time, when Sid was ranting and raving, 'Why don't we get a different daddy?' —at two and a half years old."

Sid Caesar is an alcoholic. He is recognized as a comedy genius. "Your Show of Shows" and "The Caesar Hour" rank among the top series in the history of television. Sid and his wife, Florence, live in California.

Florence Caesar

Everything Sid liked had to be a lot. He had steak in those days, a heavy big steak and a big roast beef. If one drink was good, two or three were better. So it was gradual and it started to affect him, affect his attitude, his manner. He was very different when he was drinking from when he wasn't. As he worked, he was very successful from the beginning, so there was a lot of stress there. That was his reason. He came out of the service, and we were married. He played night-clubs for a while, movies, a Broadway show, and television. He was the star, a hit. He became a star very quickly. And he drank along with it. What saved him, in a way, was that he would eat, and he took a lot of vitamins. I think that's what saved his health, although the alcohol was affecting his liver as he drank more and more.

Five or six years after we were married, he began to get very difficult when he was drinking. He'd get angry. He'd forget about it, and the next day he'd say, "What did I do? What was so terrible?" He wouldn't even remember.

Eventually, the doctor put him on pills to get him off alcohol. It started to affect him in about 1953. That's when it started to bother him physically, when they put him on pills. Then he'd sleep. He would do a lot of sleeping, which, as far as I was concerned, was much easier. He'd just fall asleep, drinking, instead of raving and ranting. It wasn't normal for the kids to see him sleeping so much, but it was a little more peaceful. I'd watch television, read, do what I wanted. He did a lot of sleeping. It was amazing. Before he opened his Broadway show, *Little Me,* in 1962, he was sleeping for hours and hours. But the opening was wonderful. The show was wonderful. He was good in it, too.

Sid Caesar was appearing in a play in Canada. It was opening night. As Sid recalls, "I did the first act, but I couldn't do the second act. I didn't know where I was." Sid missed cues, forgot lines, and couldn't remember whether to sit or stand. In his dressing room, between acts, he looked in the mirror, made his choice between life and death, and told the theater staff to "get a doctor."

Nothing says so much so briefly about alcoholism as the words of Sid Caesar. The hopelessness, lethargy, and slow suicide of the final months of his drinking in 1978, stand in stark contrast to the zest, vitality, and enthusiasm in his life today.

Sid Caesar

I lay in bed for practically four months. I never left the house. Just lay in bed and read and read and read. A big thing was to go out and get a haircut. That was really a big achievement, if I could make it. I didn't care anymore. I had given up on myself. I was thinking about doing terrible things to myself. I could never bring myself to it. I never got dressed. I remember very well just walking around in pajamas. Never left the house.

I was a lump, just walking around in a stupor all the time. All the pills, the beer, the wine, it didn't make any difference.

I had given up. I didn't believe in myself

anymore. It was just too painful to get through a day, because I was just killing time, wasn't doing anything. I didn't care to do anything. I had reached a point where I was just doing it slowly instead of quickly.

What do you think drinking is? For people who can't control it, like me, it's slow suicide.

Today, I walk around my garden and look at the flowers. I watch the gardener. I look at the house. I say, "Gee, I'm a lucky guy." Let me get out in the morning. I get the paper and stop and smell the roses. I do. I appreciate things.

I'm positive now. I don't say, "This is no good and that's no good." It's so much easier to live by saying, "Isn't that nice?"

As much as I intended to destroy myself physically and mentally, that's how much I'm devoted to turning it around 180 degrees. I look forward to working out. I really do. I enjoy it. As addicted as I was to alcohol, that's how I am to working out. You take a good workout and a good steam and a shower. Oh, boy! Little lay-down for about twenty minutes. You get up. You feel like a trillion dollars. That's it! That's what I look forward to now.

So I built myself up. I take pride in myself. And I'm good to myself because I deserve it. I went through a lot with the other guy. I'm with this guy now.

I watch what I eat. I don't drink anymore. You couldn't pay me to take a drink.

I go out and have fun—real fun. Really. I look

at myself and say, "What a lucky guy I am. I caught myself."

―――――――――――――――――――――

Lois Robards thought she was headed for a nervous breakdown and would end up in a psychiatric ward. She would wake up in the morning and begin to cry. She couldn't take it any longer and made the decision to leave.

She had thought that the birth of their second child—a son whom Jason desperately wanted— would change everything; but immediately thereafter it was life as usual. After discussing escape money with their accountant and lining up a job in Canada, she told Jason of her plans to leave—and she meant it.

Jason Robards is an alcoholic. He is considered to be one of America's finest actors. On the Broadway stage, on television, and in film, he has won all the major acting prizes, including two Academy Awards. He and his wife, Lois, and their two children live in Connecticut.

Lois Robards
What I knew about Jason was that he was a totally good person. It wasn't as if he was a real rotter. He didn't chase women or beat me. I thought of him as someone who never could really accept love. He just didn't believe somebody could love him completely, and in his

266

drinking behavior he would drive you away to prove that love didn't exist. That's really how I saw him. I remember when we were first married, he got up after dinner one evening and declared, "Work is the only thing. It's the absolute. The only thing that really means anything to me is when the curtain goes up and I'm working in the theater." My sister was there, and she was dumbfounded that I did not believe that Jason really meant it. She said, "He declared to everyone at the dinner table that he did not care about his children, his wife, anyone, as much as he did work." I said, "I don't believe it."

From the very beginning, when his mother left, I think he had the feeling that if he did love somebody, that person would go away. So he was not willing to express that. He might tell me how much he loved me and everything like that, but there were moments when he was drinking when he would say how the theater was all that was important to him. It hurt, but I still didn't believe it was true. Maybe something in me would say, "I can prove to him that he's wrong." I don't know.

We met in 1966, when we were working on a show called *Noon Wine,* a Katherine Anne Porter short story. I was in TV and film production, and I was the associate producer on the show. I worked for the Suskind and Melnick Company at the time. Oddly enough, I didn't really see Jason at all when we were working. It was after that he called me up and asked me to go out to dinner. I said all right. Then my secretary, a great big, long, tall, spindly Englishwoman said, "Oh, he's divine. He's married to Lauren Bacall." I said, "What?" I absolutely didn't know that. So I said, "Oh, my gosh, he's married. Call up the studio and leave a message that I can't go." He was working over at Twentieth at the time and I was at CBS. She left word at the gate because we couldn't get through to the studio where they were shooting. So I went home and I was in my bathrobe, and guess what? Knock, knock at the door at nine o'clock. "Gee, sorry I'm late," he says. "Why aren't you dressed and ready?" It was one of those situations where you go, "Ah, ah, ah . . . You didn't get my message? Ah, ah, ah . . ." So I went out with him, and that was the beginning.

I suppose when you're going out with some-one, you think of drinking as just having a good time. You never think that it's going to stay that way all the time. You think, Well, when he is working that doesn't happen, right? But then I did know, because I went with him to Europe before we were married, and I realized that he had a terrible drinking problem. But by that time I was very much in love with him. I had every intention of not marrying him because of his drinking problem. But I did anyhow.

At that time, he could go along for a week or so and work and do whatever he was doing, but then he'd come for the weekend and he might just be drunk all day Saturday or Sunday. We'd go out to dinner on Saturday night and he'd start drinking brandy after dinner; then we'd play music into the morning and carry on and sing, and he'd be really out of it. Never an unhappy drunk. There was just no tomorrow. It was all wonderful. The world was wonderful. But I knew this man had a very serious problem.

We'd start out drinking and I'd think, Well, this is going to be a perfectly wonderful evening. We'd have a couple of drinks and we'd have wine with dinner and I'd think that was going to be it. But it wasn't. It'd be a drink after dinner and then drinks all night. Some nights he would have no drinks, or just a drink with dinner, and everything would be perfectly fine. He could go along for months in which he wouldn't get terribly drunk. But then, suddenly, it was out of control, especially whenever there were any money problems or any kind of emotional problem, such as with his ex-wife or children. There were always problems with alimony. He would get very upset and that would always mean two days drunk. It would definitely mean that.

When I see someone doing that sort of thing, I think I have more concern for their sake than I do for the embarrassment of the situation. Embarrassment never had anything to do with my feelings about his drinking, even if we were in a restaurant with someone and he was singing very loudly or if I had to look for him in bars, asking for him by name. Those things did not bother me as much as my concern for him.

I never ever discussed it with my family. Don't ask me why. That's one of those areas that I could not discuss with my family. I didn't want them to feel sorry for me or think less of Jason. Most of the time, after we were married, we were under enormous stress. I did not want them to know. I just felt that I was an adult, I had made the choice. Even with my brothers and sisters, I could not share it.

My parents were staying with us in Connecticut at one point, and Jason had not come home overnight. They knew he was in *Moon for the Misbegotten,* and they were getting up to go on a trip with my other sister in the morning. I called her and said, "Carol, could you please pick up Mom and Dad by eight-thirty?" Someone had found Jason. He had been out overnight in a bar and had been located. I had been on the phone all night. My parents got up and were tiptoeing around to make sure, just as they always did, that Jason would not be awakened, because he'd had a terribly tough night doing *Moon for the Misbegotten.* To this day, they still do not know that he was never home. They left and then the other car came with Jason. Just a half-hour in between cars. I had to make sure they didn't see the sad scene of this man singing away, gone to the world. They never saw that.

He quit when Shannon was three. She was accustomed to being quiet while Daddy slept because he had been in a lot of plays when she was small. His sleeping late wasn't a big problem with her, particularly. But one time Jason did not show up from the theater. It was when he was doing *Country Girl*. I had to wheel Shannon through the rain in her stroller, in and out of bars on the West Side until it was her naptime, looking for him. He eventually showed up with a package of sausage and an off-duty New York policeman who had decided to bring him home. The policeman had heard from one of the bartenders along the route that we were looking for him.

I wouldn't say these things were common, only maybe every three to four months. You just never knew when it was going to happen. Never any idea.

I don't think his drinking got worse. I think his ability to drink got worse. His tolerance was less and less. I think his intent was, Oh, I'll just have a couple of drinks. But once he started, he'd be standing in a bar someplace and he would remember an old song or the old baseball games and he'd just keep right on going. I don't think he ever had any conscious intent, saying "Oh boy, I'm going to lay one on tonight and forget my troubles."

What I used to say most of all was, "Why do you do this to yourself?" I would always wait until a hangover was over—because he always felt very guilty when he had done something like that. He'd be the one, rather than us, tiptoeing around the house, saying, "Oh, no, no, don't bother, I'll get my own breakfast," whenever he happened to get up. "No, no, no, I don't need anything," he'd say. "No, that will do." Everything was perfect, no matter what was going on. He'd try to melt into the woodwork. I knew that I couldn't say anything because the guilt was so heavy already—especially toward the end, when he was doing *Moon,* right before and after Jake was born.

We had gone to see a psychiatrist. Jason really had gotten particularly bad on *Moon*. He was carrying a heavy role in a heavy play and it seemed that his ability to drink was gone. He had already had his car accident, and he had quit drinking for a while. Then it was just a little wine, then heavier drinking. And then it was just as if nothing had ever happened. It was so reckless of him to do at that particular time, a man who had just come so close to losing his life. And he was in a play that no one expected to be worth anything. They expected no more than a five-week run. He was into it almost a year when he really started drinking heavily.

I realized I was going to leave him when I began to think I was having a nervous breakdown. And I was, I am sure. It wasn't any pretend part at all. I was pregnant with Jake. I was told I was going to have complications with the delivery. And here I was with this man who had absolutely no will to take care of himself, to fulfill life for himself, let alone care about what was happening with his family. This child was something he had wanted very much. Here this child is about to be born and I can't even find him at night after the show. I think he realized that I meant it when I said to him, "Jason, I cannot worry about you and about me and these children, too. I can only worry about them at this point, so I am leaving when this child is born. I am going. I have to."

He disappeared again right after Jake was born. I'd been driving down to the theater when I should have been breast-feeding our child. The milk would be pouring out of me. I would go right into his dressing room and say, "You're coming home with me." Often he'd dismiss the driver and then the driver would call me and say, "He's done it again." I'd say, "I told you to stay there at that curb until he came out." And he'd say, "But he won't get into the car with me." So I would have to go storming down there and say, "O.K., you're coming home." I wasn't embarrassed when the stage manager and the doorman and everybody stood right there, listening to my harangue until he came out. The policeman outside got accustomed to my car being double-parked outside the theater.

At that time Jason was still doing *Moon*. I don't know how much subconsciously, as an actor, Jason began to feel as though he was destined to be that character, Jim Tyrone, that he was going to booze himself to death.

I really never wanted to leave Jason, but when I got up every morning I would start to cry. I was breast-feeding a newborn child, and I couldn't look at the day because I was in such emotional pain. I thought that I might have a breakdown. I don't know what I'll do with these two little children, I thought. If I don't do something, I may end up in a psychiatric ward at Norwalk Hospital. That's where I'm heading. It would terrorize me to think about it, the fact that I might end up in a mental hospital soon if I didn't do something to change my life. I would be driving the car, going to the station to pick up somebody, or I would be alone, and I would cry. I would get up in the morning and have to wash away the tears. I began to feel very unstable. I felt I had to change this. It was not the time for me to fall apart, because I would leave two children behind.

I think that Jason probably recognized, too, what was happening. He made an appointment to see a hypnotherapist. After the first appointment, he called me up and said, "Your mumbo-jumbo man worked and I'll never take a drink again." Of course I thought this had to be too much of a miracle. It couldn't happen in one time. But he came home that night and said, "I feel like a great weight has been lifted off my shoulders. I will never drink again. My son will never see me drunk."

I said to myself, "I've got to believe. I've got to believe. I've got to see this, but I've got to believe." I'd never ever heard him say, "I will never be drunk again."

I think actually leaving does a lot more than saying, "I'm leaving." I had spoken to our accountant about the financial arrangements, and I had called to find out if I might be able to get a production job in Canada, which I could. I realized that I was going to have to support myself. If I were going to disappear, I wasn't going to move down the block from Jason. If I was going to move out, I was going to move. I was going to leave, definitely. I don't think there was any doubt in Jason's mind. But he stopped drinking, and I stayed.

Jason Robards never set out to get drunk, and he remembers that some of his drinking was fun. But he also says some of it was "madness" and "paranoia" and he sometimes drank to handle problems and worries. When an alcoholic quits drinking and then goes back again, he picks up where he left off. It's as if he had continued to drink. At one time, Jason quit for a year and a half, then went back to drinking as usual. Later, after a car accident that nearly cost him his life and necessitated plastic surgery, he resumed drinking at the same level, and then worse.

Until that moment of truth when the alcoholic comes to grips with his alcoholism and realizes he cannot drink anymore, the revolving door keeps on spinning.

Jason Robards
In the early years, I never could afford to drink. I

had a wife, and we were barely getting by, living in a cold-water flat. I was trying to be an actor and was not terribly successful until I was thirty-five years old. It was eleven years of struggle. During those years, my twenties and early thirties, I was not really a drinker. I had a beer, once in a while, a nickel beer. It was not a question of alcohol being a daily occurrence. At Christmas we would buy a bottle of PM, the cheapest whiskey we could get, and make a punch for our guests. We never had whiskey or wine, just beer once in a while, when we could. I never had any problems with drinking.

It was during the run of *A Long Day's Journey into Night* that I really started to drink on a daily basis. I don't mean getting drunk, falling down. I couldn't have. I was doing a play and I never drank before a performance.

In those days the curtain was at 8:30. You didn't get out of the theater until close to midnight. In New York, in those days, everything stayed open. All the great restaurants were open until two, three in the morning. And so it became routine. "I'll meet you at Frankie and Johnnie's. We'll have a steak. We'll have drinks." "I'll meet you at Downey's. We'll have hamburgers, drinks." It's in the profession, in a way. I'm not blaming the profession. But so many people in it, at that time, met and drank and ate and went home to bed about four, because the whole workday begins at night.

I noticed it during *Long Day's Journey into*

Night, which I played for two years. I played the older brother, who is really dead the minute you see him. I found the longer I played it, the harder and harder it was to separate myself from him, off stage, when I was finished. I was getting praise, which I didn't know how to accept at all. I didn't accept the warnings about being unable to shake a character that you are playing—and he's a devastating character. O'Neill knew the classic case of the guy who was unable to face things and was killing himself through drink. He takes that man ten years later through another play, *Moon for the Misbegotten,* which I also did, and shows you his demise. He doesn't die physically on the stage, but he is dead the minute he leaves at the end of the play. So here we're dealing with a real classic. I was that guy. I know now. Later I went into a play called *The Disenchanted,* in which I did Scott Fitzgerald, and I died on the stage from drink.

I don't do a role and just learn lines and go back to the hotel. I still have the residue of that play and cannot throw it off that easily.

My life was disintegrating. So were my marriage and my drinking. My first wife drank along and she became an alcoholic, much worse than I. It was also compounded with mental illness. The depression of alcohol on top of her own depression kept her in hospitals, off and on, for almost fifteen years. Most of the time I raised my oldest children by myself. I would hope for a job so I could get a baby sitter, but by the time I paid the baby sitter I came out with nothing.

I'd pick up empty bottles. You could trade them in for a nickel to get food. It was that kind of existence. My wife would come home from the hospital, but then she would get sick again and go back. At first I didn't connect it with alcohol. I thought it was just a mental condition. But the two combined finished her. She died about six years ago.

I never missed a performance as the old man in *Long Day's Journey*. I never missed a show, just like the character, who is a drunk and who's also never missed a performance. I was always on time. I didn't drink before I went on. I have gone on with hangovers, but I never had a drink less than twelve hours before a show. That came much later. I had youth, when your enzymes are working for you. You have everything making it go, so you're not even having hangovers most of the time. You feel like a million bucks. I was a distance runner. I had great endurance. Great energy and power were natural to me. I'd think, What the hell—wait for the weekend and we'll get shit-faced, and then we'll sober up—Sunday. We'll perform Monday and we'll be fine, and we were. We were fine.

My wife and I broke up. I went with another girl, got married, but was married only about three weeks. Wonderful girl, and I was drunk the whole time. I didn't know what the hell was going on. She got wise and pulled out. I don't blame her.

Then I married Betty, and she said, "Oh, I'm used to heavy drinkers. Bogey was a heavy drinker, but not an alcoholic." I could never figure that one out. It killed him. She thought there was a correct way to drink. There was no way for me to handle a drug like that. And you can't handle an alcoholic by strident behavior. You can't just yell at a guy. I was constantly moving to a hotel room. I loved to go to a goddamn hotel and lock the door. At least I got peace and quiet. I kept checking into hotels. When I heard the doors slam in some of those toilet hotels I stayed in, I thought I was in a Cagney picture. I'd be sitting on the bed and the priest, Pat O'Brien, would be giving me the last rites. The cell door would slam. But it was still better than being badgered at home. I thought everybody was badgering.

I made great attempts at being a nice fellow. I tried very hard to be a father to my stepchildren, Bogey's kids. It lasted for about eight years, I guess, that relationship.

Every girl I went with, I married. Completely in love. When I was getting divorced for the second time, I had only one day to fly to Juarez to get the divorce, because I was getting married and I had a show Monday night. My father, who was in the play with me, said, "You know, Jason, I think you ought to take the weekend off. Your marriages are overlapping."

Having to be married was another strange thing that came from lack of self-esteem. If I didn't marry a girl, I was sure I was going to lose her. You can't keep a girl, I thought. Each one was the ideal of my dreams. So I married. Again and again. You do that three times and you see the destruction and the death of relationships. It's the death of a person, an ideal person. I felt it as a death.

I married Lois when I was really starting on the way down. I don't know how she took the first five years. That's something she has to explain. I wouldn't have taken it had I been she. I couldn't take that kind of thing. A couple of times it came very close to falling apart, and the last time it came close is when I quit. That and the problems with work did it.

The last thing to go is work. It's always the last thing to go. The family, your health, everything can go, but work remains. When the work goes, you hit the bottom. Rock bottom. That's it.

I could not face my problems, my children, my wife. The only thing that kept me anchored was the work, to the point where I said that the only thing that mattered in the world to me was the theater. It was a haven. I went to the dressing room earlier and earlier every day, so I could stay there longer. I left later and later at night. Usually you spend four and a half hours in the theater. I would spend eight to ten. Never leave. I don't mean for the audience. That's only the two and a half to three hours. I would go in earlier and earlier, get the feel of the theater, walk around, talk with the stagehands, be part of that womb.

That dark womb. Those empty seats. All that is left after the show are crushed orange drink cartons and the programs with your face stepped on by a million people.

You can't play a drunk drunk. There's where you get into trouble. I tried. I wasn't shit-faced, but I had had a few. When that happened, I had the choice of life or death—that and the threat of Lois leaving both happened simultaneously.

With Lois it was never really a threat, just straight. I saw her cracking. Psychologically finished.

Isn't it odd that this guy in *Moon for the Misbegotten* is a dying drunk, seeking forgiveness, love, and understanding, but he is too far gone? Isn't it odd that the character I played as a young man, I played many years later as an older character who dies? I made the choice not to die. I let him die and I began. That was ten years ago. I let him die. I never drank again. I played that role another eight months, and I was better than ever.

Colleen Dewhurst said, "I will never forget that performance. You were Jamie, Jim Tyrone. You were that man dying in my arms that day. I have never seen truth like that before." It was the truth of knowing that I was finished. I thought I was really finished in life, as an actor, as a husband, a father, lover, knowing that I was going to my death and trying not to do it, not to die. It was the culmination of thirty years of technique that got me through that performance, but what was going on way underneath was the classic case of the alcoholic. Everything destroyed. All you could give him/me was pity and forgiveness, which is what is said in the last line of the play. The character and I became one. And that isn't acting. Because otherwise, if you do Othello you have to be arrested for murder. You have to get a new actor to kill Desdemona every night. Colleen didn't mean what she said as a compliment. She meant it as terrifying truth.

At the same time this happened, a psychiatrist whom I saw sent me to a hypnotherapist. He was a little guy named Nat Fleischer, on Fifth Avenue in the Village. I could see the son of a bitch was in some kind of trim. He said, "I'm sixty-four years old and a diabetic. Look at me, I'm healthy." He was. He was terrific. "I'm going to give you two hours here," he said, "and it's going to cost you nothing because I work with drug addicts. I work in hospitals all around the world. I have just come from France, where I did four major operations using hypnosis, where people cannot use any anesthesia."

I went to him three times, once a week. Finished. I was completely ready. I admitted that I was an alcoholic. I got the reenforcement at the moment that I admitted it. So it helped. I never drank again.

I cannot take a drink, and I'm not interested in it. It doesn't even cross my mind. It's a different stage of my life now. I have no desire. I can sit in bars and sit at dinners and love it. I get emotionally drunk.

We were in France, at a castle friends of ours rented. They had wine with dinner every night, and I was not drinking. It was as if I were . . . The mood was wonderful.

9 Are You an Alcoholic?

The questions "Am I an alcoholic?" or "Do I really have a drinking problem?" never occur to normal drinkers. These questions never cross their minds, even if they get drunk on New Year's Eve or at their sister's wedding.

Alcoholics already know deep down inside that something is wrong, but because denial is an essential element of the disease, they fail miserably to see that the problem in their lives is alcohol.

Often alcoholics compare their drinking with the stereotype of the bum on skid row. The truth is, only 3 percent of alcoholics fall into that category.

If you can identify with the stories in this book, you do have a problem. To check out the validity of this statement, try the following ninety-day experiment.

Today set a reasonable limit on the number of drinks you will have every day for the next ninety days. The number—as long as it is reasonable— doesn't really matter: it could be two or three or even four. Regardless of what happens in your life for the next three months, stay with that number. (Death, birth, wedding, change of jobs, graduation, your birthday, or Saint Patrick's Day). If you go over the number you have chosen, you have an alcohol problem. No excuses, no denial.

The following test may also help you decide if you have a drinking problem.

Are You an Alcoholic?

To answer this question, ask yourself the following 20 questions and answer them as honestly as you can.

1	Do you lose time from work due to drinking?	Yes	No
2	Is drinking making your home life unhappy?	Yes	No
3	Do you drink because you are shy with other people?	Yes	No
4	Is drinking affecting your reputation?	Yes	No
5	Have you ever felt remorse after drinking?	Yes	No
6	Have you gotten into financial difficulties as a result of drinking?	Yes	No
7	Do you turn to lower companions and an inferior environment when drinking?	Yes	No
8	Does your drinking make you carcless of your family's welfare?	Yes	No
9	Has your ambition decreased since drinking?	Yes	No
10	Do you crave a drink at a definite time daily?	Yes	No

11 Do you want a drink the next morning?	Yes	No
12 Does drinking cause you to have difficulty in sleeping?	Yes	No
13 Has your efficiency decreased since drinking?	Yes	No
14 Is drinking jeopardizing your job or business?	Yes	No
15 Do you drink to escape from worries or trouble?	Yes	No
16 Do you drink alone?	Yes	No
17 Have you ever had a complete loss of memory as a result of drinking?	Yes	No
18 Do you resent the advice of others who try to get you to stop drinking?	Yes	No
19 Do you drink to build up your self-confidence?	Yes	No
20 Have you ever been to a hospital or institution on account of drinking?	Yes	No

If you have answered yes to any one of the questions, there is a definite warning that you may be an alcoholic.

If you have answered yes to any two, the chances are that you are an alcoholic.

The foregoing test questions were developed at Johns Hopkins University Hospital, Baltimore, Maryland, to help determine whether or not a patient is an alcoholic. Reprinted by permission.

Some of the contributors to this book offer their help in answering the question "Are you an alcoholic?"

Grace Slick

If you think you have a problem with alcohol, you probably do. Because people who don't have a problem with alcohol don't think they have a problem with alcohol. I think that's real simple.

Billy Carter

If you think you have a drinking problem, you've got one. And everybody else knows about it.

Jason Robards

Each alcoholic is so different. That is why we have such terrible times pinpointing or helping people. People can take the slightest amount and be alcoholics or they can have two or three drinks and never be alcoholics. It's very mysterious.

Joan Pheney DeFer

Alcoholics don't understand why they can stop at a bar one night and have three drinks and control their drinking and on another night go to the same bar and end up having twelve. What they don't realize is that they are experiencing a symptom of alcoholism, a very early symptom, called loss of control. Very rarely will you talk to alcoholics who get drunk every single time they drink. But then there will be times when they have every intention of having only three drinks and are not able to stop at that. Some new research tells us that there is a very interesting biochemical reaction that takes over and does not allow the alcoholic to quit drinking.

Dan Anderson

An alcoholic is a person who is unable consistently to control either the start of drinking or the amount consumed or both, and because of that experiences harmful consequences. All you really need is the loss of control. You don't need a bunch of automobile accidents and wife beatings. The loss of control, I think, is the most essential part of the definition.

I think every alcoholic lives with a dilemma and denies both aspects of it. Every person who comes into Hazenden's front door has a terrible fear: "My God, they're going to take my alcohol away from me and I can't live without it." At the same time they say, "I really don't need to be there. I can control my drinking if I really want to," even though the evidence is that they can't. There is a double whammy there, a double burden of, "My God, I can't live with it and I can't live without it. What can I do?" That's a horrible dilemma. No matter which way you turn, the anxiety level goes up, and that's a terrible, terrible fear.

Doug Talbott

The most significant difference between a problem drinker or abusive drinker and the individual with the true disease of alcoholism is the presence of compulsivity. That means illog-

291

ical, irresponsible, irrational, continued use of the drug as it destroys his or her life. Not stopping. Every alcoholic I've ever known has been able to stop. It's staying stopped. As an alcoholic myself, who now has a considerable number of years of recovery, I realize that I stopped a hundred times. My problem, when I crossed the wall from the abusive stage into the addictive stage, was that I couldn't stay stopped. That is what compulsivity is. It's not staying stopped. It's the continued use of the drug as it destroys your life.

Jean Kirkpatrick
We can't really say that an alcoholic drinks because the alcoholic is unhappy, because sometimes that isn't true. Through happy periods of my life I was as much addicted to alcohol as I was in periods when I was sad.

Pete Townshend
The first person who told me I had a drinking problem was my wife. I disregarded what she said. You should listen to what people tell you.

Ryne Duren
How important is alcohol in your lifestyle? Ask your best friend if he thinks you drink too much. Tell him to give you an honest answer. Ask your wife. Ask your mother-in-law. Ask them, "Am I behaving differently?" Ask your kids. What is the group consensus? What do the people who are important in your life think

about your drinking?

Shecky Greene
You can't be a drunk without hurting people. I'm sure I hurt my family. I'm sure I hurt everybody around me.

Sid Caesar
Let's face it, alcohol is a depressant. It takes all the negative thoughts in your mind and magnifies them a trillion times. You imagine things that aren't even there. You make up things. You get used to it. Alcohol starts as a habit. You feel you have to have it. The habit becomes a physical need. Once it becomes a physical need, you have to stop. That's it!

When you get into drinking, you have got to understand you're responsible for it—if you hurt anybody, if you hurt yourself. Look at the chance you're taking. You don't think about this when you're drinking every night. You know you're going to have a hangover in the morning. You know that. And in spite of that, you go on. That's punishment.

Admit that nobody is pushing you to do it. It's happening because you let it happen. You want it to happen.

"Look at the drunk I am. Look how I fall down. Look how I vomit. Look at the foul language I use. Look at the fights I get into. Look how I punish myself. Look at what I'm doing." This is calling attention to yourself in a

293

negative way. Do you want to go through this? Do you want to debase yourself like this? For what? Is it worth what you are doing? Who are you getting even with? Who are you showing? What are you doing? Get up and do something with your life again.

You can't blame it on anybody. Look at yourself. Nobody is doing it to you. Nobody is forcing you to take the drink, and if you want to stop drinking, take the responsibility for your own life. Forget about the people you're with. Don't do it for anybody else. Just for yourself.

Verbalize it. "I'm an alcoholic." It's out. You've said it. You have actually said the words you dreaded. Once you say it, it goes away. It's like a big sore; it breaks and all the pus comes out.

When you yell for help you are admitting, "I need help." I don't want that other personality. I don't want him. I've had enough punishment, and from now on he's going to listen to me. I'm going to be the boss here. No more of this. No more self-punishment. No more. If you have anything left in yourself, you have just got to turn yourself around. No more. That's it. Once and for all. Know what you're going to go through. Be prepared. It's gonna be tough. Gonna shake and rattle and roll. But it's worth it, boy. A couple hours of shaking, that's not bad. Especially if you're in the hospital. They take care of you.

I couldn't take it anymore. It's not worth it.

It's really not worth the pain. It truly isn't. I can see it now, but at that time I couldn't see it. The pain is horrendous, and I was doing it to me. Nobody was doing it to me. I did it.

You've got to hang on to yourself. Believe in yourself. That's what I had to do.

When I go out now to have fun, I enjoy myself because I appreciate it. I found out that enjoyment is appreciation of where you were and where you are now. That's enjoyment, and I appreciate it all.

Gale Storm

Alcoholism is a disease. It is not a character weakness. It's a legitimate disease. It's an O.K. disease. You don't have to be ashamed of it. It has nothing whatsoever to do with will power. If I had diabetes, would people tell me to use my will power to get rid of it? No, they wouldn't.

Wilbur Mills

The alcoholic has to realize that he is an alcoholic. It's very important for a person to listen to his inner voice. I have heard so many alcoholics say that they knew they were alcoholics.

Every once in a while an inner voice said, "You're drinking too much. You ought to quit drinking." My own opinion is that whenever that happens to you, you already have a problem. You're already an alcoholic. I never knew of a social drinker who had to worry about taking too much to drink or quitting. Whenever that voice says something to you, that's coming from way inside and it would be well to think about it.

If people are beginning to say something to you like, "Do you feel good today?" and do that every day, they are saying that they are noticing something about you. Maybe they don't have the nerve to say directly to you what they think, but look at yourself a little.

Alcoholism is a progressive thing. It creeps up on you without your knowing anything about it. You can be an alcoholic and be the last one to know it. Begin to look at yourself, look at what you are doing. Ask people around you, "Have I changed any? Am I doing things differently?" Make some inquiries about yourself. Remember, alcoholism has a fatal design. The bottom floor of the elevator lets you out at the insane asylum or the cemetery, one or the other. I've seen people in asylums who have lost their minds completely from drinking alcohol, and I have seen people die of alcoholism. It's a horrible death. That's the final floor. You don't have to wait to get off on the final floor if you just look at yourself and analyze yourself a little bit. You have to be honest with yourself.

I think an alcoholic needs to have a good physical examination for one thing, but don't go to a doctor just for that. Get his opinion. Be honest with him. Tell him how much you drink, the reaction, the feeling you get from it, and what's happened to you. Then he'll have an opportunity, because you are honest with him, to diagnose your case properly. Go to a doctor who understands alcoholism. The doctor can determine whether you need to be hospitalized, whether you need to go through a treatment facility, or whether you can do it on your own, with or without Antabuse.

There should be no more embarrassment about being an alcoholic than about having TB.

Anybody who is trying to get sober in the beginning needs hope that he can do something that somebody else has done. He needs to know that it is possible to quit drinking a day at a time. Not for life, but a day at a time. He needs to know that people out there have done it, and because they have done it, he can have hope that he can do it. It is a highly treatable disease, the most easily treated of all our diseases, once a person makes up his mind that he wants to quit drinking and asks for help. That's all he has to do. The rest of it can be taken care of. He can then be shown how to stay sober the rest of his life.

Gary Crosby

Alcoholics are afraid to change because they're always looking at the glass as half empty instead of half full. No matter how miserable their situation is, they feel if they change it's going to be worse. Alcoholics never think it's going to be better. They always look at change as moving toward something worse. Somebody says he has to quit drinking. The first thing he thinks is No, I can't change. Never does it dawn on drinking alcoholics to say, "Hey, it might be good." Alcoholics are very negative. That's what alcoholics dwell on.

Robert Bauman
A lot of people ask, "How do you manage in a social situation when you stop drinking? How do you manage not to drink?" Well, it's amazingly simple—I just don't drink. No problem.

Don Newcombe
It's very evident that people don't go to AA or even think about AA because they don't think they're alcoholics.

Gerry Spence
Human beings are lost. We don't know where we are so we don't know who we are. To help understand ourselves, we label. With the label *alcoholic,* the question is whether or not it's useful. I think generally it is because accepting it is a way by which a man can say, "I have a constellation of problems that surround the use of alcohol." So the label of alcoholism may have some benefit to people dealing with that problem.

If I can admit that I am an alcoholic, I have taken the first step toward dealing with my problem. If I can't accept that I have an alcohol problem, if I can't make that initial admission, then there is no way for me to begin to deal with that problem or to find an answer for it. A person certainly can't climb up the stairs from the basement unless he recognizes that he is in the basement.

Elmore Leonard

(An excerpt from his book Unknown Man No. 89)

He watched her, after a moment, take another sip of wine.

"You want to get there, what're you fooling around with wine for?"

She didn't answer him.

"I used to drink mostly bourbon, over crushed ice, fill up a lowball glass. I also drank beer, wine, gin, vodka, Cuba Libres, Diet-Rite and scotch, and rye with red pop, but I preferred bourbon. Early Times. I knew a guy who drank only Fresca and chartreuse. I took a sip one time, I said to him, 'Jesus, this is the worst drink I ever tasted in my life.' He said, 'I know it is. It's so bad you can't drink very many of them.' A real alcoholic, though, can drink anything right? . . . What time you start in the morning?"

Without looking at him the girl said, "Fuck off."

There was a silence. He watched her raise the glass.

"Okay, then, how much you drink a day?"

"I don't know," the girl said. "What do you think would be about right?"

"If you're not working, have the time, I'd say

a gallon, gallon and a half. Depends what time you start."

"Early," the girl said.

"Right before you throw up?"

"Before," the girl said, looking directly at him now. "Before I get out of bed. Then I might throw up or I might piss in the bed, whichever comes first. You want to come home with me? You're so fucking interested, I'll show you what I did this morning."

"I've seen it," Ryan said. "I've been there. And you know what? I don't ever want to go back."

The girl turned to her glass of wine, subdued. She stared at it for a while before saying, "I'm not ready for you yet."

"Why put it off? Because you're having so much fun?"

"I'm not *ready*."

"You're close enough," Ryan said. "Every day you put it off you're going to hit harder when you quit. Maybe you want to crash and burn first, end up in detox. It's your choice, I'm not going to argue with you, try and convince you of anything. But listen"—he took one of his business cards out of his wallet and placed it on the bar next to her glass—"you've got to have a very good reason to want to kill yourself. Have you got one?"

The girl, staring at her glass, didn't answer. Ryan got up from the bar and left.

Doc Severinsen

You either quit drinking or you die or you have a wet brain. Those are the three options for an alcoholic. There are no others. That's it. There is no pope for drunks. You are or you aren't, and there is nobody to rescue you but yourself.

10 The Families of Alcoholics

Throughout his alcoholism, the alcoholic is surrounded by family, friends, and coworkers who tolerate his insecure personality and his drinking behavior. They become "co-alcoholics," and they are also affected by the disease. To the degree of their closeness, they develop a manner of thinking, a way of reacting, and emotional scars which they will carry for life. They have a problem, which they believe is the alcoholic and the alcoholic's drinking. They are wrong to place the blame where they do.

The first thing they must learn is that there is absolutely nothing they can do about the alcoholic and his drinking. Arguments, control, threats, bribes, favors—all that appears to be well-motivated and helpful—will fail. They must seek help for themselves. They must wait for the alcoholic to hit bottom or force it to happen.

The lives of those close to a drinking alcoholic are lives of anger, frustration, self-pity, and depression. The co-alcoholics—whether the alcoholic in their lives is drinking or not—must get down to the business of living their own lives. In seeking help for themselves and not the alcoholic, toward whom they previously directed their energy, they will begin to discover a new sense of peace and happiness. When they focus on their own needs and wants, their lives are transformed.

When those around the alcoholic seek help for themselves, they quickly learn how they are helping the alcoholic to continue his drinking. By helping themselves, they change their own behavior. This ultimately will affect the alcoholic, who in turn may seek help for himself.

If there are 20 million alcoholics in America, minimally 80 million Americans are directly affected by alcoholic behavior. This figure— which represents more than one third of the entire population—includes the alcoholics themselves, and the husbands and wives, brothers and sisters, children and parents of alcoholics.

Society has a long way to go in truly accepting alcoholism as a disease, and that is doubly true of accepting alcoholism as a family disease.

However, Dr. Conway Hunter, Jr., is hopeful when he says that enlightened people nowadays recognize the impact of one family member on another. Dr. Hunter does not mince words when he says, "You show me the child of an alcoholic and I'll show you a sick child."

Conway Hunter, Jr., M.D., is an alcoholic. He serves on the board of directors of the International Council of Alcohol and Addiction, an organization that advises the World

*Health Organization and the United Nations.
He is a physician in private practice in
Atlanta, Georgia.*

Conway Hunter, Jr., M.D.

When an alcoholic drinks, he or she changes into a different personality, a different being. The whole family is involved in the process.

Enlightened people know that in families each individual's life is involved with the others'. This is not just true with alcoholism. It's true with any major illness in any family. For example, when somebody is dying of cancer or having a serious surgical operation, the entire family is affected by it. But these things have an end point. Alcoholism or drug addiction goes on and on and on and on. It waxes and it wanes, and it gets better and it gets worse. It's the complete instability of the disease process, with apparently no known causes, that becomes so undermining to the entire family. It's very difficult for the family members to regard themselves as having part of this illness, to think that there is anything wrong with them. More often than not they develop a martyr role that is supported by their friends. Rather than thinking of the family members of the alcoholic as sick people, we think of them as deprived, depressed, poor, suffering individuals.

Alcoholism becomes a way of life, for the family members as well as the alcoholic. They live a life of total deceit. They deceive themselves by trying to rationalize that they are in a normal situation. There isn't anything normal about it. They develop all kinds of schemes to cope. They start game-playing and role-changing. They become protectors. As the alcoholic slowly descends into a childlike personality, the other family members assume parental and protective roles. They protect many different things: themselves, the integrity of the family, the economic structure of the family, and, of course, family pride. As they enter into this alliance of deceit, they become very untrustworthy. They become unreliable and physically and emotionally sick themselves. They become enablers. They make up stories to explain abnormal behavior in the alcoholic. They make up excuses for an absence. They hide. They cover up. They rationalize. They justify. They forgive over and over and over again and assume that it's not going to happen the next time.

In our society today, the pillar of strength in the home is the mother. When she becomes a victim of alcoholism or drug addiction, it is devastating to the entire family, especially the children. They are horribly embarrassed by her. They are mortified. They are ashamed. They blame themselves. This is a very significant event. Almost 100 percent of children of alcoholic mothers blame themselves for their mother's illness.

Paternal alcoholism is more socially acceptable. The whole family unites. The father is usually removed from the house and does much of his drinking away from home. The impact, though not as great as with the mother, is still devastating to the children and the family. They become victims of living in a very abnormal situation. They make excuses. They become deceitful. They all accept the blame for their father's illness. They suffer greatly from lack of their own identity and self-expression because so much of their lives are involved in their father's illness. How are they going to explain it? What are they going to do with it?

I often hear stories about children hiding under the bed or in the closet. The children gather together and go up into the attic and sit, waiting for Father to come home, not knowing how he's going to be. Is he going to love them or is he going to beat them? There is no in-between. It is one way or the other, and it produces such an unstable situation that these kids never get on an even keel.

You find that they become, more often than not, overachievers rather than underachievers. They need to excel. They need to find a source for their own re-enforcement. And often their energy is devoted to making top grades in school. They're in the glee club, the band, they work on the school paper, and things like that. They're overachievers, involved in many activities. They are often isolationists and do not mix well with the other kids. They become leaders, but they become loners.

Children of alcoholics quickly learn not to

bring friends home. Because of the instability of the situation, they don't know what it's going to be like when they get there. The fear is there all the time, plus the shame, so they do everything they can to avoid embarrassing episodes.

The long-term effect will probably be the same, whether for boys or girls. Most of these children will live abnormal lives. Many of them will become alcoholics themselves. A large number of them will marry alcoholics. Almost all of them will experience very difficult living situations. They just do not turn out to be really rounded individuals. Adult children of alcoholics will have to deal with low self-esteem, difficulty in trusting other people, hostility, anger, fear, shame, guilt. Guilt for everything, completely unfounded guilt. They often assume responsibility for everything negative, including their parents' alcoholism. They will experience a distorted view of marriage, difficulty in achieving satisfying relationships, and all manner of sexual deviation problems, real and imagined.

Children of alcoholics grow up with not only a negative role model, but an incredible amount of verbal abuse, physical abuse, and often sexual abuse. They're all people-pleasers. Their abnormal growing up is an abnormal way of life. Not until they get beyond that, get out and away from home, do they find that other people don't live that way.

Husbands or wives of alcoholics are prisoners of the alcoholic. They come under the spell of the disease of alcoholism. The spouses don't know whether to be loving or to have defenses up and be ready to go to war. They have to stay that way all the time because they never know in what state the alcoholic is going to be. They are prisoners of this imbalance that keeps them teetering and tottering. There's no one more loving, more generous, more kind, more empathetic, and more passionate than a sober alcoholic. On the other hand, no one can be as bitter and cruel and selfish as the drinking alcoholic. So the spouses who live with it are caught in that turmoil. Is it going to be up or down? They don't know. They keep coming back. It seems that there's a greater power pulling them to the alcoholic than the one that's pulling the alcoholic to drink.

The most mysterious thing to me, which I have never been able to solve, is this: We take the worst possible situation, which is the daughter of an alcoholic father, and nine times out of ten she will marry an alcoholic, even if she doesn't know her own father, her blood father. If she divorces an alcoholic, nine times out of ten she will find herself another alcoholic, who may not even be drinking at the time she gets involved in marriage. This happens over and over and over, about 90 percent of the time. It seems that this negative re-enforcement, this slap in the face, may be part of the answer. She seems to thrive on it.

Every form of sexual dysfunction, from bestiality to incest to adultery, can surface in alcoholic marriages. Seeking companionship with members of the opposite sex outside of marriage is probably one of the most commonplace events that occurs in an alcoholic's life—predominantly with males, but with females, too, especially now, with the so-called liberation of women. More women work; more women are outside the home. Infidelity is also prevalent among the spouses of alcoholics. The alcoholic becomes isolated and, to a degree, unlovable and unreceptive. Often the alcoholic is demanding and really obnoxious in the bedroom. The spouse then begins to seek understanding and compassion and romance wherever it can be found.

Close friends, employers, and coworkers also become victimized by the alcoholic to a degree, depending on their closeness to the alcoholic and to the unnatural environment. This is very important. The brother who lives thousands of miles away is not going to be as affected by his sister's alcoholism as her sister, who lives in the house next door. The brother is somewhat protected by the distance. Yet he's still affected because the family network holds together. "What are we going to do about Joan?" It is an embarrassment for the entire family that they can't get away from. But the closer they are to the alcoholic, the more severe is the impact of the disease process.

Some of the sickest people and the most enabling people are the parents of alcoholics. Their son, their daughter, can do no wrong, and they will love them to their graves. They will enable them to their grave's edge and then push them in. Parents are very difficult people to deal with because it's hard to break down their denial.

You show me the child of an alcoholic and I'll show you a sick child. You show me the wife of an alcoholic and I'll show you a sick wife. You show me the mother of an alcoholic and I'll show you a sick mother.

Family members of an alcoholic need to get treatment for themselves. They may or may not survive without it. In order for them to become totally complete, self-sufficient individuals, they need treatment for themselves, not to help the alcoholic. If they get better, the alcoholic will get better, too. It is from their own wellness that the alcoholic reaps the benefit.

Lee Bonnell, the husband of Gale Storm, is specifically included in this section because he so clearly recognizes what he did right and wrong in dealing with Gale's alcoholism. Looking back on those years of Gale's drinking, Lee realizes how he enabled her to hide from her own responsibilities and continue drinking. At home and on the road, when Gale was appearing in theaters, Lee often bought alcohol for her, even though he says, "I knew that it was not the smart thing to be doing, but I did it." At times he felt like a failure, even though he realized that he was not to blame.

The best thing Lee did, he says, was to attend

Al-Anon meetings. It was there he realized, "There just wasn't anything I could do about it." He let go.

Lee's story is a powerful message to the spouses and family members of alcoholics to seek help for themselves.

Lee Bonnell is a former top insurance executive. Lee and Gale Storm have been married forty-three years and are the parents of four children.

Lee Bonnell

There was a conspiracy of silence. No one wanted to talk about it. We all knew that Gale was an alcoholic, but we just didn't like to think about it. Maybe that was the whole thing. Our son Peter said he just thought that she'd drink until she killed herself, and I got to a place where I was of the same mind. I didn't want that to happen, but I realized that there wasn't anything I could do. I would turn it over to God, and it was up to him to work it out. But I had to get out of the picture in the sense of trying to run her life.

The thing I think I did wrong, and in a sense it enabled her to go on drinking, was not really facing up to the fact that she was an alcoholic. I knew she was an alcoholic three years before she did, but I didn't do anything about it except needle her and cause friction in our relationship. Our daughter, Susie, got me to go to Al-Anon, which began to help me realize what I was doing.

What I did right was to go to Al-Anon, and when I went there I realized that I had been helping her to drink instead of helping her to stop.

I enabled her by catering to her, by doing things for her, by not being up-front with her with my feelings about her drinking, by not explaining to her that I thought her self-worth was going down because of how she deprecated herself and let me make all the decisions. I thought I was doing right, but, in retrospect, I know I was an enabler. I did all the wrong things. She should have been standing on her own feet. She should have been making decisions. She should have been aware that she was drinking too much. But I protected her. I knew she was drinking at home. I'd come home and know that she'd drunk an awful lot of liquor. I could tell that she had been drinking because her personality would change. She would become very antagonistic and very angry very quickly. We could no longer talk. We could no longer communicate.

She never really went on a bender per se. I begged off from social situations many times because I knew that she wasn't up to going. She was sick, so we couldn't go out. I would become very angry. I knew that our life could have been a lot more rewarding socially for both of us if she hadn't been drinking. So I resented that.

But I never was embarrassed about the fact that she was an alcoholic. A lot of people are, I think. But I never felt that way. I guess I loved her so much it didn't make any difference to me what other people thought.

Sometime after Gale quit drinking, she said she wanted to go public and tell other people about her alcoholism, to help them, and that was the most exciting thing that I think could have happened. I think God has used her in a marvelous way to help a lot of alcoholics get sober who wouldn't have gotten sober otherwise. I have heard people come to her and say, "You saved my life." That's a thrill for her, and it's a thrill for me too.

After forty-three years together, you begin to read each other's minds. And that happens a lot with us. I'll be thinking of something and she'll say, "Are you thinking what I'm thinking?" I'll say, "What are you thinking? . . . Yup, that's it." We do have a great relationship now. We've had a marvelous marriage. We've had a lot of ups and downs, lots of screaming and yelling over the years, but, believe me, I really love her, and she really loves me. We have a warm relationship. I don't know what I would do without her, and I'm sure she feels the same about me.

Children of alcoholics experience feast or famine, all or nothing, protection or neglect.

The Reverend Jerry Falwell's father was an alcoholic who died from cirrhosis of the liver when Jerry was fifteen years old.

Jerry says, "I never recall a time when my

father was not drinking—not a single day.'' Reflecting back on his own lack of knowledge about alcoholism, he says, ''We had no perception of the problem he was facing, and we had no concept of how to help him.''

Like so many children of alcoholics, he wished that his father would stop drinking, and shame and embarrassment about his father's unpredictable behavior prevented him from bringing friends and dates home or talking with them about his father's alcoholism.

Reverend Falwell believes that his father's guilt feelings played a large role in why he was given so much at such a young age.

Reverend Jerry Falwell is the pastor of the Thomas Road Baptist Church in Lynchburg, Virginia, and president of the Moral Majority. His father, Cary Falwell, was an alcoholic. In his father's memory, Falwell started the Elim Home for Alcoholics in Lynchburg.

The Reverend Jerry Falwell
My father was a successful businessman. He was about five ten, 210 to 215 pounds, a big, rotund fellow with a bay-window stomach, and very aggressive and volatile. He was very kind to us children and gave us everything. I have a twin brother, Gene, an older brother, Lewis, and an older sister, Virginia. Gene and I are both fifty now. We had an older brother who died last year

who was eight years older than Lewis. My father was very considerate to us all, probably gave us too much, lavished things on us—automobiles, money, whatever—without our having to work or assume responsibility to obtain them.

In my first memories of my father, when I was a little boy, he was already drinking quite heavily. He was running the Power Oil Company, the Mary Garden nightclub, and a large motel/restaurant. During Prohibition, he ran a liquor business, illegal moonshine, and sold it to distributors. Though he was well known as a lawbreaker, he never had any trouble over it. Dad made a lot of money selling liquor. Everybody in our town, of course, knew that. We lived in a big house up on a hill, and you could either get your oil or whiskey there or someone would deliver it to you. The nightclub was a very rough place. My father also, back in those days, would stage dog fights and chicken fights. They were all illegal, but they were on our farm and everybody came. They would gather in a big circle, betting. My father never had any problems at all with the law because he was so powerful in the county. It was just part of life. I grew up that way.

In 1931, two years before I was born, my father and his younger brother, Garland, who was quite a wild fellow, quite a reckless guy, had gotten into an extremely violent argument. There was a shoot-out, and my father killed him. There was never any trial over it. It was all in self-defense.

I guess that Garland was in his early twenties. My father would have been thirty-eight. There was quite a range between them. Garland had been in a lot of trouble and actually gone to jail. He had been unmanageable by any member of the family. They couldn't handle him. I don't know all the circumstances of that day, only hearsay. Garland was on drugs. He was wild. Completely out of it. Someone had called the police about his throwing firecrackers next door to our restaurant, right there in the city. It was a neighbor who'd called, but since Father owned the restaurant, Garland thought it was my father who had called. When Dad drove up, I am told, Garland came out of the restaurant with a pistol in each hand, cursing and screaming and yelling at my dad. Dad was very hot-tempered, so he drove to our house immediately, a mile away from there. Mother said she knew he was very upset when he came in. He got the shotgun, .12-gauge double-barreled shotgun, and told my mother he was going back up there to see what Garland was doing. She pleaded with him not to go, but he went anyway. He parked and walked in the door, and Garland came out with his two guns again; Dad shot from the hip. I think Garland was hit in the chest or the neck and was killed instantly. My mother said it was the key incident in my father's life, with which he could not cope.

Nobody was bitter with Dad about it. But that incident precipitated his excessive drinking, and

319

he never stopped. Seventeen years later he was dead from cirrhosis.

I was fifteen when my father died. He didn't believe in hospitals or churches, and he never set foot inside either one. He died at home. Doctors treated him there. Cirrhosis causes your liver to stop working. You swell up and then they tap you, draw off the fluid so many times until you are out. You turn very yellow. Jaundice. I remember, as a boy, watching that.

Three weeks before Dad died a man named Josh Alvis, now long since dead, had come by the house. I remember his coming in to see Dad a lot toward the end. He spent some time reading the Scriptures to Dad, giving him the biblical plan of salvation, the story of the gospel of Christ. Dad accepted Christ. It was not until years later that I was able to put all the pieces together and connect his conversion experience and his last days on earth with what happened and the way he reacted. The last several weeks of his life, probably three, his language and his attitude were greatly changed. Very little hostility there, I recall. I detected that he was ready to die.

Dad used to come home after a long day, really loaded, yelling and screaming, and upset everything. Mother was never disturbed by it, and because she wasn't, we never paid any attention to it. He never struck any of us. He never hurt his family. He was never violent to us. But very noisy. He'd go to bed early every night and get up at four o'clock every morning. By the time everyone else was up and around, he had long since been at the office. I do remember, about the last five years of his life, that he would sleep a lot because the drinking was beginning to take a real toll on him, to debilitate him and deteriorate his faculties. By that time, my older brother, Lewis, was involved in the business, and things were going on without Dad's personal involvement.

Dad never drank to the point where he couldn't run his business, but several fifths of whiskey a day were not unusual for him. He got to where it didn't intoxicate him, where you couldn't notice it, except for the smell on his breath.

Dad had made enough money in his life, even while he was drinking heavily, that we never had to do without anything. It was nothing, back in those days, for me, a twelve- to fifteen-year-old kid, to walk around with a hundred dollars in my pocket. To the kids I ran with then, that was a mammoth amount of money. It was nothing unusual for money to be piled up on the table. I'd say, "Dad, you got any money?" And he'd say, "Get your hand full." He didn't know what I took. He didn't care. I had an automobile by the time I was twelve. My father gave me one. He signed a driver's application saying I was fifteen.

With the license, I didn't have to stay at home. But I didn't dare bring a girlfriend or anybody refined to the house because Dad was totally unpredictable. I brought a friend into the house one day. Dad was sitting at the table. A fifth of whiskey and a .38 Smith and Wesson were lying on the table. He carried a .38 with him all the time. My dad picked up the gun and said, "Don't move, boy." And he put the gun down to his feet. "I've been trying to kill that fly all day." He shot a hole in the kitchen floor, right between his feet. That was the last time I ever got my friend onto the property. Mother just couldn't believe it.

When Mother saw a storm arising, she would just get us out of the house, just tell us to go. Whenever it was just Dad and Mom, he got quiet, because he knew he would never get a rise out of her. There was no point in starting an argument if it was going to be a one-way street. The only time he would put on a show was when he was really upset and a crowd was there. Mother very wisely would say, "Why don't you find something to do? Go somewhere, play with somebody." We always had something going. I was very active, into everything, and all that fit into Mom's way of handling the problem. She made the situation as harmonious as it could be under the circumstances, but rather than bringing a crowd of buddies to our house, I would hang out in the town where the gang was.

The refrigerator was filled with liquor all the time. Dad usually kept a fifty-five-gallon keg of wine in the basement. Good wine, usually several cases of beer, and always cases of whiskey. The refrigerator would be full of it. He wouldn't have cared if we drank it. We never did. I suppose seeing what it was doing to him, instead of tempting us to drink, caused us to hate it. I have drunk some whiskey and beer in my life, wine as a youngster, just piddling with the guys, just to act big. But I never enjoyed it. Never wanted to do it. I think it was because I saw the bad side of it.

Dad would go to bed very early and, of course, young people don't go to bed at eight o'clock, so we would have to get out of the house and do things, which we did a lot.

We couldn't say anything. Couldn't knock on doors. Couldn't let the phone ring. That type of thing. He was shielded, protected all the time, and he had enough money that he was never deprived.

I knew a lot of kids at school who probably didn't have the money we had, but they had very happy family relationships. Their parents, family, were all close together. We were always careful to cover up, to pretend we had the same thing, talk about it as if we did. I doubt if any of our friends knew that Dad had a serious drinking problem until he was dead.

We had lots of buddies and friends. We just busied ourselves, staying out of the house, staying away from Dad because the situation was definitely uncontrollable. Very few people in our school knew that he had a problem. We never talked about it, and it was really a well-kept secret inside the family and the business that he was deteriorating and diminishing on a regular basis.

Because of Mother, we always had big Christmases, and Dad would unload any amount of money she wanted to buy things. We got big gifts. Big everything. It was all a part of the guilt complex, I'm sure. Thanksgiving, no matter what, we'd always have a big Thanksgiving dinner. To his credit he would really try, until the last year or two, to be straight for the holidays because people would be coming in. It would usually be late in the evenings before he got a little bit difficult. On holidays he might have a little bit. He drank enough that when he drank a little, you wouldn't know it. As a matter of fact, he had to drink a little to stay steady. He'd sip all day. The big citizens around the area would be in during the day. Everybody who was anybody. Dad would take a little drink here and there throughout the evening until he got ready for bed.

Every morning he'd get up, break two raw eggs, sometimes three, into a glass and swallow them. Very often I would see him mix raw oysters with vinegar, salt, and pepper, and then take the bowl and swallow them. I couldn't imagine anybody drinking raw eggs and oysters. But that was his Maalox, the way he kept his stomach livable. He couldn't eat anything until he had those eggs or oysters, and a little drink after that.

I know that I wished that he would stop, that he would not drink. I saw it getting worse. Yes, sir, I saw him physically going downhill. There was obviously a medical problem. And I saw his personality, his will, weakening. I saw him sleeping more. I saw him coming home during the day. I even saw him a few times at his place of business, when he would have his office locked. When I would go look in the window of the office, he would be asleep on the floor, just taking a nap there.

I think we had more pity than contempt. Because it would be nothing for him, sitting in a chair, to fall asleep in the middle of the day, just fall out of it. Toward the last, he really lost control.

I was so much into life, having the money and not having to work, that I didn't have time to feel neglected or sit down and analyze how bad things were. I have a feeling that if Dad had lived until I was seventeen, eighteen, or twenty, I would have begun to build up those resentments. I think maybe I would have come to the place where I really would have resented what he was doing to Mother. I think my biggest concern, the only thing that gave me any bad feelings toward Dad at all, was his making life so miserable for Mom. She would never leave home. She was very much a homebody. I do recall feeling very strongly about the uncomfortable, miserable conditions Mom was in.

She never took on a martyr's complex. She never retaliated against him, and she worked very hard to prevent our ever resenting him. She never allowed an altercation. She took all the burden on herself. It must have been a tremendous burden, but, as a result of it, we don't have any bad memories of being unkind to Dad. She would always tell us, "He just can't keep drinking, he'll stop." She would try to give us a ray of hope. I don't think I ever had any hope that he would stop. I don't think I ever believed what she was saying. He died at the age of fifty-five of cirrhosis of the liver, right in the spring of his life. He was victimized by alcohol.

"There were unlit Christmas trees and cold houses and no dinners." This simple statement says so much about the alcoholic home. Rod Steiger's mother was an alcoholic, and his early years profoundly influenced his life. The beauty of Rod Steiger's story is its positiveness and his joy for his mother, who found sobriety through Alcoholics Anonymous. Rod Steiger's love for his mother and his understanding of alcoholism are inspiring.

Rod Steiger, one of America's most distinguished actors, received an Academy Award for his performance in In the Heat of the Night. *Some of his other films include* On the Waterfront, The Harder They Fall, *and* The Pawnbroker.

Rod Steiger

I'm an only child, and I was born in West Hampton, Long Island. I think my mother's basic problem was the fact that she was a very attractive woman physically; she also had great mental spirit.

We took a trip to California when I was a child. I don't remember this incident, but the story is in the family. My mother was on the beach in a bathing suit, and she was offered a contract by a movie company. That's how attractive she was. Soon after that, she got an infection or a disease in, I believe, her right leg and they did an operation. In those days they were not technically where they are today, and the operation backfired. The leg became stiff for the rest of her life. At one time she wanted to be a singer. She had a very good voice, which is passed on to my daughter, who is now an opera singer in Britain. I think out of that incident she began to fortify her courage, to lose her disappointment, through the use of alcohol. It got to a point where alcohol finally took her over instead of her having any control of it.

When I was a young boy, before my family broke up when I was twelve or fourteen years of age, she was to the point where she was hiding bottles around the house and under mattresses. It was like *The Lost Weekend*. I didn't understand at the time that alcoholism was a disease that could take over a person's nervous system or central operating mechanisms. We had quite a few fights, some of them physical.

One day my stepfather left a note saying, "I'm going down to the corner." He left a little money on the table—and he didn't come back. He was a wonderful, wonderful, wonderful man; I could not have had a better father had he been my real one. I never knew my real father.

My mother used to disappear for days at a time, and things were pretty rough. We had verbal shouting matches and fights and arguments and struggles over bottles of liquor. There were unlit Christmas trees and cold houses and no dinners. My most embarrassing memories are of being called up by people in local saloons and told to come and get my mother when she was making a nuisance of herself. I didn't bring many friends home after a while because I didn't know if anybody was going to be home or who was going to be home. When she went through her worst periods there would be all sorts of strange people in the house and they'd be drinking.

When I was a child I didn't know that an alcoholic needs guidance and professional help. A child can't understand why a parent doesn't stop something that's hurting the child, and hurting herself. You become confused and angry; you don't understand at all.

When I was sixteen and a half years old, I went looking for my mother and, in a sense, physically forced her to sign a paper saying I was seventeen, so I could go into the navy. While I was in the navy, my mother tried to pull herself together and had a little flat for me to come home to. She begged me to come back after the navy. I came back, and I was old enough and I had seen enough in the navy and had learned enough of life and death to be grown up. I began to look at her differently. Very quietly, without even telling me, she joined Alcoholics Anonymous, and through AA she pulled herself out for the last eleven years of her life. She became a sponsor of other people, and she worked very hard. She never had another drop of drink for the rest of her life and became a wonderful person again. I loved her again, instead of thinking I hated her, which had been because I hadn't been an old enough or wise enough or mature enough person to understand her problem. It was through her own efforts—that's what makes me proud of her and her ability to face her problems—that she finally conquered it.

I loved my mother very much when she died, but it was only because of my own problems and what I had seen in the navy that I began to realize that alcoholism is a disease and can be treated, and a person can pull out. My mother certainly did, and she was splendid and well loved at the time of her unfortunate death, of a coronary.

I understand my mother better now because I've had major surgery, which put me into depression. I didn't go into alcohol, I went into a depression, which is another form of chemical imbalance. When you have a major operation, your hormone balance is knocked off, and I could easily have gone into drinking to ease the pain of depression. Having seen what it did to my mother, I didn't. I went for therapeutic help, but I can see how quickly one could go to alcohol.

I think that for a great deal of time my mother's drinking made me distrust any intimate relationship with anybody; it made me into too much of a loner. It may also have affected my relationships in marriage; I've been married three times, and I'm not very good at it. That was the unconscious effect it might have had on me psychologically.

I learned that my mother had a disease that could be handled, and I learned to have compassion for her rather than anger. I realized that she was fighting a very bitter and desperate battle and, happily, she won. I can't say words enough about such organizations as Alcoholics Anonymous. No organization is 100 percent, but whatever they do, it's wonderful. I've seen in action what happens when human beings are given reaffirmation in their self-respect and a little love. Nothing bathes you more in happiness than to see those you love regain their self-respect. The glow of their pride coats you like a new God-given sunshine. If you love them, nothing makes you feel better than when you see them hurdle a fence that they swore before they could never get over. They become Olympic champions in your eyes and in their eyes. I saw that change in my mother and I remembered it. Because my mother gained her self-respect, I found the ability to love her again. An ability to create love is one of the greatest treasures on the face of the earth.

11 Help for the Families

Something can be done about an alcoholic's drinking. Intervention is the process by which those close to the alcoholic—family, employer, friends, and coworkers—confront the alcoholic. The goal of the intervention is to force the alcoholic to seek treatment.

Widespread use of intervention today is responsible for many alcoholics' facing their alcoholism and now living happy lives. Though there is risk and the stakes are high, an intervention—guided by a trained professional —can be highly successful. Joan Pheney DeFer's message is: You don't have to live the way you are living anymore, and intervention is the loving thing to do for an alcoholic.

Joan Pheney DeFer, M.S.W., is an alcoholic. She is the former director of Counseling Services and of the Outpatient Department at Brighton Hospital, an alcoholism treatment facility in Brighton, Michigan. She now counsels recovering alcoholics and cocaine addicts, in private practice.

Joan Pheney DeFer, M.S.W.

When alcoholics are confronted about their drinking, on a one-to-one basis, they react angrily or deny it or discount it.

Families tend to get very, very resentful of the alcoholic's behavior. They think alcoholics can quit if they want to, but most alcoholics cannot quit without some kind of intervention, without some kind of treatment, without some kind of realization of the problem.

Each individual who knows an alcoholic has a pearl of wisdom about that person's alcoholism that can really help get the alcoholic into treatment. One little pearl does not make a necklace, but you put all those together and you have to have something. And it is harder for an alcoholic to deny what you say when you have other people to back up your story.

Intervention is a group of concerned, caring people whose goal is to confront the alcoholic to get him or her to agree to go to treatment.

You confront the alcoholic with the reality of his or her situation. When you consider that this person can die from the disease—and will, if he or she doesn't go insane first—what you are saying is, "We love you. We care about you. You're sick and we want you to get help and we will help you. We don't want you to bomb out. We don't want you to end up losing your job, your spouse, all the things that alcoholics can lose." What we're doing in intervention is

334

creating a situation in which, we hope, the alcoholic will feel there is too much to lose not to go into treatment.

I wouldn't even ask an alcoholic to admit he's alcoholic. I would ask him to be willing to go through a treatment, period. I'd say, "You're having trouble with alcohol. Go and see. Go and learn something about alcohol. See if you're an alcoholic. We think you are. Agree to go to treatment. Take three weeks out of your life."

A professional, like an alcoholism counselor or a therapist, really needs to run the intervention. It is a skill that takes coordination of the various players. It takes experience to be able to handle these situations, which can be very difficult, to make sure everything turns out the way you want and does not turn into a yelling match. Anything can happen when you get a nonobjective person at a very emotional time. You need someone who can have objectivity and conduct the intervention so the outcome is good for the family members and the alcoholic.

Usually what happens is that one person close to the alcoholic comes and says something like, "I'm very concerned about my husband. His drinking is getting out of control. He hit me for the first time." So the counselor asks that person to pick the key people in the alcoholic's life. That person will go to the key people and say, "I'd like you to come to a meeting about Bill's drinking. We're all concerned about him. I'd like you to come and get some education. There is a process we may do called intervention. Here are some things to read." So then that group comes in and we educate them about the disease of alcoholism. We tell them exactly what an intervention is like. Then we ask them to go home, saying, "This is your task. We would like you to write down specifically the last three times that Bill, our alcoholic, has hurt you or embarrassed you or caused you concern. Write down the date, the time, and how you felt about it." They come back after they have done their task and meet as many times as they need to to make sure that they understand what they're doing and why they're doing it.

It's going to be a tense encounter. The alcoholic will be there. Each person is concerned about what the alcoholic is going to think about him or her, so their experiences are put in writing after being thought about at a calm time. That way the person doesn't have a chance to forget it. Sometimes people don't respond as well under pressure. It's also a good exercise for the person who's writing it to realize which alcoholic behavior bothers him or her. That starts to get the person used to the fact that this is alcoholic behavior. It's the beginning of the healing of the family. These issues and the hurt within the family need to be dealt with, but at a later date. An intervention should not open wounds and leave them open. The family also has to make a commitment in the intervention to seek further help themselves.

The key persons in the alcoholic's life include all the family members. We encourage all ages. Some people say, "My child is only five." That child is still part of the alcoholic system, even if he's just sitting there. He needs to be able to say his piece. It is also very important to have the employer in there. Some people hesitate about that. But the employer knows. I don't care what the alcoholic says, the employer knows that he's having a problem with alcohol.

If a clergyman is important to the alcoholic, invite him to participate. Remember, everyone has key people in their lives.

A best friend is real good, even if the best friend drinks. Even alcoholics can see in other people what they cannot see in themselves.

If the alcoholism counselor feels there is a person in the group who is so angry that he or she can't pull off the intervention, the counselor will ask that person not to be involved in the intervention, and explain why. Some people are so enraged by the alcoholic's behavior that they can't put that aside. Part of the assessment of the alcoholism counselor is to make sure the people are all set, so someone doesn't sabotage it or get angry. The alcoholic will pick up on that right away. Alcoholics are perceptive people. They are very sensitive. They can feel the mood of anybody in a room. If they walk into a room and it's hostile, they can feel it. The love has to be there. If we have a family so angry that they can't confront the alcoholic, we'll work with them around that so they can do it eventually.

We like people to come to the intervention with a plan of what they will do if the intervention is not successful, if the person refuses to go into treatment, remembering that this is done with love and caring. You must be willing to say what you are going to do and follow through on it. Sometimes that means a temporary marital separation. These things are very serious. We are talking about someone who could leave, go to a bar, get into an accident, and get killed. Even though this may sound a little heavy-handed, intervention works. A lot of people stay sober because of intervention.

The intervention is not done at home, not on the alcoholic's turf. The alcoholic is too comfortable there. If you don't think you can get the alcoholic to go to a treatment center, go to a doctor's office or someplace that's neutral. That's decided in your pre-intervention sessions with the therapist. You decide where you'll meet, what time you'll meet, and you actually do a rehearsal of the intervention. You have your little piece of paper with your facts and your dates and your feelings. It's one person's job to bring the alcoholic to the intervention. In the meantime, we have called the hospital. We have a bed ready for him, and his bag is packed. It's in the car. We don't want the alcoholic going home from the intervention to pack. We have met with his employer. His coworkers are helping out. Everything is all set. His options are closed. His reality is narrowed down. His employer is going to say to him, "Fine. Forget about that case. We've got someone taking care of it." The alcoholic is not going to be thrilled about this, you understand.

Bill, our alcoholic, walks in. He looks round. The alcoholism counselor is the first to speak. "Bill, we have all asked you to come here today. We have some things we'd like you to hear, and when we're through you may ask some questions. We'd like your cooperation right now. We like to ask you not to interrupt until we're through." If Bill does interrupt, the alcoholism counselor will intervene and say, "Bill, our agreement was that you can ask questions. You probably have a lot of legitimate questions right now, and I know that this is a real stressful time. We'll talk about it after everyone is through."

Then you systematically go around the room and each person tells his or her story about their concern for him and their love for him. Many times the alcoholic will say, "Well, what do you want me to do?" Then the alcoholism counselor, or whoever is coached to do this, will say, "We'd like you to agree to go to Hazelden or Brighton for three or four weeks." If the alcoholic says yes, that's it. The intervention is over. Then we say, "O.K., we've got your bed. Your bags are in the car." Boom—the alcoholic is in treatment before you know it. That doesn't mean that the alcoholism counselor won't come back and answer questions for him. We've had interventions where people walk into the room, look around, and say, "O.K., what's the deal?" They know. They start laughing. The counselor says, "We want you to go for treatment." The alcoholic agrees. Then the intervention is over. They can be that simple. We rarely have people stomping out.

You have that person's world sitting in the room. You have the most powerful people in that person's life, and all you ask the alcoholic to do, at least for the first ten minutes, is to listen. That's pretty hard for someone to turn down. Now, you take a middle-stage alcoholic with symptoms like marital discord, problems on the job, drinking in the morning, drinking before a party. He still has a lot to lose. He still has his wife and kids and dog and cat and job. Your chance of getting him into treatment is about 80 percent, which is very high.

The alcoholic can feel the caring in the room. That's why it's so important during the intervention process to make sure the family can set aside their anger and resentment. This must be dealt with in their own treatment, or while the alcoholic is in therapy, so they can do their own recovering. Alcoholism is a family disease, not one just affecting the alcoholic. The family has been wounded by the alcoholism, and they need to be repaired just as the alcoholic needs to be repaired.

Basically, an intervention would sound like this. The wife's best friend, Gloria: "Bill, on

Saturday night you came over to our house for dinner. It was our anniversary and I was really looking forward to it. You fell and you broke a piece of my crystal. I asked you about it the next day, and you didn't even remember. I was very hurt because that crystal is something my mother gave me." That is an actual description of what happened. That's not judging it. Gloria is talking about her own feelings: "I felt hurt. I felt concerned about you."

Gloria's husband, Fred: "When you drove us home after the hockey game in January, I was afraid we would all be killed."

John, the alcoholic's best friend: "You know, when we went on vacation, Bill, you drank an awful lot, especially the Saturday night that we planned to go out for dinner. We were going to surprise you and we went to pick you up in your room and no one could wake you up. We couldn't. We tried everything. We splashed water. You were like a dead man. I thought, What's happening to my friend? Where is my friend?"

The alcoholic's daughter, Sally, may say (and it can be very emotional): "You were supposed to come and see me in a school play, and you called and said you were going to be a few minutes late because you were having a drink with a friend, but you would be home, and you never came home. You stayed out all night and you missed the play. I wanted you to be there and you promised me you'd be there. I cried."

His twelve-year-old son, Dick, may be more

aloof because he's had more years of this: "You asked me last Saturday night why I always stay over at Mike's house. The reason is, I won't bring any of my friends over to the house because you get drunk and you start saying real weird stuff about girls and I can't stand it. It makes me sick. I don't know why Mom doesn't leave you."

The wife, Jane, might say: "Bill, you used to be such an affectionate person when we first got married. Last Friday night you came home and you were so drunk. I was trying to help you upstairs and I went to put my arm around you and you turned around and called me a fucking whore. I'd never heard you call me something like that before. I was so hurt. I went to talk to you about it the next day, and you acted as though I was crazy, as though you had never said it."

The counselor keeps order, keeps things running smoothly. If someone gets too emotional, the counselor can go over and put a hand on that person. The counselor orchestrates the intervention.

The father of the alcoholic might say: "You know, Bill, I have always been so proud of the way you have been with your mother and me. You have always been such a good person. But when we hear you talk the way you do, like you did when you were over to our house for the birthday party, it was as though you were a different person. I was shocked at the language you used, calling your mother a dumb old broad.

We had heard your wife say that you had been using some of that language, but we had never heard it. We were just shocked. You had been drinking."

The mother of the alcoholic might say: "The other night, when you stopped by, you'd obviously been drinking. And while you were at our house you drank four beers. I begged you not to take the fourth one, and when I wouldn't give it to you, you just took it and told me that I didn't know what I was talking about and that I had always been an interfering person. You hurt me a great deal."

The boss would say: "Bill, you have been an asset to our company. You are very talented. However, you have been missing a lot of work. The quality of your work has gone down. What projects we used to give you, you would finish a week early, with no help. Now we always give the junior partner part of your work because you are so erratic. We don't know if you are going to finish or not. These clients are important people. Our obligation is to them. We like you very much. We think you're outstanding. But if you don't get treatment and stay sober, we can't keep you on the staff anymore. We just can't do it. We've had complaints from our clients. You reek of alcohol and don't follow through on things. You're rude on the phone. We can't tolerate that. We want you to get help. We'll support you and let you take this time. We've got someone who will do your work for you while you're gone.

When you come back, no problem; but if you drink again, you're out."

Some alcoholics become angry. Some are very relieved because they have been fighting this. Now the jig is up. When alcoholics come to treatment, they may be angry, but by the time they leave, they are so grateful to this group of people. People feel that the risk of participating in an intervention is enormous. They are afraid that the alcoholic isn't going to like them anymore. They are afraid they're going to lose their husband or their son or their best friend or a very good employee. But the alcoholic sees their love. I have very rarely seen an alcoholic leave treatment who hasn't come full circle.

Don't forget the family has been through the intervention training and they have decided what the consequences are if the alcoholic does not go into treatment. The commitment must be there. We will work with people for however long it takes to get some kind of commitment. If the alcoholic has nothing to lose, there is no point in having intervention because then you have no clout. You need the clout. You need the clout of people who love him. You need the employer. You need the wife. You need the kids. They have to be willing to follow through. All the key people ask the alcoholic to go into treatment. If the alcoholic refuses treatment, we ask him to go to AA and remain sober. If he is able to do that, God bless him. If he isn't, the agreement is that he'll go into treatment.

Intervention is a primary tool for helping alcoholics nowadays. The National Council on Alcoholism in your state can give you the names of people in your area who conduct interventions, or AA is in every phone book. Their people will know, or they'll find out for you, what treatment centers are available and who is doing intervention.

Al-Anon: Is It for You?

Millions of people are affected by the excessive drinking of someone close. The following twenty questions are designed to help you decide whether or not you need Al-Anon.

1 Do you worry about how much someone else drinks?   Yes No
2 Do you have money problems because of someone else's drinking?   Yes No
3 Do you tell lies to cover up for someone else's drinking?   Yes No
4 Do you feel that drinking is more important to your loved one than you are?   Yes No
5 Do you think that the drinker's behavior is caused by his or her companions?   Yes No
6 Are mealtimes frequently delayed because of the drinker?   Yes No
7 Do you make threats, such as, "If you don't stop drinking I'll leave you?"   Yes No

8 When you kiss the drinker hello, do you secretly try to smell his or her breath?   Yes No

9 Are you afraid to upset someone for fear it will set off a drinking bout?   Yes No

10 Have you been hurt or embarrassed by a drinker's behavior?   Yes No

11 Does it seem as if every holiday is spoiled because of drinking?   Yes No

12 Have you considered calling the police because of drinking behavior?   Yes No

13 Do you find yourself searching for hidden liquor?   Yes No

14 Do you feel that if the drinker loved you, he or she would stop drinking to please you?   Yes No

15 Have you refused social invitations out of fear or anxiety?   Yes No

16 Do you sometimes feel guilty when you think of the lengths you have gone to control the drinker?   Yes No

17 Do you think that if the drinker stopped drinking, your other problems would be solved?   Yes No

18 Do you ever threaten to hurt yourself to scare the drinker into saying, "I'm sorry" or "I love you"?   Yes No

19 Do you ever treat people (children, employees, parents, coworkers, etc.) unjustly because you are angry at someone else for drinking too much?   Yes No

20 Do you feel there is no one who understands your problems?   Yes No

If you have answered yes to three or more of these questions, Al-Anon or Alateen may help.

346

You can contact Al-Anon or Alateen by looking in your local telephone directory.*

Many who have lived with alcoholism offer their advice to family members, friends, co-workers, and employers of alcoholics.

Ryne Duren

Alcohol is a drug. Most of us have been taught from childhood that a person who can't drink is a weak person, rather than that alcohol is a drug and if you use it you will act out drug behavior.

The word *alcoholic* doesn't mean anything unless you understand what you are saying. The alcoholic is a drug addict. One of the things about the addict is that he doesn't always have to use it, but he always has to have it available, just in case the urge comes up. Most people don't understand the alcoholic's relationship with the drug. It becomes the most important thing in his life, more important than his wife or his children.

In my case, my wife would say, "Your mother and dad are coming over and it's Steve's birthday, so be home at six o'clock." I wouldn't show up until midnight, drunker than a hoot. The folks had gone home, disgusted with me. She would say, "How could you possibly do that under those circumstances?" The most important thing

*From *Al-Anon—Is It for You?* Copyright © 1983 by Al-Anon Family Group Headquarters. Reprinted by permission of Al-Anon Family Group Headquarters, Inc.

to me at that time was my relationship with the drug. That is how it is with a drug addict. That's the mistake that people make. I was having a relationship with a chemical that surpassed any other thing. That's what drug addiction is all about.

When the alcoholic wants that fix and gets involved in it, nothing else has any importance.

Shecky Greene

One of our top entertainers is a very close friend of mine. He has tremendous success and tremendous love of the public, and I see him drinking more and more and more. He doesn't realize what he's doing. His wife said to me one day, "I know you had a problem with alcoholism. I'm having trouble with him. Maybe you can help."

Then we were all three having dinner, and she said, "Waiter, will you please bring my husband a double martini, two olives, and I'll have the same thing?" She had said to me, "He's getting crazy with this drinking and I don't know what to do about it."

But the minute they finished their drinks she said, "Waiter, would you bring my husband another one, double, two olives, and I'll have the same." Later I said, "You're doing this to him. You don't realize what you're doing. He didn't ask for the drinks. I was sitting here for an hour and a half and didn't hear him ask for a drink. You automatically think that when you sit with people, that's the thing to do, to drink. You're the one doing this. You have as much of a problem as he has."

Wilbur Mills

The wife will call on Monday and say that her husband can't be in because he's going to the dentist's office to have a tooth pulled. You check back on the records and find that he's had seventy-six teeth pulled. She'll go to the liquor store to buy him something to drink because he can't go himself. She's doing it out of love. She thinks she's helping him. All she's doing is helping him to the grave.

You learn at Al-Anon not to do those things. You've got to give them tough love, rather than the kind you've been giving. Love is more caring. You want him to live; you don't want to love him into the grave. It's awfully hard—for a wife, particularly.

On one occasion, a woman called me and asked me to come see her husband. He didn't call me. I don't normally do that, but I did. He was not there. She wanted to know what to do about him. He would get drunk at home and then go across the street to an apartment where he had a drinking buddy. When he had run out of liquor himself, he went over there to drink the buddy's liquor. He wouldn't listen to her. He wouldn't do anything about it. She wanted to know what to do. I said, "Call the police and have him arrested for drunkenness." "Oh, I wouldn't think of that,"

she said. "They'd throw my poor husband in jail."
I said that closing the jail door sometimes
awakens a man to the fact that he's got a
problem. "Something has got to happen to your
husband to cause him to want to be sober, to
recognize he's got a problem." She did, finally.

The Arlington police picked him up. He
identified himself as a District policeman. So they
got the District police and told them that they had
one of their men over in jail. They sent over to
get him and put him in a facility. They got him
sober. He wouldn't have gotten sober otherwise,
frankly; he couldn't take the coddling. He
probably would have died.

Sometimes you have to be tough. They live
longer if you're tougher with them. I would
recommend that any wife living with a drunk
husband, or a husband living with a drunk wife,
go to Al-Anon. Learn how to cope with life and
living in the environment of a drunk. Your own
happiness and your own life are what you learn
to preserve under those circumstances. It's tough.

The hard thing for the family is not to be a
helper, not to love an alcoholic into the grave. It's
just hard not to do it. You are going to do it
either because you love him or because of the
embarrassment of somebody's finding out his
true condition. Members of the family are the last
people in the world who are going to influence a
drunk to quit drinking. A stranger could do more
with a drunk than the family could do. The
family is too close to him.

Billy Carter

I would probably have quit drinking a year or so before I did if I hadn't been protected so much by my friends. I think Sybil will admit that if she had to do it over again she wouldn't have protected me for the last year or so of my drinking, which she did. I was overly protected. Lord, when I was on the road I had two people with me, keeping me sober enough to do what I was supposed to do. Everybody has a tendency to be overprotective.

Today, if I saw somebody drinking on the job, I would immediately report him or go to him and talk to him and say, "All right, straighten up your act. Go get treatment or your ass is gone." In both industry and business we have a tendency to refuse to try to make them face it. I wouldn't face it. I think if Sybil had said, "The hell with it, I'm not going to protect you anymore, get out," I'd probably have quit earlier.

Personally, I have no sympathy for somebody who gets caught driving drunk the first time. I used to go out of my way to help such people keep their drivers' licenses. I've made a complete turnaround. I think a bastard can kill somebody when he's drunk. If he does, he ought to go to the electric chair, like somebody who murders somebody with a damn gun. We just overprotect the alcoholic. The drunk-driving laws should be a lot heavier.

Sybil Carter

If you love them and you think they are worth it, stay with them, stick by them, help them when you can, but tear them loose. Let them go with love. Let them make their own mistakes and take the responsibility for it, as badly as it hurts. In some ways alcoholics are very capable of taking care of themselves. They are not helpless and they are not weaklings. I didn't know this back then, before I had treatment. I know now that you must let them fall flat on their faces. You have to let them go. You can do it with love or you can cut the strings completely and say, "O.K., I have had enough. I'm through. Go to hell. I don't care what happens to you. Die." Or you can let them go and still be with them, love them all the time. But if they fall, they have to pick themselves up. They have to be responsible for what they do and what they say, and it's the hardest thing to watch.

You have to take yourself away from the situation and think about yourself first. It sounds selfish, but it's not. If the ship is going to go down and you can save yourself, why not try to? Why should you go down with it? That's two lives gone. If you are a husband or wife and there are children involved, you have an obligation and responsibility to those children, especially if they are younger, to be the best person you can for them. Above all, you have a responsibility to yourself to be the person that you want and need to be.

You don't really want to admit you need

help, but you do.

Pete Townshend

My wife, Karen, told me she didn't want me to be that way, and she was right. The best thing of all that she did was to tell me to get the fuck out. If there was an alcoholic who worked for me, and he wouldn't stop drinking after I had asked him politely a few times, I would fire him. If he was working with me, I would refuse to go on, even if it was a great humanitarian work we were involved in. I think you have to stop being complicitous in an alcoholic's demise. It's the old lifeboat adage. Don't drag somebody into the lifeboat who's already sinking. Let him finish it off. If he wants to swim, he'll swim.

I was talking to a friend of mine who is in a new band. One of the guys has a drinking problem. The boy is worried about him and said to me, "I really want to help him. The band is about to get a record deal, but he drinks too much. He knows he's got a problem, but only the other day I saw him come in and he had a bottle of vodka. He didn't think I saw it, but I did." I said, "No, he knew you saw him. He put that bottle of vodka there for you. You are an accomplice in his alcoholism. Now he can drink more because of you. You will be there when he falls down the stairs, to take him to hospital. Leave him. Kick him out. Regroup. Wait. Be there when he comes out, or let him know you are waiting, but don't be complicitous. Don't be a part of it."

Stop whatever you're doing. It doesn't matter how important it seems. Stop using the excuses you come up with: Well, we can't do it now because the kids are in the middle of exams. Fuck the exams. It's better that the children have two parents who love one another than a few passing grades. You've got to get your priorities right. Talk to people. Talk to everybody. Make it public. Let the world know. So much absurd pride is caught up in this. There is so much shame attached to it. Save the shame for later, for when we've got this guy or this woman straight.

Don Newcombe

Families should get treatment for their own disease before they start worrying about the alcoholic. They are contributing to the alcoholic's disease by covering and protecting him or her. They furnish him or her all the things needed to continue the sickness. As a result, they are suffering from the sickness more than the alcoholic is.

If you have an alcoholic wife or husband, you ought to learn something about alcoholism by going to Al-Anon meetings or getting involved in a treatment modality. Learn something about alcoholism, then use the information you get in your own treatment with the alcoholic whom you love and care about. As long as you condone his drinking, as long as a wife protects her husband from the boss on the job, lies for him, cheats for him, protects him, he's going to keep on drinking. He's not going to stop. He's going to keep on lying to the boss and he's going to keep on lying to his wife. He's going to keep doing all the things that alcoholics do because we're devious people when we're drinking.

Stop protecting that alcoholic. You know the alcoholic is sick, but you're not a professional. You're not a doctor. You're not an alcoholic yourself, and I don't know anyone who can diagnose alcoholism besides an alcoholic or a medical person. If you're not one of those, how are you going to diagnose it? How do you know? Are you going to deal with it by constantly telling a person that he's a "goddamned drunk" or she's a "goddamned alcoholic"? Find out about it. Learn what this person is suffering from. You'd be amazed at the transformation that takes place when families learn something about the sickness. It's a very insidious sickness, a sickness that even we alcoholics don't fully understand.

Lois Robards

One of the most important things is not to criticize alcoholics, because they are really no different from someone who is suffering from pneumonia, has a high fever, or is very ill. Try to look at it that way. It's very difficult because they are functioning human beings and you think it's just their lack of will. It isn't that easy. Do not malign their character. Always keep an attitude of respect for the person as a human being.

It is very difficult, under trying circumstances, not to say, "You are a no-good son of a bitch. You are unworthy of the love I have given." If you have truly given it, they must have it. You've got to remember that no matter how bad it gets, even if your lives are going to be apart and separated because of the alcohol, you musn't hurt the alcoholic by what you say because of the pain you are suffering. That will never help him. I really believe that. I think that's probably the one thing that helped Jason and me in our relationship. It just so happened that I loved him very much, and I think he knew that in the end.

Conway Hunter

The one who suffers the most is the child who lives in the home with an alcoholic parent. We have spent time, money, research, and done volumes on the fetal alcohol syndrome and the effects of alcohol on the unborn child. This is very important and it's all true. But that does not compare one percent to the damage that is done to children who live in a home with an alcoholic mother or father.

Wilbur Mills

I knew one child who committed suicide because his father was an alcoholic. He hung himself in the high school gym. Couldn't live with his father being an alcoholic.

Robert Bauman

Al-Anon will teach you how to live as a human being even if you have an alcoholic in the family who won't do anything about it. There is lots of good help available. Look under Alcoholism in the Yellow Pages—now.

Rod Steiger

You can't do it by yourself. Contact Alcoholics Anonymous or Al-Anon; contact your local counseling centers. Let them guide you to a place where there are people who are trained to help the person who is a victim of alcohol and let them help you. Let them help strengthen the glue of your relationship by giving you the correct knowledge, not friendly advice from neighbors. Above all, do not lose your self-respect or respect for the person who has the problem because that person is dealing with and fighting a disease. You can always put a dime into a telephone and call the psychology department of any university, and they will tell you places to go. Call your religious center if you are a religious person. Get your information from people who are informed about alcoholism. That's a very cheap and rewarding phone call to make.

Knowledge gives you strength. Knowledge gives you courage. Without courage there can be no progress; without progress there is no solution.

12 Members of Alcoholics Anonymous

Alcoholics Anonymous is an organization of men and women who have a common goal—to stop drinking and to stay stopped. The common bond of membership, which brings them together and keeps them together, is the negative experience of alcoholism. They help each other accept the fact that they cannot drink. They also help each other to cope with daily living and grow. Medical professionals agree that AA is the most readily available, and in sheer numbers the most successful, way of quitting drinking. The worldwide membership of AA exceeds one million "recovering" alcoholics.

AA is unstructured and has no rules, regulations, dues, affiliations, or membership cards. Some of the general public sees AA as a secret organization of down-and-outers. On the contrary, AA is made up of doctors, dentists, lawyers, factory workers, college students, judges, policemen, housewives, bank clerks, secretaries, shoe salesmen, ball players, nuns, librarians, actresses, nurses, butchers and bakers, and people from every other profession. Only 3 percent of alcoholics live on the streets, conforming to the stereotype of the alcoholic in many people's minds. Men and women, young and old, rich and poor, from every station in life, representing all races, creeds, and religions, sit together as equals. The stories of horror and miraculous change told by AA members are electrifying.

AA makes no bones about the medical aspects or consequences of alcoholism. It is to the point. For an alcoholic, drinking is a life-or-death situation, now or down the road. Some members are quick to say that they did not get a divorce, they did not end up in a car accident, or they did not hit a financial bottom, but they know these things await them if they do drink.

A frequent question from an outsider or new member is, "How does the AA program work?" The answer is most often, "The program works fine." The philosophy of AA, which becomes a way of life, is called "the program" by its members. That entire philosophy is contained in the twelve steps, or principles, which change remarkably the course and quality of a member's life.

Meetings are held daily and nightly all over the world. They are either "open" or "closed," and the format varies only slightly in different groups and in different parts of the country. Open meetings are open to the general public, to anyone who has any interest in alcoholism. Open meetings consist of one or two speakers who tell their personal stories. These talks follow a traditional pattern of what it was like as a drinking alcoholic, what brought the alcoholic to his or her knees, and how life is better today without alcohol. In some parts of the country, this is the entire meeting. In other places the speakers are followed by members sharing their thoughts and feelings on anything that has been triggered by the talk. Closed meetings are for alcoholics only. A particular topic is suggested or a particular "step" is chosen as the focal point. Members may speak to the subject or not, as they choose. In some parts of the country, regardless of the size of these closed meetings, the group splits up into subgroups of eight to twelve, often called "tables."

Although alcoholism is the common bond that weaves its way in and out of the members' comments, often a meeting will be devoted to subjects like anger, procrastination, impatience, or keeping life simple. It is through these meetings that members grow. However, the primary purpose of the meetings is to remind the alcoholic that he or she cannot drink. Most members do outside reading, which is totally optional, and are in touch with one another as friends. Helping other alcoholics plays a key role in sobriety.

Newcomers are encouraged to sit back and relax and listen. They are never told that they are alcoholics. That is their own decision. They are told that if they think they do have a drinking problem, they are in the right place. Often, it is suggested that they give the program a chance for sixty to ninety days and not drink. At the end of that time, if they decide they are not alcoholics, "all of your misery will be refunded." Newcomers are advised to go to as many meetings as necessary in order to stay away from drinking. Regular members of AA with some sobriety usually go to several meetings a week. It is their choice.

The traditions of AA suggest that it is a program of attraction and not promotion, consequently the public rarely sees AA advertised. It is the philosophy of AA that when a person is ready and willing to do something about his or her drinking, the program is readily available.

Another tradition of AA focuses on anonymity. A variety of reasons is given for anonymity at a public level. In the early days of AA, there were so few members that they could not help all of the alcoholics who were seeking help. Also in the early days, some members wrapped themselves in a cloak of AA and tried to promote themselves or certain causes. It has also been of concern that certain members might set themselves up as "experts," and it is essential to the spirit of AA that everyone be equal. AA believes that false pride has already caused the alcoholic enough problems in life. There is also concern that members would be identified with AA and then begin drinking again, thus setting a bad example. What seems to have evolved is that anonymity is up to the individual. Among the well-known contributors to this book, many have been helped by AA. Some choose to mention it; some choose to omit it. It is a personal decision.

The newcomer can be well assured that his or her anonymity will be protected by all of the membership. Indeed, it is clear to all members that many people, because of the stigma of alcoholism, would not attend a meeting if anonymity were not guaranteed. Newcomers can feel secure about their own anonymity.

As a group of people, AA members are positive, happy, tolerant, giving, and loving. An observer cannot help but notice the fun and humor that exists in AA. AA members appear to have a very clear idea of who they are and what life is all about. Regardless of their religion, or whether they are atheist or agnostic, AA members develop a spiritual dimension to their lives. AA members strongly believe that spirituality is the key to life. The most striking thing about AA members is their sense of inner peace.

Members of Alcoholics Anonymous have contributed the following essays.

Ed

Maybe it did have something to do with alcohol. Family and friends said it did; the experts agreed. I agreed. So I went with them. I went to a meeting, a meeting that was supposed to change my life. I was afraid to go to the meeting. So there was a prior meeting among four of us. One of the men I knew; the other two were strangers, strangers in the sense of never having met before. Like the man I already knew, I also grew to love the other two because they knew me. They knew me because I was part of a fellowship I had not realized existed; so they taught me and I began to grow.

When I went to that meeting, I met others like them, others like me. They saw the rage I felt, but they were not angry with me. They felt the pain I knew, but they would not cuddle me—they said we could bear the pain together. They knew it had something to do with alcohol, but even more, they knew it had something to do with me. They knew that the invisible bonds of human love that once held my life together had been shattered. They implied that they knew of a way to mend them, a way to make me whole again and therefore free from drink. I did not believe them. Loved ones had lied to me before. So I lacked faith.

They said if I stayed they would show me. I was reluctant, but I had nothing left. Nothing—no hope, no image, no pride, no God, no love. I felt like Robert Frost's hired man, "Nothing to look backward on with pride and nothing to look forward to with hope," so I stayed. I went to meetings. I talked. I cried. I was hugged. I was afraid. I was trusted. They believed me because they said they knew, and slowly a healing took place. No magic. No cure. But a very slow healing occurred around tables, among people who had experienced great pain, great sickness, much emptiness. Collectively we were being healed. It was the same and different for each of us. I began to know that it had something to do with alcohol, but more to do with me.

They touched my soul when it was time. I knew I would keep going to the tables to try and describe the touch of a soul, the feel of it, the freedom of it, the adventure of it. If that meant I could not drink today, then today I would not drink. If that meant I had to go to a meeting, then I would go. It was all I ever wanted—to touch the soul of another. Again, again, and again. Do it again, God, and again and again.

Helen

I started drinking at about eighteen years of age, like all my friends, socially. I don't know just when it started to change. There was no happiness left in alcohol, just depression. I didn't really know what was wrong, didn't know it was alcohol. I tried vitamins, exercise, self-help books, meditation, my church. Nothing seemed to work. I did think that if I cut down on my drinking I could lose some weight and then everything would be all right.

I went to my first AA meeting very secretly. It had to be an all-women meeting because I was ashamed to go where there were men, ashamed to even think I might be an alcoholic. I was so confused, depressed, envious of people, including my husband (with no cause). I felt worthless and very lonely in spite of ten children coming and going in the house.

A drink did seem to help, but then there were nights I didn't remember how I got to bed or how much I'd drunk. I would hurry and check the bottles the next morning. I was sneaking drinks when my husband left the room and going to different stores to buy bottles. If I wasn't drinking, I was thinking about when I could.

I never knew anything about alcoholics or alcoholism, nor did I know any alcoholic—or so I thought. To me it just seemed that some people drank a little too much and should cut down.

One of the reasons I went to AA was vanity. Also, I was sick and tired of being sick and tired. But still I thought I couldn't be one of those people. I went three months to the women's meeting before I told my husband or before I really even told myself. That was the summer of 1977. I was fifty when I came in and I'm fifty-seven now. I like to say I was fifty-seven when I came in and I'm fifty now.

I attended AA for twelve days and drank again for a weekend. I went back to the fellowship for twelve weeks and again tried to drink, but AA had spoiled my drinking. I felt ashamed and worthless again. I wanted what I saw at the meetings, so I went back to AA for seven years of quality living. One day at a time.

Today I go to about five meetings a week because it makes me feel good. I'm taking tap-dancing and roller-skating lessons, I'm bowling, playing good golf, doing Yoga, helping to start new meetings, and sharing hope with the newer members. Today I find that what I am shouts louder than most anything I can say.

They told me at my first meeting that alcoholism is like a roller coaster to hell, but I could get off anytime I wanted. I guess you could say I had a high bottom, but it was as low mentally as I want to go. All the other things would have come in time: car accidents, jail, losing my husband and family, institutions.

Today I turn down a drink by saying, "No, thanks, I'm allergic. I break out in a drunk," and then we all laugh. Living is beautiful. I need a lot of humor in my program today because I cried for so many years.

Tom

To this alcoholic, staying sober without AA would be a lot like a right-handed person playing eighteen holes of golf with left-handed clubs. I could probably get around the course, but it sure wouldn't be any fun!

I don't personally subscribe to the idea that "it's great to be an alcoholic" any more than I feel it's terrific to be a diabetic or have heart disease. The fact remains, I have a disease called alcoholism and have to deal with it the best way I know how—through AA.

Life can be tough for alcoholics and nonalcoholics alike. There are plenty of legitimate demands made on us in the areas of job, family, and marriage, but the idea is more than just to "get through life." We should get something out of it! As we "get through life," why not enjoy a sense of accomplishment, a feeling of belonging, the pleasures of sharing and love?

I made the decision years ago that if I was going to pursue quality life through sobriety in AA, then, by God, I was going to take all the AA program had to offer. All the benefits are available to me in exchange for following a few simple suggestions found in the AA program, not the least of which is found, in part, in our twelfth step, which says that we "carry the message to the suffering alcoholic."

It seems to me that "charity" today is O.K. for many people if it's tax deductible; it's all right to help your fellow man if the "payback" is right. Only in AA have I seen so much so freely given with so little expected in return. The gifts of compassion, understanding, and help are just a few. This can be found in one alcoholic's helping another alcoholic. So it goes—sharing the "secrets" of sobriety with relative strangers, many of whom become very close friends. It's truly incredible when you consider the unselfish motives.

We may "give" at first only because it's one of the suggested steps to recovery outlined in the AA program. In my own case, this soon gave way to giving and sharing purely for the good feeling I got when I saw another alcoholic begin his own recovery. To watch (not judge) the progress in someone I helped get started has to be one of life's great paybacks.

Jan
I had absolutely no confidence, but today I can dare to be myself.

I grew up just outside of San Francisco in a middle-class neighborhood. The oldest of three children, I did well in school and was always involved in extracurricular activities. The only really unhappy times of my life were always alcohol related. My father is an alcoholic, and aunts and grandparents on both sides of my family are alcoholics. I remember thinking it was a wonderful holiday if the family had gotten together and not had an alcohol-induced argument.

When I married at twenty, after a brief time in a convent, we did not have alcohol in the house. Most of the people we ran around with didn't drink or brought their own when they came to our house. We had two children within our first two years of marriage. We also started on the long trail of many moves around the country to further my husband's career. Before our third child was born, I had a terribly traumatic experience that I didn't think I could ever handle. I quickly learned that having a drink occasionally relieved some of the pain. I also found out that it gave me an added bit of confidence, more energy, and seemed to make me more relaxed. I was just beginning my long road of escape with alcohol and prescription drugs.

By the time I made my first call to AA, some twenty years later, I had gone from an outgoing, efficient, loving, well-groomed person to someone who couldn't answer the door or the phone, make a bed, paint a room, go to a tennis match to see one of the kids play, do the bills, take a bath, or just about anything, without a drink! I no longer cared how I looked or what people thought about me.

I phoned AA six years ago—at the same time that Betty Ford went into treatment.

It has been five and a half years since I had my last drink and took my last pill. Today there are very few things that I am not willing to try. I love to be around people again. I feel and look great. Best of all, I can respect myself again. AA has taught me how to live a sometimes not too easy life without the use of chemicals. I have a great feeling of excitement when I start another day and so much gratitude at that day's end. Now I know that I can jump into life's waters with both feet.

Bill

When I first met these AA people it was so important that they understand and accept me, and they did. Deep inside I had felt that all of life was grinding to a close, that there was no hope for anyone at all, and that the good feelings for which I had once lived were thorough illusions. And yet, after a number of meetings, I soon became enamored of these uncanny people whose wise insights came not from study hall surveys but from their own anguish and survival.

I feel a bond with them unique from even the love for my own family. We share one another's victories and pain, laughter and tears, and they show what really works for them in life. I've come to recognize a remarkable spirit in their eyes, their words, their company. In time, I, too, came to believe that the steps they took could work for me. By their example, I've become able to do what was impossible. I have come to revel in my life just as it is, and the thought of drink has no appeal today. From one sunrise to the next I have the sure sense that I am cared for and a useful part of the fantastic experience of life. It's become important that I accept and understand others as they did me, and I do.

Veronica

Today I am living a rewarding and meaningful life. I have a myriad of interests and am pursuing many of them. I work as a substance-abuse therapist with chemically dependent men and women, and I am currently a graduate student at a local university, pursuing a master of social work degree.

I am the wife of an attorney, the mother of four children who range in age from fourteen to twenty years old. I am also a member of Alcoholics Anonymous, and this has made all the difference in the world. Recently I celebrated my tenth anniversary in the AA program, ten years of a very hope-filled, quality sobriety. I accept each day as a special gift and have grown in the ability to accept myself as a unique, loving, and lovable human being.

Life wasn't always this way. I pray that I will never forget how sick I became as my alcoholism progressed to the point of terrible confusion, emotional chaos, and near despair.

I grew up in a family that was loving, hard-working, and responsible. There was very little drinking. It simply did not fit into the family lifestyle. I started to drink in college, like most of my peers at the time. It was the late fifties and early sixties. Not only was it acceptable to drink, it was expected. The legal drinking age was twenty-one, but most of my friends and I had fake I.D.'s. We drank mostly beer, enjoyed making the rounds of college bars, and drank at football games and the usual weekend parties. I found that drinking loosened me up, helped me relax, and I wondered why I had waited so long to begin using alcohol.

At age twenty-two, after graduating from college, I married and settled down to the task of raising a family. My husband worked full time during the day, attending law school in the evenings. We had three sons, each fourteen months apart. I found my life constantly revolving around taking care of others' needs. We always had sufficient income to live on, but none to spare for any luxuries. My lifestyle became that of a full-time wife and mother, as well as jack-of-all-trades around the house. Weekends away and vacations were not in the picture. My husband worked very hard and spent his "leisure" time studying. For recreation, we attended the law school parties on Saturday nights.

I found that I could drink an increasing amount of alcohol. I would often have one or two mixed drinks before I went to a social event. I also found that I was drinking wine in the evening after I had put the boys to bed. I looked forward to this "reward" at the end of a busy, often monotonous day. This was the beginning of a pattern of drinking that I had never known but which, at the time, seemed very normal. Today I recognize that my "denial" of what was actually happening was symptomatic of my progressing alcoholism.

Our daughter was born a year after my husband finished law school and passed the bar exam. Our oldest son was starting first grade. Our life was really beginning to change. There was more time for my husband and me to be together, and there were more opportunities to enjoy life. We were now able to afford a few luxuries, take time for vacations and travel, and I finally got a car of my own. Our dreams seemed to be coming true. There was really only one black cloud on our horizon—my drinking. The so-called nectar of the gods, which had always offered me the means to relax and have fun, was now an ever-increasing need. Four more years elapsed as my early stage of alcoholism progressed into the middle stage with devastating consequences. I was deteriorating physically, mentally, emotionally, socially, spiritually. I felt disoriented, fragmented. My marriage was on shaky ground; my husband and I were growing apart; my life offered little fulfillment; and I no longer knew who I was. I had no real awareness that I had become alcoholic, nor that my alcoholism was causing or exacerbating most of my life's problems. In my own distorted alcoholic thinking, I believed that the pressures of managing a home and family were causing my increased drinking and subsequent loss of control. I felt hopeless. It was as if I were being sucked into a dark, terror-filled tunnel. The emotional pain and alienation were too great to bear. I could stand no more. I cried out for help.

Then there was a moment of truth. I knew I had to stop drinking—completely—totally! I remembered that a friend of my husband's was a member of Alcoholics Anonymous. He had been sober for nearly five years and seemed so happy and well-adjusted. My denial and false pride were shattered. I called this man, and he took me to my first Alcoholics Anonymous meeting. I left that meeting with a very precious gift, the gift of hope. I had admitted to my alcoholism. I had identified with each one who sat around the first-step table that evening and shared their experience, strength, and hope with me. I still remember their faces. I remember how varied their backgrounds and life experiences were.

Mostly, I remember how they cared about me, how they accepted me as one of them—a human being with the disease of alcoholism. I believed what they told me when they offered the hope of recovery. Why wouldn't I believe them? They were living examples of recovery—men and women who were sober and who understood that they had been given a new life "one day at a time." That was my first of countless AA meetings. I never drank again.

Alcoholics Anonymous—its people and its program—saved my life. It was in this program that I learned to accept myself as a woman with an illness, as a woman who could recover. It was here that I experienced the caring and healing of a loving, compassionate God who restored me to sanity. I continue to participate in AA and to work the twelve steps of its program. I continue to accept the gift of sobriety one day at a time. Today I live with the hope, the gratitude, and the joy shared by so many others who have known the bondage of addiction and have experienced the liberation and new life of sobriety found in Alcoholics Anonymous. Today I am living my new life deeply.

Remi
In 1970 my wife got sick. She overdosed (which is what I like to call it) four different times. In May of 1973, she made the grade. I then began drinking more heavily. I was going to show her that she couldn't do that to me. I broke my ankle in

December of 1974 and received a medical retirement from the auto company I worked for. While I was in the hospital I went through the D.T.'s for twelve days, but continued drinking after leaving. I broke my hip in September of 1977, drunk, and went through the D.T.'s again. I went through all the same things that many alcoholics go through: car wrecks, jail a few times, being drunk two to three times a day, sleeping with all kinds of women (married or not), spending too much money, losing the respect of my family and worst of all, my self-respect.

Sometime in September 1978 I made the decision to shit or get off the pot. I called AA and went to a meeting. At first I went there to learn how to drink, but I kept going back because they had something I wanted. I went to a lot of meetings and found out I had to live the program for myself, but give it away also. The family is back together. I have a new granddaughter. Things are good. Just one day at a time.

Mike

AA is a fellowship that slowly but surely circles you with hope and love. Reaching this fellowship is a gift of God. I call it a gift because I had no willingness in the beginning.

Slowly the AA program replaced the incapacitating fear with a faith that continues to grow on a daily basis. When I say slowly, there is no exaggeration in my case—eighteen months passed before I succeeded and accepted God's will and realized the total helplessness the next drink would bring.

Out of the surrender came a limited amount of freedom. However, the discipline of the AA program brings more freedom each day as the program becomes a way of life. As the days pass, positive thinking and spirituality continue to grow to levels I never dreamed possible.

As the big book of AA states, "It's easy to let up on the spiritual program of action and rest on our laurels." We are headed for trouble if we do, for alcohol is a subtle foe. We are not cured of alcoholism. What we have is a daily reprieve contingent on the maintenance of our spiritual condition. Every day is a day when we must carry the vision of God's will into all of our activities.

Mary

I came to AA at age thirty-two. After fifteen years of drinking, I got tired of running away from myself. I was lost. I had always been afraid.

When I was a child, I would lie awake at night and listen to my parents arguing. My father would be drunk, yelling at my mother. She silently took all the abuse he gave her and prayed a lot. She would say, "He does not mean it. He's an alcoholic, he's sick." I heard the word *alcoholic* and knew that there was something dreadfully wrong with him. It was something very important. When he was drunk he was somehow not responsible. He couldn't help himself. He didn't have to do anything. He wasn't capable. Our world revolved around this sickness. I escaped to the beach and into books.

One by one my brothers and my sister left. By age thirteen I was the only child at home, and it was decided that I would go to a boarding school. I was sent off and felt sad. The nuns tried to save my soul, but it was already too late. There was something wrong with me. My feelings got stuck inside. I became very shy and started writing poetry. There was no way out of these feelings until I discovered drinking. Alcohol let me come out of myself and feel good.

I went to college and started to drink seriously. I never studied and was constantly falling in love. I was always looking for someone to love me and take care of me and make decisions for me. My insecurities overwhelmed me. I quit school, went back, then started in the world of work. I never could stay in a job. I didn't think I deserved to succeed and didn't want to try.

By the time I got to AA, I was not much of a human being. I was hanging out in bars, playing pool, picking up men, looking for love, and having no idea what love was. I was dying of loneliness. My brother called me up one day and told me he had found out what his problem was, that it was alcohol. Both of us had been in therapy for many years. I had also tried meditation, but stopped. I couldn't be still.

The day I went to my first AA meeting I was a very frightened, depressed, angry, immature person. My anger was all inside. On the outside, I was sad, full of self-pity, and hopeless. I hated the word *God*. I had turned away from everything that was good and healthy and normal. I had turned away from life.

I went to AA meetings once a week for about six months. I didn't talk. I didn't get to know anyone and didn't want anyone to know me. It was too risky. I didn't want AA to work. I didn't want to change. In a way, I didn't think I was capable of ever getting better. I didn't think I was really an alcoholic. I knew what a real alcoholic was—that was my father. I was never like him.

I was very lost. I didn't belong in AA, but I was afraid to drink. I was afraid to make a move either way. I was paralyzed with fear. I quit AA and retreated into my own safe world. It was a world where nothing ever happened except I managed to get to work. I would get up and go to work and come home and go to bed. I hid under the covers and avoided most people. I was very depressed, but I didn't drink. I was in limbo.

Meanwhile, my brother continued to get better. He was involved in AA and was starting to feel pretty good. I thought he had become a fanatic. He couldn't hold a conversation with me without talking about AA. I felt betrayed. I had lost my brother to AA. If that was what happened to people in AA, I never wanted to be like them. I got more and more angry at him, but it didn't seem to bother him. He kept feeling good, and I kept feeling bad. One day I got desperate again and went crying to my mother, hoping she would tell me I was O.K. She didn't. She said, "Why don't you try AA again? Look at what it's done for your brother." I was furious. I was without hope.

I did try AA again. I went back, and the second time it was different. I was still depressed and confused. It took me about four months to do more than say hello to anyone. When I did start to talk about myself, all I could do was cry. I thought I was really a bad person, and I had a lot of doubts that AA could work for me. I knew it worked because I could see people all around me who were feeling pretty good. I was not sure if I could get better, but luckily I was not sure I couldn't. I kept going to meetings. After two years of not drinking, I finally decided to trust someone. I called up a woman and started telling my story. She listened, didn't judge, and accepted me. She became my sponsor. She said I was going to be O.K. and that, in fact, I was O.K. just the way I was. This was the real beginning of recovery for me.

It's hard to walk in the door to your first AA meeting. It's very hard to put down the drink and take a look at what a mess you have made of your life. It's hard to admit you can't do it alone and you need people to help you. It's hard to give up pretending you're O.K. and say how you feel. But it's worth it. I have been involved in AA for real for about a year now. Sometimes I look at myself and can't believe I am the same person.

Today I am not depressed. Today I laugh and meet people and have a very good time. After almost twenty years of depression, I now feel good. It wasn't staying away from booze that did it, although that was the first important step.

What is AA all about? AA people know how to live sober, and the only thing they want to do is help you. The fellowship of AA is full of people who know how you feel because they have been there. What drew me back to AA was the laughter. There is no point to getting sober if we don't learn how to laugh.

I didn't see much to laugh about when I first got sober. I do now. I let myself be cared for. I let people know me. I found out I was no different from the rest of the human race. I don't have to be perfect. I have learned to make mistakes, fall, get back up again. I have learned to tell the truth. I have learned to face my problems. I don't wake up in the morning dreading the day. I wake up and wonder what's going to happen. Life isn't a tragedy. I don't have to drink anymore to feel good, or to not feel. I don't have to drive around drunk with no place to go. My father did that. I ended up just like my father in so many ways.

After walking around in a fog for so many years, I have come back to life. I believe alcoholism is a sickness and that recovery is not only possible but inevitable for anyone who is willing to try.

I have been, and continue to be, healed by the power of love and laughter. This I found in the halls of AA.

Joe

The setting does not matter. It could happen anywhere and often does. I drank alcohol for many years, most of the time with control. Later on, in my middle and late fifties, I began losing control. Those terrible morning hangovers sometimes resulted from two- and three-day drinking bouts. Toward the end I virtually lost all control.

My business was selling. I began working after World War II with a nationally known blue-chip company on a lower level and worked up to executive status. My contacts and acquaintances, both business and social, were many. And, of course, the cocktails were always present.

I had married a beautiful, patient girl, and over the years we acquired a large family. We were a happy family. We had the usual family cares and problems. We were healthy. We always had good food and clothes. We had a comfortable home. My wife and I took good vacations both with and without the kids. Life was work and fun.

I drank, most of the time with control—this sentence tells a lot. There were warnings during this period that went unheeded. There were episodes, at times, when I drank and knew, somewhere deep inside, that alcohol and I were not compatible. Reasoning said, "You ought to stop." Emotions said no.

At a young forty-five years of age, my wife contracted cancer. This was a blow to all of us.

After two successful operations, she was her old self again, and that continued for five years thereafter. I continued drinking "moderately," I made myself believe.

Business was good. Income was excellent. My wife was again in good health. The children were growing, some were even in college. Life was good.

Then tragedy struck. The cancer returned, and within a short time my wife died, young at fifty years. I was fifty-nine. The drinking sprees became longer and more frequent. My family was frightened. My wife's death was an excuse to continue. Her illness and death were not the cause, but I used them for that. Self-pity, guilt, remorse. Another shot will pick me up. And another, and another.

Coming off a bad bout, lying fully clothed in bed, sick, shaking, nauseated, realizing I had lost all control, I said, "God, help me." A friend said, "You are making life a living hell for your children." My son said, "Dad, you are going to have to do something. Do you want my help?" The answer was a weak yes.

I was introduced to a Catholic priest who related his problems with alcohol. He made no condemnation, which I had fully expected he would. He later introduced me to a small group of men, who, it turned out, were having an AA meeting. The men in the group, all successful in various careers, were impressive, to say the least. These men certainly are not all alcoholics, I thought. They were clean-cut, well-groomed, well-dressed, poised, well-spoken—but all were alcoholics in recovery. That was ten years ago. I have not had a drink since. Nor do I want one. Nor do I crave one. I was not unique. I am not unique. There are millions of recovering alcoholics. The doors to AA meetings are open everywhere.

Through the grace of God, I found AA and sobriety. How my life has changed. What a joy to be living. "Recovering alcoholics are such charming people," writes Fulton Oursler. How true! I have met them by the hundreds.

Mark

From the outside looking in, it seemed that I had everything—family, friends, and a very comfortable living. But from the inside, I was void of all feelings that make this life worthwhile. I lived most of my childhood as a lonely child and didn't find any relief until I was twelve years old. At that time, I discovered the easiest, fastest way to feel good. I discovered drugs and alcohol. From the time I drank my first drink and smoked my first joint, I was hooked. I loved the feelings these chemicals gave me.

I went from beer and pot to pills and hard liquor to cocaine and LSD, and before I was old enough to drink, I was in jail for possession and distribution of marijuana. I built walls between me and everyone around me, except my closest "friends." I went from wanting to get loaded to needing to get loaded. I started experimenting with harder drugs and eventually became a full-time professional drug dealer. I was constantly running away from home and all too frequently overdosing on various drugs. When I was sixteen, I ate enough psychedelic mushrooms to get ten people high, and I almost killed myself.

On February 11, 1981, I went from a jail cell to a police car to a drug rehabilitation hospital in Baton Rouge, Louisiana. I haven't had a pill, a fix, or a drink since then.

Letting go of my drug and alcohol addiction and allowing myself the chance to sober up and live a new, healthier life was one of the hardest things I have ever done. The chemicals I used were my crutch, and now I had to find healthier crutches to lean on. Some people call it weakness. I call it being humble. I had never asked for help in my whole life, and now my life depended on whether I accepted help. I was in the hospital for two months, and then I was sent to a halfway house in Minnesota for six months. I changed more in those eight months than I had in my five years of using chemicals. I learned that there was more to me than my physical being. I learned to like myself and then even to love myself. I also learned of a thing called spirituality, which was completely new to me. I came to believe in a power greater than myself. Eventually I learned to trust this power for guidance in everything I did.

For the first nine months of my sobriety I was pretty much taken care of. After that I had to start taking care of myself. I went from my halfway house back to living with my family and began going to AA. During my first year home I went to at least three, and sometimes seven, meetings a week. I got to know the people in the meetings and later made friendships that will last a lifetime.

Today it has been almost three years since I have had any kind of mood-altering chemical. I have gone from a high school dropout to a B+ college student. I have real friends today, all over the United States. I have come to trust in the will of my higher power, whom I choose to call God. I am not a religious person but a spiritual one. I work a spiritual program by asking God to do for me what I cannot do for myself. Today I feel that if I worry, why pray? And if I pray, why worry? I had my turn at running my life; now I choose to let God run my life, and everything is at its best. Today my problems are my opportunities. Everything that happens to me that doesn't feel good can be turned around and used as another steppingstone of growth for me. I have everything to gain and nothing to lose by staying sober.

Tom

My impression of AA before I became a follower was that it was a rigid and formalistic organization making imprudent demands on one's conduct and behavior. Experience has shown that, on the contrary, the fellowship helps one to stop drinking and allows one to grow along the path of personal awareness. Instead of being ritualistic and personally burdensome, AA is the path to unloosening one's innermost values.

Barbara

I am an alcoholic in my early fifties with three grown children. For thirty years, alcohol and then tranquilizers were woven into the fabric of my life. There was a time when our family was considered to be successful. We had a beautiful home in the suburbs, two cars in the garage, we belonged to country clubs, took vacations, and had good friends. At one point I said to my husband, "We have everything that anyone could ever want." He left shortly thereafter for a younger woman. I was devastated. My world had fallen apart. Because I was a dependent person, I began to depend more and more on alcohol. It helped to kill the pain and bury the feelings that I could not handle.

During the last ten years of drinking, I had to keep alcohol in my system. I could not stop. The doctor found that I had a fatty liver, the beginning of cirrhosis. I suffered blackouts, drove while drinking, had a traffic accident, and was jailed.

I joined AA because of fear and left six months later. The next two years, as my disease progressed, I developed many phobias, had chronic back problems and constant "flu" symptoms. Life to me was futile.

Through the intervention of my daughter,

working with my first AA sponsor, I was put into Maplegrove. I had a rough time with detox. During the twenty-eight days, the counselors worked very hard with me to make me feel at my gut level that I was an alcoholic. It was one thing to say it and quite another to feel it and know it. I came into Maplegrove beaten by the drugs. I finally surrendered and accepted the fact that I was an alcoholic. With a strong desire to turn my life around, I made a decision to do everything that the people at Maplegrove told me to do, which involved aftercare, Antabuse, classes in assertiveness training, and most of all, AA.

For two and a half years I have not taken a drink or a pill or any other mind-altering drug. This is truly a miracle because it is the most normal thing in the world for an alcoholic to drink. That is why there are so many "slips." I do not ever want to go back to where I came from. Because of this, I keep it simple and remember to do two things: I do not take the first drink and I go to meetings.

The foundation and framework of my life is AA. The Twelve Steps are truly inspired and they teach me how to live comfortably. I know that acceptance was always a difficult thing for me in any part of my life. I wanted what I wanted immediately and was defiant, rebellious, quietly resentful. Through the program I am learning to accept things in my life and to grow from a childlike state to an adult state.

We laugh a lot at meetings, as well as being

serious. My humor and joy are at an all-time high. I have an opening and a closure to each day. In the morning, I put my life and my will in my Higher Power's care, asking only for the wisdom of his will for me. At night, I thank him for another day of sobriety.

I graduated from college, but last year I went back, earned twenty credits and am now enjoying an exciting job. I still have many old friends and now have many new ones. I have a sense of well-being, even though I have had to face big problems in the last two and a half years and know that there will be many in my future. I will continue to attend meetings and solve my problems with the tools of the program.

Now I know what self-esteem means. I have the respect of my children, which is one of the most important things in my life. I won both because I put the cork in the bottle.

Joe

For me, the worst part of being alcoholic is the loneliness. Stopping my drinking didn't change this, but, gradually, my membership in AA did.

One of my many justifications for drinking was that I was able to mix with people more comfortably when I was drinking than when I wasn't. I was more social. Alcohol was the lubricant that minimized the friction in all my relationships.

It worked, too. With enough alcohol, I could tolerate anyone and almost anything. I could and did associate with people who would not have interested me in the least, or whom I probably would have actually disliked with good reason, if I hadn't been drinking. I would go places, do things, and say things I never would have gone to, done, or said but for the lubrication. Alcohol overrode the inhibitions that kept me from going to those places and doing or saying those things when I hadn't been drinking. Unless I had a drink or two, I was uncomfortable with anyone anywhere.

I think it was, quite simply, that I didn't really like anyone. I was also sure no one liked me, and I couldn't blame them. I didn't like me, either. The only "craving" I experienced was for relief from the constant pain of having to associate with people I didn't like, people who didn't like me. Even more, I craved relief from the pain of being me. I discovered that alcohol would ease that constant pain. I let myself become totally dependent on it for that purpose.

I ignored the possibility that there might be other ways to ease my pain. I ignored the possibility that I might actually enjoy being fully aware of the sensations of a relationship with someone I could respect if I worked hard enough to make it a pleasant one for everyone involved —not just for me. I ignored the possibility that I might even like myself if I did the things I would respect anyone for doing. I ignored the fact that I had reached a point where the only relationships I had left were with people as dependent on the lubrication as I was. I also ignored the fact that not every relationship is always pleasant. I ignored these things for so long and so completely that I destroyed every important relationship in my life—with my wife, with my children, in my employment, socially—and I destroyed every ounce of respect I had for myself. When it hurt, alcohol eased the pain.

When the alcohol finally exacted its toll, as it always does, physically, mentally, and emotionally, it was not difficult for me, in a brief God-given moment of sanity, to admit that I was powerless over alcohol and that my life had become unmanageable. That was obvious. I admitted myself to a treatment center, thinking it would solve my problems. It didn't.

I'm not sure now what my plans were when I first got out of the treatment center, but I do recall that AA did not figure prominently in them. The twelve steps, the slogans, the spirituality, the readings, and the stories of other people's drinking escapades and disaster all seemed too simplistic to me. I went to my first few AA meetings simply because there happened to be a meeting immediately following a lecture series on alcoholism I wanted to hear. I thought enough education about alcoholism would enable me to overcome it. But that didn't solve my problems, either.

I remember being surprised to find that my family still cared enough to take an active part in my treatment program, but I was also surprised by how much our relationship had changed. They had adapted to my easing myself out of every uncomfortable situation, and there was a vacant spot in all our lives—in theirs where I was supposed to be, and in mine where they were supposed to be. They were happy that I was trying to change, and I was happy that they cared, but none of us could successfully pretend nothing had happened and pick up the loose ends where they had been so selfishly severed so long ago. I was still very much alone.

Work was no better. Taking the easy way out for so long had pointed my professional life toward disaster, and I knew it. I was deeply in debt, the prospect for immediate income was bleak, and simply not drinking did not effect a miraculous change in my work habits or my attitudes. I still didn't like people and I knew a good many of them didn't—or wouldn't —like me. There I was, facing these problems alone, and with no alcohol to ease the pain. I was not prepared for this loneliness.

Somewhere along the line I began to notice a change in what I was seeing and hearing at those AA meetings. The meetings didn't change, I'm sure, but what I heard did. Through some miracle, because it wasn't anything I consciously did, I came out of my self-imposed shell long enough to hear that other people were actually exposing the fact that they felt the same fears, the same insecurities, and the same loneliness that I felt. Some people used the present tense, and that made me feel less alone. Others used the past tense to describe these feelings and the present tense to describe something they called serenity. They gave me hope.

I began to look hardest at those people who could use the past tense to describe what I was feeling so painfully in the present, to see what they had done that I wasn't doing. I discovered that they were doing those things that I had thought were too simplistic to work for me—working the twelve steps, following the platitudinous slogans, and sharing their experiences.

By sharing their experiences, AA members gave me new meaning for slogans like "one day at a time." It doesn't, I've learned, mean just don't drink for that day. It also means to live each day to the fullest potential, without borrowing either good or bad from tomorrow, and without carrying any of yesterday's baggage. Other trite slogans took on entirely new meanings for me, too, when AA members explained how the slogans worked for them.

I now study the twelve steps, too, in the anonymously written books available through AA. I am absolutely amazed at how precisely the same fears, doubts, and self-pity I feel have been felt by other alcoholics. As I stumble up these steps, trying so many times before I make it, I am equally amazed how the promised changes do occur. No "presto-chango," instant friends, and riches, but real, lasting, identifiable changes for the better. Some small, some not so small, have really happened.

I've got a long way to go to achieve the serenity all alcoholics pray for, but I am more grateful to the successful men and women of AA for sharing the secrets of their success with me than I've ever been for anything in my life. With their advice and God's help, I'm sure that someday I'll be able to use the past tense and, by doing so, give the same hope to some lonely alcoholic they've given me. I've learned—from them—that only by sharing this hope can I keep it. Until then, I pray, with millions of people just like me, and with equal emphasis on all three requests: God grant me the serenity to accept the things I cannot change, the courage to change the things I can, and the wisdom to know the difference.

Georgette

At the age of twenty-six I walked into my first AA meeting, alone and feeling like a zombie. There was a small voice in the back of my head saying, "Please, God, let there be something here for me." What I heard at that meeting made my head drop to my feet—I was getting the message that in order to control my drunkenness I was going to have to stop drinking completely. What I know now, and didn't then, was that I had just walked into a perfect support system that could help me do just that.

I kept going to meetings, in spite of my inner resistance, because, for the first time in my life, I was hearing other people speak of the anguish, despair, shame, and guilt that I had felt and kept to myself for years. When I started drinking alcohol, at the age of thirteen, I thought it was the most wonderful thing in the world. I had had polio as a kid and went back to school after four years in hospitals and home tutoring. My re-entry into society was excruciatingly painful, and I discovered that alcohol was the perfect outlet for all that emotional pain I'd built up inside. It was the perfect solution to life's difficulties and disappointments. When I encountered people with obvious problems, when I sensed or knew someone didn't drink, I thought they were strange or stupid. Drinking over problems came as naturally as breathing to me.

The one catch, however, was that once I had the first drink, I didn't stop until I reached oblivion. I thought surely I'd grow out of this compulsive drinking behavior. At the age of twenty-three, I looked at myself in the mirror and thought, melodramatically but truthfully, You're a drunk, you've always been a drunk, and you'll always be a drunk. I had no idea that I was battling a powerful addiction, one in which control is a total self-delusion. There were many times in my fifteen years of alcoholic drinking when I said to myself, "I think I'll have a drink," as if it were a choice I had.

I felt during all those years of drinking that I drank because I had personality problems, never knowing that the drinking itself produced a terrible corrosion in my self-esteem, my self-confidence. Instead of coming to grips with the self-pity I felt, alcohol allowed me to wallow in it. I had years of suicidal thinking, years of self-loathing; I was internally programmed for failure. All my achievements were dismissed by me as "too easy," yet I strove constantly to over-achieve. I wanted to and did become a visual artist, and I thought that my creativity flowed from my insanity. I thought that great paintings were born only of anguish.

When I reached the halls of AA, I thought that my previous thirteen years of drinking had been hell. But the next two years of going to AA meetings and not being able to stop drinking for any longer than a few months were even worse, because now I knew there was a solution and I didn't seem to be able to catch on to it. But something was happening to me. I was coming out of the alcoholic fog and growing in under-standing of what alcohol was doing to me, how it controlled me and not me it, how I could no longer hide in it. I also learned, by continuing to go to AA, that there were things other than myself and booze in which I could believe and trust. After two years of desperately trying to catch on to the AA program, the gift of surrender to my powerlessness over alcohol came, and I miraculously stayed sober.

Part of what AA did for me was to expose my self-deceptive thinking. I thought I drank because I was handicapped, then later, when I tired of

that excuse, others came along, just as logical. I thought I drank because I felt, as a woman, weak and fearful of taking care of myself. I thought that if I was pretty or rich I would not have to drink. I saw all kinds of people in AA. They had been stricken by the same horrible set of symptoms I had, and I began to realize that there was no excuse for drinking, but that there was a reason—alcoholism.

I've come to believe that life is a spiritual journey, simply because I have grown in spiritual awareness through repeatedly practicing AA's twelve steps of recovery and by passing through, in the last sixteen years, a good number of situations in life that seemed like the end, situations of tragedy, terrible decisions, and growth, which I went through kicking and screaming. I don't want to grow this way, I thought many times. It's too bloody painful. I feel I have transcended the pain of my alcoholism and have triumphed over it. The AA program and other recovering alcoholics have been my constant guides and sources of strength through the years. Like other sober alcoholics in AA, I am in a unique position to pass this gift of sobriety and growth on to others because I can share what happened to me.

Ted

I'm of Irish parents, and I arrived in the United States when I was three years old. My mother brought me and my two sisters to Pontiac, Michigan. My father had been shot and killed, and my mother remarried. Her husband adopted us three, and we moved to Portland. As I grew up, my stepfather avoided me at all opportunities, and he and my mother started to have children of their own. He took his children everyplace he could, but I was always left out. He treated my sisters fine, though. My mother objected to the way he treated me, but there was nothing she could do. It was during the depression and she had to have a home for us children. Consequently, I was very bitter and I quit school in the fourth grade and became nothing but a street urchin.

At the age of thirteen I had a chance to ship out. Under the Maritime Commission, a captain could hire and fire as he saw fit. So before I was fourteen I had been in Central and South America. Being a seaman, I followed the group and started drinking.

At the age of fifteen, I was home from a trip to see my mother. Late one night I was seen standing over the body of a man who was bleeding profusely. I do not recall being there. At 2:00 or 3:00 A.M. my mother came to my room and said that the police were there and wanted to talk to me. The police arrested me for assault and battery. Later that day the man passed away, so I was brought back and charged with murder. I was found guilty and sentenced to ninety-nine years. I entered prison at the age of fifteen, the youngest person in the United States to be sentenced like that, I've been told.

A fine educational and sports director explained to me I could make out of life what I wanted to in prison. He recommended that I get an education because whatever knowledge a person has can't be taken away. I graduated from grammar school with an institutional diploma, which is of no value. I graduated from high school with an institutional diploma, also of no value.

Lifers are allowed to choose their own place of work; I chose automotive and the machine shop. Anyone who was qualified was allowed to take a National Correspondence School course free of charge. I graduated from that and finally had a diploma that wasn't "institutional." After finishing that course, I was allowed a second one. I took diesel engineering and received a second diploma.

After twelve years, the son of a former mayor arrived in prison for manslaughter—two and a half to five years for drunken driving, hitting and killing two sailors who were walking along the highway. We were the same age, and I got him assigned to work in the machine shop with me, since he was from my hometown. His parents were very interested in me because I had helped out their son.

His father started an investigation of my case. He was a thirty-third-degree Mason and got the Shriners and the Odd Fellows involved. Through this investigation, it was found that the man I had supposedly murdered was seen lying in the doorway an hour and a half before I was seen standing over him, but nobody had paid any attention to that. With this evidence, they went to the governor and I was exonerated. They gave me seven thousand dollars and let me out of prison. Seven thousand dollars was a lot of money at that time. I came out, bought a new car, and lived high, enjoying women and wine. In nine months the car was gone, the money was gone, and I had no choice but to start working.

Back to sea I went. This time, going to sea was different because I had a trade, diesel engineer. I shipped for a number of years, and I met the lady I married. We had three children, a lovely home, two cars, and a sizable bank account. She couldn't stand my going to sea and being away from the children, so I took a job in the shipyard as a foreman, then a supervisor, and then a trouble-shooter. As a trouble-shooter I was sent on different ships to different places, so I was away from home at least four to six months out of the year. When I was home, I wasn't spending time with my family.

I did not consider myself an alcoholic, because I had a home, a good job, and was maintaining the family. As I look back on it now, though, my wife was father and mother to my children. It came to where she was threatening to do this or that if I didn't stop drinking, but I would control my drinking to a certain extent and let it pass over. Soon, however, I was back into the same act again. One day the threat was fulfilled. My wife divorced me. I couldn't believe it. Since ours was community property, I gave my share of the property to my three boys. The bank account was split up, and I came to Puerto Rico.

I arrived in Puerto Rico at approximately 5:00 P.M. At eleven o'clock I woke up in the street with no suitcase, no money, no watch—just the clothes on my back. Then I realized that I was an alcoholic. I was in a strange place. I did not speak the language, and I did not know a living soul. I felt sorry for myself, disliking everyone and, above all, disliking myself.

For two and a half years I slept in the streets, in the cemetery, on the beaches of San Juan, figuring this was my destiny. There was nothing more left for me.

A lady who passed me on her way to work every morning would give me a sandwich or a pack of cigarettes. The prostitutes would go to the Salvation Army, now and then, and get me a clean shirt, a clean pair of pants, a pair of shoes. None of them ever offered me anything to drink. They would buy me a sandwich, once in a while, or take me up to their rooms so I could take a shower and shave and put on the clean clothes.

Then, one day, the lady who gave me the sandwiches and cigarettes took me by the hand, wanting me to follow her. She couldn't speak English, and I couldn't speak Spanish. But I followed her. We wound up at the police court. Standing before the judge, drunk as always, I thought she was entering a complaint against me.

Instead, I walked out of the courtroom married. Why, I do not know.

It was my first time inside a home in approximately two and a half years, sitting down to a meal or having a bed to sleep in.

My wife continued to work at her job, and I continued to drink. She went to many doctors to see what could be done about my drinking. No doctor could give her any solution until she got to one doctor who wrote out a prescription for AA.

My wife took me to my first meeting, sixteen and a half years ago. At that meeting I met my unsolicited sponsor, who took it on himself to see what he could do for me. For fourteen months I never touched a drop. But still not believing that I couldn't drink at all, I tried it again for a one-night stand, and my sponsor had me back in again.

In the meantime I had gone to the Coast Guard, at my sponsor's insistence, and got my license renewed. My sponsor insisted that I start going back to sea because that was my only occupation. But before I got back to sea, I had another three-day stand. He told me that he would not put up with it any longer, that there were other people who needed help and that if I didn't do something I would have to find another sponsor. Knowing that no one else would want to take over the responsibility of being my sponsor, I started working this program to the best of my ability, and I did get back to sea. I was at sea when I had a heart attack. I was in the hospital. I had two more heart attacks within five months. They finally retired me and pensioned me off.

I was full of self-pity because I had projected a new home again and things that I had always wanted. My sponsor informed me that I was the most ungrateful son of a bitch he had ever met. His words were, "You're still alive. Can't you understand that you're alive for a reason?" I wanted to know what the reason was. He said, "Did you ever think that maybe you could help people who have been in similar situations?" He said, "You're supposed to grow in this program, but I don't see where you have grown one bit."

The AA program has been a lifesaver because I was drowning in booze, self-pity, misery, hate— just a derelict floating around. Since then I have worked this program to the best of my ability, and I have found a reasonable amount of peace and comfort because, in helping other people as best I can, I also found out that I'm helping myself. I'm helping myself in my attitude, my disposition, my feelings toward other people. Today I do not know anyone I dislike. I have found comfort in this program. I do not come to attend meetings today to please other people. If they are pleased with me, that's nice. I come here to keep my sobriety, and I have peace and comfort with myself. I only do it one day at a time. I do not work this program to please my wife, my children, or anyone else, because when I start pleasing them with this program I am only making excuses, and then possibly I'd pick up another drink. If I work it for myself, I have no excuses. As of today I have had no excuse or any reason to pick up a drink.

On arriving in Puerto Rico many years ago with no finances, I was panhandling and begging to get by and eating out of trash barrels. Before I arrived I had drunk royally—Lord Calvert, Seagram's, Johnny Walker—but on arrival my drinking dropped to industrial alcohol, which was forty-five cents a quart. A group of what eventually became fourteen of us, including two women, would meet every morning in Plaza Colón and would start our tour for the day to get money to drink. We would get two or three quarts of industrial alcohol. If we couldn't get that there was always a place where we could buy formaldehyde for a dollar a gallon. The industrial alcohol had to be split. The formula was to pour water into the industrial, not industrial into the water. If you poured industrial into the water it would get so hot that you couldn't drink it. The smoke would come out of the neck of the bottle. I can look back at this now and laugh, but at that time it was a necessity. I was drinking to live.

The group diminished little by little until today only two of us are alive. One incident I remember very clearly. We were in back of the Tapia Theater, where there is a wall which is forty feet from the top to the street below. One of the fellows—he wasn't in the crowd drinking with us that day—appeared at the top of the wall. We asked him to come down to have a drink. He said, no, it was a good day to go for a swim. The water was beautiful and calm. We tried to entice him to come down. Then he took a big dive and landed head first on the concrete below. His head broke open like a coconut. We just picked up our bottles and cups and went to the old railroad depot. The man lay there for nearly three hours before his body was removed. That was his last drink. Because of this program two of us who are left, thank God, didn't have to follow the same path.

José

I grew up in Brooklyn, New York. At the age of twelve I started to experiment with marijuana and drinking a little beer. This was the beginning of my battle with alcohol. I drank for almost nine years.

In the eighth grade I made the basketball team as a reserve player. As I look back I see how the progression of alcoholism had already set in. I remember being late to my first basketball game on a Friday night because I had been drinking. On another occasion I was going to the local school dance but never made it because I had gotten drunk on wine with my cousin. We had waited by the liquor store for someone to buy us some wine, and once we started, we didn't stop until we were drunk. I was only fourteen years old at the time, and already alcohol had become one of my priorities.

I graduated from junior high school and continued on to high school. The first year in high school I passed my courses. In my second year school was no longer of any interest to me, so I would go just to meet friends and get high. I became a daily drinker and used my lunch money for alcohol.

After two years of this type of drinking, I was held back as a sophomore for the second time. So I quit school and went to work in a warehouse. It wasn't long before I got fired from the job because of my drinking. I would come in late and hung over almost every day, and miss work on Mondays.

Being a high school dropout and having no skills, I tried "the geographical cure" we speak of in AA, joining the Marine Corps Reserve. For the first time in a long time I was dry for three months, during boot camp. After training I went right back to drinking, and the progression continued. I found another job and lost that, too, because of drinking, but I denied it had anything to do with the alcohol. I told myself I could stop whenever I wanted to. My excuse was that I just didn't want to stop. Besides, I was young.

My alcoholism had progressed tremendously through these years, and everyone told me I had a problem. But, no, I wouldn't listen to anyone. I isolated myself from people more and more and drank every day.

I ended up going into the Veterans Hospital psychiatric ward for alcoholics, but I still wasn't ready to get honest. I left and continued to drink.

That same year, 1978, I was taken to Cumberland Hospital in Brooklyn for treatment. This time I went for the right reason, to get help. It was there I had my first experience with AA. I realized I was an alcoholic after listening to a man from AA speak. I had run out of excuses and I was hurting, so I listened. This was the beginning of a new life.

After leaving the hospital, I was taken to my first AA meeting, in Bay Ridge, Brooklyn. I have been sober ever since. It's going on six years of continued sobriety, with no drugs or mood changers of any kind. The obsession and compulsion I had daily for years was lifted. I couldn't believe it. A power greater than myself, whom I choose to call God, relieved me.

The AA program has changed my life entirely, from a mere existence to a life full of meaning. Today I feel as though I belong to the human race. I realize I have a fatal disease and that the program is the only thing that has worked for me. I've been able to get my GED and get into college. I'm in my junior year at New York University, and that's only one of the many fringe benefits sobriety has given me. I've made many friends, and people in the program have helped me tremendously. I'm very grateful for a chance at a new way of living. It's the best thing that ever happened to me.

Ann

My life was in flux. I felt buried alive because of another divorce, because of unreconciled relationships with my children, with my father who, because of my drinking, had taken me out of his will, and with friends who were not happy to have me around. My paramount responsibility, to my four daughters, was not carried out. The two oldest children, fourteen and sixteen years of age, left and went with their father, my first husband. The two youngest, four and six years old, were in the care of their nanny and their father, who sometimes had to take the younger one to work with him. I was incapable of taking care of myself—I was drinking around the clock at this point. The role of a drunken mother isn't pretty. I had lost everyone's trust and respect. It isn't a secure feeling for children to have policemen at their home because of all the fighting and arguing that takes place. All of this in a lovely suburban home.

I had no self-respect. I felt like a moral degenerate, worthless and full of remorse. Why was all this happening to me? Who was I? Was it true, as my doctor told me, that if I continued to drink I would be dead in six months? "Who cares," was my reply to him, the man who had delivered my fourth child and whom I had greatly respected. But the truth is, I did care, and I was so scared that I drank even more. Many times I swore to my family that I would stop drinking, and I believe that at the moment I meant it, but

410

as soon as I felt better I would be off again.

I never thought that I would go into a bar alone, but let me tell you, it didn't take long to accomplish that. I went to one bar where I knew the owners and there I played many parts—an engineer, a dancer, or whatever seemed to fit the script—while at home my family was wondering where their mother was.

My husband took away the car, but that didn't keep me home. Sometimes I rode my bike in the afternoon to my favorite haunt—needless to say I came home, bike and all, in a cab. There were times when the cab driver refused to take me because he said I didn't know where I lived. I nearly killed my husband in a blackout once. Every ideal I had was stamped on when I was abusing alcohol. Every major event in my life—loss of virginity, marriage—was influenced by alcohol.

I was born in New York and raised in Westchester by my paternal grandparents because my mother had died when I was born. I was watched carefully, given every advantage that money or culture could confer. I attended all-girl Catholic schools in Manhattan. I was loved very dearly, spoiled, and yet it was a very strict, proper household. I was not permitted to do many of the things my peers could, but I did them anyway and lied my way out. In high school a few of the girls experimented with drinking; I was among them. The crowd I went with drank at parties, football games, and baseball games. At eighteen I got drunk at the Stork Club. It was all fun and games.

World War II arrived, and I was engaged to be married to a marine. He was killed at Guadalcanal, and I could not accept it. How could this happen, when I went to church and prayed every day for his safety? I damned God and drank— drink and be merry, for tomorrow you die.

Two years later I met a young lieutenant at a cocktail lounge. We were married in New York and I came to Detroit as the newest member of one of the leading structural steel company families. We were very social, and drinking was the big thing. After nine years of marriage and two children, we divorced. Not believing in divorce, I could not accept the situation, so I drank. Now I had full responsibility for making a living and raising my two girls.

Very shortly after my divorce I met my second husband in a bar and was married out of the church. Again, I was overwhelmed with guilt and fear at what I had done, so I'd have a few drinks to forget. Two children were born. With the pressure and responsibility of my family, I began to join my husband in a nightly drink before dinner to relax. If I was out with lady friends and it was suggested that we stop and have a drink, I would do so, mindless of my family at home.

The progression of alcoholism left me completely bankrupt and unable to function. The terror of having no control—wanting to stop, knowing I needed to drink—was a nightmare! When I think about it now, I feel as if I am looking down on a stage at someone else—but no, it's me.

It was in this condition that I was introduced to AA. I didn't call them but came in through a divorce lawyer—little did I know that he was an AA member. I thank God for that one moment of sanity. People in AA welcomed this wretched wreck. They seemed to understand, and I was no longer alone. They told me to keep coming to meetings and not to take that first drink. In retrospect, that is all I did, struggling to grasp their simple concepts. I found out that alcohol was but a symptom of what was wrong. The real problem was that "growing up" is painful. It wasn't easy to be willing to open my confused mind, to be honest with myself. I had a progressive disease—alcoholism. Looking back on my life, it has been a learning process—and a process of unlearning so many preconceived ideas. Gradually, these negative feelings of false pride, depression, self-pity, anger, and hate were replaced with hope. I was a sick person trying to get well, not a bad person trying to be good. They told me I was a human being—no better, no worse than anyone else, and no matter what anyone did, I had no control over them or their behavior. That was and is a major step in deflating my whining and self-pity. Stripping away a lifelong facade—like peeling an onion—I was beginning to feel better. No one was responsible for making me drink. No one ever poured a drink down my throat. No more pretense. I had so much self-hate, striking out at others to cover up my feelings of inadequacy, people-pleasing to cover up my feelings of inferiority. I had submerged all my feelings. All of my rationalizations had to go.

Today I like myself, so consequently I do not hate anyone. I found out the true meaning of love and joy in living each day. I have replaced fear with faith in a Higher Power. All of my needs are taken care of. I feel worthy and deserving of good things. I can be self-expressing, I can care about my health, can see the best in others, can be affectionate without expectation of return. My life is changing, and I can be receptive and open to change without anxiety. I can face reality without a drink. I have dignity and function as a responsible person. I have the love and respect of my family, and I have a restored sense of humor. I learned to be grateful in AA for what I am today, a contented, recovering alcoholic. AA took care of me when I was not able to take care of myself. I have options now, and I live each day full of hope. I am free to be the person God wants me to be. I'm no saint, but I can strive to do my best each day. It's such a relief not to live in the past or worry about what's ahead—all I have is now.

Paul

I feel and live through my participation in the program. AA is an opportunity for me to participate with others in an open and honest atmosphere, sharing the common problem of alcoholism and living without alcohol. AA allows me to gain self-esteem at the physical, emotional, and spiritual levels of my life. This is made possible through my trust in, and reliance on, the other members. I believe in their unselfish and genuine concern for me.

Through the self-discipline that the program demands, I gain the freedom from self that allows me to be a meaningful participant in life, a life I now live with respect for God, myself, and my fellow man. I now accept responsibility and enjoy the benefits that flow therefrom. Life now is directed by a desire to do what God wills for me—out of love for God rather than fear of him. As a result of my desire to live a God-directed life, my daily activity is more meaningful and satisfying. AA has provided me with the tools and hope to bring about this better life.

Today I enjoy a life that promises me the opportunity for happiness. When I was drinking I was unable to respond in a manner other than one of self-seeking. Fear of failure was paramount, and a general feeling of inadequacy was the norm. I existed on a steady diet of worry and conflict.

There were extended periods of loneliness and separateness. At the end of my drinking career I had lapsed into complete despair. When I came to AA I was totally beaten, without any feeling of purpose or direction.

AA has given me the opportunity to discover

myself. I have a feeling of belonging and a willingness to respond to life with my fellow man. I wish to continue to change and grow. AA allows me the fulfillment of myself.

On Drinking

We drank for happiness and became unhappy.
We drank for joy and became miserable.
We drank for sociability and became
      argumentative.
We drank for sophistication and became
      obnoxious.
We drank for friendship and made enemies.
We drank for sleep and awakened without rest.
We drank for strength and felt weak.
We drank medicinally and acquired health
      problems.
We drank for relaxation and got the shakes.
We drank for bravery and became afraid.
We drank for confidence and became doubtful.
We drank to make conversation easier and
      slurred our speech.
We drank to feel heavenly and ended up feeling
      like hell.
We drank to forget and were forever haunted.
We drank for freedom and became slaves.
We drank to erase problems and saw them
      multiply.
We drank to cope with life and invited death.

—Anonymous

416

13 Say Yes to Life

An alcoholic could be called an egomaniac with an inferiority complex.

The drinking alcoholic believes that he is the center of the universe and the rest of the world revolves around him. At the same time, he has no confidence and lives in fear. In sobriety the alcoholic joins the human race and becomes a participant in life.

The now sober alcoholic has work to do.

Father Vaughan Quinn lays down a blueprint for a positive life—not only for the alcoholic, but for everyone. The major stumbling block to happiness, he says, is preoccupation with self. The happiest recovering alcoholics are those who have not only quit drinking, but have changed their attitude about themselves, others in their lives, and the world around them.

The Reverend Vaughan Quinn, O.M.I., is an alcoholic. He is the executive director of Sacred Heart Rehabilitation Center, an alcohol treatment facility in Detroit and Memphis, Michigan.

The Reverend Vaughan Quinn, O.M.I.

The person who is given over to alcohol is very negative and the hallmarks of that are worry, anger, self-pity, and depression. One or two of those negative emotions can totally immobilize a person. In that state, he is unable to make any lifegrowing, mature, unselfish decisions for himself. The rest of the world is pushing his buttons. Continually working out of a negative situation because of guilt, that person is continually forced to act in a way that is tremendously manipulative of other people. He tries to ingratiate himself with other people by his presence, doing all kinds of good things excessively and compulsively to gain other people's approval.

Alcoholism is not a symptom of other, deeper character disorders. It is a primary disease with its own etiology, symptomatology, and fatality, if nothing is done about it. Alcoholism is a chemical problem. There are millions of people who drink. The effect of alcohol on alcoholics is totally different from what it is on social drinkers, and measurably so, speaking clinically and pharmacologically.

Alcoholics adopt a cluster of behavior patterns to protect their drinking and their position in life so that they don't go below the threshold of pain. So the lying comes in, the sneaking of drinks, the egocentricity and the narcissism, the "to hell with the rest of the world" and "me, me, me" attitude. All of the self-centeredness comes in because the people who are closest to us reflect back our own self-disgust and we respond in anger. That has to change. We have to learn to deal with those people differently. We cannot play the same games we were playing with those people before. When the alcoholic quits drinking, he's got a lot of work to do because of the cluster of behavior patterns he adopted for self-protection while the drinking was going on.

The real purpose of sobriety is for the alcoholic to change from a selfish to an unselfish person. The whole business is to turn the negative into something positive. Author Father John Powell says, "If our basket of life is filled with nothing but worry, anger, self-pity, depression, resentments, and hostility, that's the way we're going to relate to people." The philosophy of recovery, and here I'm making direct reference to the philosophy of Alcoholics Anonymous, is being able to change all that negativity into a positive acceptance of the human condition. There cannot be anything negative about it. There cannot be any crying, "Poor me, poor me, I can't drink. Everybody else is able to drink but I'm not."

The cause of the fear and pain that block every human being—not just alcoholics—from growing is preoccupation with self. The further a person regresses in the addiction process, the more he becomes self-occupied, self-centered. His world becomes no bigger than himself.

The goals of recovery are freedom, happiness,

peace, and serenity—that is quoted directly from the philosophy of AA. That cannot be arrived at as long as there is any amount of alcohol or addictive drug, any type of foreign chemical in the system. The first step is to free the person from dependency on chemistry so he is able to experience the growth process that gives life some zest. This demands continued therapy, regular attendance at AA, so the person doesn't slide back into the old negative frame of reference. It's a pity today that we find so many people—and I even see them in some AA groups—who find their comradeship, their fellowship, their sense of belonging, by being negative, by voicing what I call proclamations of protestation. They are not being present to one another, reflecting back one another's goodness and dignity and sense of divine origin.

I feel very strongly that the AA philosophy and the whole recovery process consist of sharing how we get well, sharing with other people the experiences of the present and the hope of the future. That hope is the personal commitment to the not yet certain. None of us has answers to what is going to happen five years, or even five days, down the road.

Through the philosophy of recovery and the philosophy of AA, there are people who live in the now and enjoy a meaningful, purposeful life in an enthusiastic way. That is the reason AA is so successful. What makes a person stop drinking is always a negative thing, and that's valid. I'm going to lose something. I'm going to lose my health, my liver, my spleen, my wife, my car, my job, or in my case, my priesthood. That's valid for the initial stage of recovery.

But the human brain is a thinking brain, and we can always rethink things and look into our memories for the positive things. All of a sudden, after the pain, the guilt, the shame, the remorse disappear—and they all do, in time, or we'd all be looking for a bridge to throw ourselves off —all of a sudden, it's "Well, drinking really wasn't that bad" or "I think I can do it a little bit differently." This is fatal because the person has started a rationalization process that is going to defeat him in time.

What keeps a person in continued conditioning therapy, which is AA, is the realistic appreciation that life is better because of the fact that they're not drinking, not using drugs. There is more joy, more enthusiasm, more purpose. It's just a better, more positive lifestyle.

AA could stand for Altered Attitudes. A person changes from being negative into being positive, so that he becomes part of the solution instead of part of the problem. He stops reacting negatively, stops crying about what a despicable world it is, stops being a prophet of gloom and doom. The toast is burned. The coffee is too cold. The sidewalks are too narrow. The eggs are too greasy. The beautiful mountains are blocking the view. That type of world approach is very dangerous in the person who is recovering from alcoholism. What that signifies is that the infantile part of the ego is again assuming directorship of the universe. Those negative feelings will lead the alcoholic back to drinking.

When we talk about deflation in the recovery process, we're talking about the infantile part of ego. The alcoholic starts with the attitude that says, "I am king and I want what I want when I want it. Everybody else darn well better do what I want, and my wish is everybody else's command." This is an attitude he brings with him from infancy—"His Majesty the Baby." He really gets to believe, although he never really articulates it, that the sun rises and sets on him, that his own goodness and well-being are paramount. Another part of that ego deflation has to focus on tolerance of frustration. Alcoholics are notorious for waving at a taxi in a rainstorm. The taxi driver doesn't even see them, so they go in and drink for three days. Low tolerance to any type of frustration has to be worked on. That's why the "one day at a time" philosophy of Alcoholics Anonymous is very effective. It does away with sabotage concepts in which a person tries to do much more than he's capable of doing and sets up a situation where he is doomed to fail. Alcoholics also have a mania for doing everything in a hurry. We want everything to happen right now, yesterday. It takes stick-to-itiveness in general daily living, which has to be worked on, to gain serenity and peace.

Now, what is every bit as important is that the other side of the ego, which not all people are aware of, has to be built up. That's the part that deals with self-worth and self-respect, the part that deals with a sense of divine origin, the part that deals with being created on this earth for a purpose, the belief that "I am a good person." To bring out that good is certainly the purpose of AA; it isn't just looking at the negative. We know that negative things brought us into therapy. After that, what keeps us in therapy is that life has become more beautiful and there is a lot more enthusiasm.

Basically, that's what alcoholics look for in drinking. They look for the great romances, the great coups, the sense of peace, belonging, and unity. Those drives are valid. The alcohol brings total regression into their lives. That basic drive has to be directed in a more positive way so that they can participate in some significant, meaningful, joyful experiences. There certainly would be no purpose in stopping drinking if life just became as tedious and boring as it was before. The reason alcoholics drink is to change the way they feel. If a person still feels very negative, if he's not experiencing any of the positive fringe benefits of the recovery program, then he ultimately will go back and say, "Well, heck, is this all there is? I might as well just drink again."

So in the process of being involved in the AA program, that part of the ego that is involved with omnipotence, low tolerance to frustration, and impatience is deflated. The part of the ego that deals with self-worth and self-dignity has to be inflated. This part grows through service to other people, through being able to love them unconditionally, without measuring everything on a scale, without receiving any gifts in return, without the attitude, "I'll do this for you, if you do this for me. Here's my gift, and if you don't do this for me, I'll take my gift away." There can be none of that. We must learn to appreciate other people as they are, without any conditions whatsoever being laid on.

It's a continuing process of growth and change to appreciate the world, to be present to the world, to see the sacredness of things, the sacredness of other people, the sacredness of creation.

Everybody who reaches out for help has three problems: they cannot love themselves; they cannot accept themselves; and they cannot forget themselves. In AA, what we talk about is learning to accept ourselves, feeling self-worth, dignity, and self-love. This is brought about by positive actions. If a person is doing negative things, he'll suffer the negative feelings that are the consequence. The alcoholic must accept the fact that "I am a recovering alcoholic. There are certain parameters I can deal with successfully, but there are certain things I cannot do, either." The alcoholic cannot use mood-altering drugs of any nature because that would bring back the negative attitudes and make the positive sense of self-worth disappear.

Self-love deals with the journey a person takes in AA, and the morality of AA means a journey of recovery in relationship to other people. How am I getting along with the world? If we're dealing well with other people, then we receive good, positive feedback. The inventory steps of AA are there to bring out the goodness, to bring out the beauty, to bring out the lovableness, to bring out the positiveness, to bring out the creativity, to bring out the uniqueness, to bring out the fears each individual has. It's not a laundry list of all the mistakes that a person has made in life. It's intended to help a person find out what makes him tick so he can be himself and not try to be somebody else. Many people try to copy other people. They stay miserable that way. When we do copy somebody else, we invariably end up compulsively copying the negative aspects, not the healthy aspects, of that individual.

People are an unrepeatable mystery of God's creation. They're a unique creation and that's what they have to respond to, by saying yes to God, yes to the world around them, by allowing the world to challenge them and by not taking everything so seriously.

We must forget about ourselves and be about the business of being of service to other people. That is built into the mechanics of AA, through alcoholics helping other alcoholics and contributing to meetings. The only way a human being finds happiness is by getting rid of self-preoccupation. We alcoholics must rid ourselves of this selfishness or it kills us. We can't do that by ourselves; we need the help of God and other people.

What the fellowship of AA (the word fellowship means "a group of men and women called together by God") offers to the individual is an opportunity to be of service to other people, to carry that message to suffering alcoholics who are coming to the program for the first time. That gives a person a terrific sense of self-worth. What suffering alcoholics bring when they come into the fellowship is a tremendous amount of worry, anger, self-pity, depression, resentment, and even hatred, blaming other people for all the negative things that happen in their lives. There is a tremendous amount of hostility.

The whole program of AA is spiritual. It makes people aware of the spirit that is in them, a spirit that will bring them self-worth so they can experience freedom, happiness, peace, and serenity in relationship to other people.

AA is not a program in which you climb a mountain and contemplate your navel. The spiritual conversion that takes place after surrender means there's no more fighting. The person takes enough time inside himself to experience solitude and to develop peacefulness. Hostility then changes into hospitality. The person is able to perceive the stranger coming toward him as "a bearer of gifts." That's a spine-tingling phrase. This process is very difficult because it is a change in life's vision, a tremendously different approach to life. It really means a spiritual change inside the person so that other people are no longer a threat. The person doesn't go along with paranoia all the time, wondering who is out to get him. He is not continually blaming everybody else if good fortune is not happening to him. He develops a solidarity so that he is able to open up his heart, to allow other people to be present to him and share his gifts. He sees the approaching person as one who has many gifts. In the peace and happiness and tenderness the program talks about, he is able to appreciate that other person for the dignity that is in him as a bearer of gifts.

There are no more power relationships. Power relationships are taking relationships, grasping relationships, egocentric relationships. What is in it for me, me, me. I want what I want when I want it. I use other people to get what I want.

What we have in AA are relationships built on total disarmament, brought about by the common denominator of alcoholism. The only thing that's required of anybody who comes into the group is the desire to stop drinking. All of the competitiveness that we hang on to in the world, which separates us from other people and makes us different, all those little trophies we have, all those little titles before and after our names, our positions, and everything else, all of that is dropped. What brings us together is humility because of what alcoholism did to our lives. In a humble way, we become teachable. We're able to be humble enough to be taught by whoever comes to the table. We're open to them. The relationships are no longer taking relationships. They are giving relationships. In power-struggle relationships you have two people competing, each trying to force his will over the other person.

In AA the real winners, the real livers, the real laughers, the real lovers, the real creative people, the real people, are not afraid to go out and take risks and live meaningful, purposeful lives in service to other people. They don't have to direct other people all the time. They allow other people to be themselves, appreciating the goodness that is in them. The easiest way to stay sick and miserable your whole life is to make yourself responsible for other people's getting well, to make yourself responsible for other people's changing. The job is to allow people to flower at their own rate. That's what AA is. That's why it does not have any rules and regulations. Through AA a tremendous number of people are able to experience meaningful and purposeful lives.

Happy and successful recovered alcoholics are action-oriented. That's very important. If people are in AA and still living in the past, it's very debilitating. If people are there to find out why they drank, that's a total waste of time. They drank because everybody drinks. The effects of alcohol on them are different from those on social drinkers. The group that does well is able to laugh at themselves, is able to forget about themselves, is oriented to the future, is able to take risks, is able to make themselves vulnerable to situations. That's because they're not holding themselves responsible for the rest of the world's getting well.

When I talk about sobriety, I don't mean it has to be a party twenty-four hours a day. We all get knocks in the head. But at least we can avoid regressing, blaming everybody else and not living in the now. Some of the saddest people I see are those who come into my office and are emotionally on the edge of their chairs. I can see by what's emanating from them that they are living a situation created by what somebody did to them years ago. They have been allowing that person to live in their head rent-free for years, and they are totally immobilized. They can't talk about anything else. Their experience has made them very bitter. In positive recovery we've got to look upon our experiences by asking, "Are they going to make us bitter or are they going to make us better?"

The impact of AA is measurable in our relationship to other people. Are we able to be more kind to them? Are we able to be more tender to them in the way we make ourselves present to them, the way we listen to them and look at them? It's always in relationship to other people because this is where we live out our lives. It's also always in the now, and not what happened years ago. We should be at tables of AA sharing with other people how we get well. What are the joys? What are some of the hopes? What are some of the fears, real fears, that are going on right now? Then we can make an act of faith. That means a personal commitment that things will get better if we apply ourselves. It is not talking about what happened years ago. That really has no significance to what is going on now. The horror stories, the war stories abound. We all lived them and certainly it can be all right to identify that there was a loss of control, that there was a conflict between behavior and values. But what gets people well is sharing what we have now, the freedom and the joy and the happiness. When new people come to the AA program they see that. They see people laughing and relaxing and having a good time, and they say, "These people have something I want." That's important. The emphasis should be on the positive, on what's going on right now, today.

The alcoholic in sobriety can fall into two traps—pride and anger. Pride is totally taking credit for the gift of sobriety and everything else in his world. This is a type of person to whom even God will remain silent, the person who has a pride-filled heart and says, "I'm a self-made man. I've got sobriety now because I am the cause of it. I brought it into my life and I'm doing it my way and my way is working." That person is in a very hostile frame of reference to the rest of the community, to the rest of the world, and that frame of mind definitely will bring on much aggravation and many negative reactions. That person is saying sobriety is not a gift. "I am in total control of it and I am the singular efficient cause of the sobriety in my life." The sense of unstoppability in that person still remains. I have seen catastrophe and chaos in people's lives because of this. They stopped drinking and the desire was arrested for a while. Then, once again, the infantile ego came out: The sense of omnipotence, the sense of being all-powerful, the "I can do anything" attitude took over. This is a negative reaction to the human condition, one that always precedes an alcoholic's drinking.

Anger is a very real emotion. We all get mad, and that's all right, as long as it's expressed and dealt with. That's one of the redemptive factors of the AA philosophy. AA is a place where a person is able to express anger appropriately. The anger that goes unexpressed gets buried or repressed and always comes out later on, in another type of neurotic behavior that will be negative and detrimental to the person's sobriety. Anger is all right as long as we direct it to the right place, which is to ourselves, because we are responsible for doing something with our emotions. The emotions that come upon us are not always something we bring on ourselves, but they're very real, and we must do something with them. If not, we'll regress to the cluster of behavior patterns that we had before we got into AA and project the anger and blame at the people around us, most often toward the people who are closest to us. So AA presents a very good check valve for that. We can express the anger at a meeting. Once the anger is expressed, it's defused and can be dealt with in a positive, constructive way.

I am an alcoholic. There are certain things I cannot do. There are certain things I've got to do. I've got to do those things. Not my way. I've got to do what the book says, what other people say. Humility. Teachableness. I will allow myself to be taught.

God has created us in His own image and likeness because He loves us, and no matter what we do in life, He continues to love us. A cardinal of the Catholic church was once asked what was the most profound theological doctrine he had difficulty accepting. He said, "It is the fact that God loves me just the way I am." That is reality. We have to take time to really perceive that because so many of us have been brought up in the conditional way. If we are good, God will love us; if we are not good, God will punish us. God does not punish us. In His very nature, all God can do is love us. All He can do is hold us in His hand and love us. That's why He created us. He created us so that we would be able to reflect back the beauty of His creation in the twinkle of our eyes.

God isn't a General Bullmoose, up there counting everything that goes wrong. That's not what he is. So many people come to the AA program and sit around and talk about how inaccessible God seems to them. It's because they're not really opening themselves up to His work of re-creation. If we really want to see God in His creation, all we have to do is make ourselves aware of what's really going on at an AA table. Here we have men and women from all walks of life and every race, belief, creed, sitting around talking about values, spiritual values— freedom, happiness, self-worth, dignity, the presence of God in their lives. It seems very strange that in our society, in our Western culture, we think we are going to get God before he gets us, that there is some prayer we can use to change God. It is quite narcissistic when we sit back and say, "Well, I'm going to pray now. I'm going to change what God is going to do." God loves us first, and even when we get the notion to pray it is still His spirit that is working in us, bringing us back on our journey to self-worth, to our own ground center, bringing us to where our spirit is. God is not a machine up in the sky that's going to zap us. He loves us. We share the same broken human condition. We are all sinners. We need His forgiveness. He is our Father.

I think that prayer is essential to AA. A person must develop the discipline of prayer because that puts him in a relationship to the loving Father. So many of us lie when we pray. We've been given all kinds of prayer books, all kinds of rituals. Say all these words and something magical will happen. Nothing magical is going to happen.

What we do when we pray is talk to our loving Father, who loves us and knows exactly what we need in life and is willing to give it to us—if we are willing to get out of the driver's seat, if we are willing to give up our self-preoccupation. We're continually worrying about all of the negative things that go on, when we can look around and start to see the beauty and get in harmony with our own sense of divine origin that's in us, that harmonizes with the rest of creation. The whole Western culture is trying to influence God. That's such an egocentric trip. It defies any proper explanation.

Life takes discipline. Growth takes discipline. Growth takes stretch marks. People don't like that. AA meetings are tremendously important— to sit with other people, to talk about how we really feel at a particular time. What's important is what happens inside of us in between meetings.

A lot of people turn meetings into rituals. They go nineteen times a week to get out of the house so they don't have to look at other areas of their lives. Some of these other areas are our own capacity to deal with a sense of inner peace, our own sense of solitude, our own sense of silence, our own sense of prayer. We have to pray in a positive way, in a love relationship to God, our Father, who loves us. That means expressing to Him exactly how we feel. If it's anger, it's anger. That's quite all right. And if it's depression or if it's despondency or if it's a sense of nonvalue, that's all right, too. At least we're expressing that to our heavenly Father. To be able to say that is neat. "Here I am. This is what you created." Then listen. So many people just rattle off a bunch of words. You have to listen, too.

God can touch us in five different ways. He can touch our minds and put new ideas in our heads. He can touch our wills. He can touch our imaginations. He can touch our emotions. He can touch our memories. He can bring back a good thought or memory, which can motivate us to do something. But we have to listen. We have to take the time for the silence. We have to take time to meditate. In the last decade there has been a lot more interest in using meditation to get a sense of our own dignity, a sense of our ground center, a sense of our purposefulness in life.

AA is not activity for activity's sake. If a person wants quality sobriety, he should take a quiet time each day. Do some reading. Put himself in touch with God—sharing the feelings, not just words. What really ruined prayers is when we invented the printing press and made people think that if they said all these prayers they could influence God. That's ridiculous. God loves us. What we have to learn to do is respond to that love in a positive way, and we respond to that love by being of service to other people, by sharing the love He has given us with other people, unconditionally.

I get upset when people don't realize the gifts they have, when they don't realize the beauty they have, when they don't realize the lovableness they have, when they don't realize the uniqueness they have, which other people are screaming for them to share. They sit around AA tables or Al-Anon tables and just talk about negative things that happened years ago. That is not giving faith, hope, and love to other people. Young folks coming to AA now are screaming for something to believe in, something to hope for, some reason to love. Often we play games because we're old-timers, like talking about what happened to us in 1965 when we were drinking. I think we're doing them a terrific disservice. I think we're insulting their intelligence. I think we're insulting their emotions. I think that we owe an awful lot more to the sacredness of our recovery, the most sacred thing we have, the gift of sobriety.

Many alcoholics think they're the only people in the world who go through the traumatic experiences of loneliness, not having a place where they're really accepted, feeling they don't belong anywhere. Everyone else in the world has those feelings, too. It's just that we in AA are blessed with people and places where we can learn to be of service, to start having some joy.

The goal of quality sobriety is to say yes to life. That means allowing life to challenge us. When we are paranoid and fearful, we are totally preoccupied with self. That's the pain that blocks us from growing. We can't see anything. We can't see anything in front of us at all. Any type of challenge brought to us becomes a threat. What sobriety is about is joyfully to be able to say yes to life, to say yes to God, to say yes to responsibility, to allow life to challenge us—and that means that we don't take ourselves so seriously. We're all going to make mistakes. None of us is perfect. The program doesn't demand that of anybody. At least life is zest-filled and it has some enthusiasm. When I lead AA retreats, the one question I ask people is, "What makes you enthusiastic? What makes you happy?" And somebody says, "I love playing the piano." "When was the last time you played the piano?" I ask. He says, "Four years ago." That's a tragedy.

We're given so many gifts in AA. We're given opportunity. We get to where we start looking at the real values of life. All the tools are there, plus the fellowship. Life is not always going to be fantastic. It's not always going to be joyful. We all have pain, sickness and death. How are we going to respond to that? Are we going to allow life to challenge us?

If we want the good things to happen to us internally and spiritually, that demands action on our own part. We have to take the first step in faith. Then it starts making some sense. Many times people say, "I can't do that." The word *can't* is a cop-out.

Today I played hockey with the Chicago Black Hawks alumni. I am fifty years old and all these guys drilling that puck at me are twenty-eight years old. If I were to analyze everything beforehand I'd say, "My God, you're crazy." To be able to play means I run six to seven miles a day. I have the goalie pads on five times a week to practice. We were playing for a little boy who has cystic fibrosis. It gave me the feeling that I'm contributing. If they had scored ten goals on me, it would have been the best thing in the world for my humility. But I went out and gave it my best shot. And we won. The puck hit me sometimes and I never saw it, but I looked good. Everybody was screaming and clapping. I thought it was really great. If I sit back and say I can't do this, I can't do that, I can't do the other thing, then I'm not going to have any sense of celebration in my heart, any sense of self-worth, or have a positive world vision.

You can contribute to life. You can put smiles on people's faces. That's what's really meaningful. If I were back drinking, with a negative approach to life, I wouldn't be doing any of those things. To say yes to life is to get out of ourselves, get rid of the self-preoccupation, realize that God really loves us and wants us to listen to the messages He's giving us so that we can make this world a better place to live in. Too many people are afraid to live. Do not be afraid to live. You're going to make mistakes. So what? God forgives these mistakes. Live, because the gift we have is the gift of life.

14   Final Thoughts

Alcoholism is the third leading cause of death in America. Alcohol contributes to half our auto fatalities and serious car accidents and is the leading cause of death among young people. Alcoholism costs business and industry $65 billion a year through absenteeism, health costs, property damage, medical expenses, and lost production.

According to the National Council on Alcoholism, over 80 percent of fire deaths, 65 percent of drownings, 25 percent of home accidents, 77 percent of falls, and 55 percent of arrests are linked to the use of alcohol. Violent behavior attributed to alcohol use accounts for 65 percent of murders, 40 percent of assaults, 35 percent of rapes, 30 percent of suicides, 55 percent of fights or assaults in the home, and 60 percent of the cases of child abuse. Alcoholism also plays a critical role in the staggering divorce rates in America.

Some contributors to this book, because of their personal experiences, are frustrated with what they see: Rather than confront alcoholism, Americans still avoid it as an embarrassment and deny its impact on all of us.

Don Newcombe

I don't know if society will ever change its opinion about alcohol. I'm worried. The debts, the crime, the accidents, the injuries, the suicides—so many of those stem from the use or abuse of alcohol.

It's become obscene to me. If you look up the meaning of *obscene* in a dictionary, you will find very graphically outlined what Don Newcombe thinks about society and its purview of alcohol and alcoholism, and about what alcoholism has done and is going to do to so many people. Yet we totally accept it, except those of us who have been involved in it. We are the two-headed ogres in this situation. We are looked upon as if we're outcasts or lepers. "You did it to yourself. You poured the alcohol down your throat. You are supposed to be just what you are, an alcoholic." Society still misunderstands alcohol, alcoholics, and alcoholism, as it has for years. I see it in the school system. I see it in the work force. I see it in the military. I see it in sports. I see it in all society.

Society refuses to accept alcohol as a serious drug, like cocaine, marijuana, Quaalude, Valium, Darvon, Miltown, and all those other exotic drugs. People really don't think alcohol is a drug, even though it has more potency than all those other drugs put together.

Dan Anderson

Our culture loves and hates alcohol at the same time. Alcoholics learn to deny their alcoholism, not because they invented denial, but because they learned it from the culture. There is shame associated with drunkenness, not just for alcoholics. Most people who get drunk feel ashamed of what they did.

Drunkenness may bring out in us aspects of our nature that we'd all like to deny—the extremes of dependency, the extremes of defiant independence, the extremes of grandiosity or inferiority. We'd all like to make believe we were born well adjusted and we've always been that way. We hate drunks and the way they act. We can't handle that. None of us has faced up to the immaturity in ourselves. We have covered it up. Most of us drunks, not just alcoholics, regress and behave childishly and inappropriately. I feel ashamed for you, or you feel ashamed for me. We don't want to talk about it. That is the universal aspect of the denial, not just for the alcoholic, but for the whole culture.

We hate to see our beautiful socialized control stripped away. We don't want to see that in ourselves. I get drunk and meet some people at a party and I pat some professor's wife on the butt. The next morning I say, "Oh, my God, that's worse than robbing a bank."

Most of us thought the terrible problem for alcoholics was guilt. It's not guilt. They would just as soon feel guilty because then they can blame themselves. It's shame.

Grace Slick

I drove home on a Friday night about ten o'clock. It was like being in some kind of a bizarre movie, because about ten other cars were in various positions around me on the freeway, and not one of those drivers wasn't medicated. It was horrifying, the fact that that many people were that loaded. I was worried about their getting home. Everybody was weaving around on the road, and I was weaving to try to avoid the weaving, and we were all lurching around. There are a lot of people out there medicated. Hashish and marijuana and uppers and downers and sideways and alcohol—or any imaginable combination of these.

Father Vaughan Quinn

Everybody was educated to believe that an alcoholic is a bum. Brown paper bag, Sterno, canned meat, Vitalis, Yardley's, starting to drink at seven in the morning, living in a flophouse. That's what we were taught. Now we have to grow up. A person turns twenty-five and is an alcoholic and doesn't identify with that. A lot of work has to be done.

Ryne Duren

Four guys who were doing Miller Lite commercials talked to me about their own alcohol abuse.

I think a couple of them are bona fide alcoholics. But if you are offered the kind of money they are offered to make the commercials, it's pretty hard to turn it down. One of them, who had the toughest reputation of all the athletes in those commercials, collared me one day in Florida, backed me into a corner, and started talking with me. He said, "How do you say no to a drink?" So I asked him, "Why would you want to know that?" He said, "When I go out there to do the commercial I don't want to drink. I can't handle it anymore. That's not what I want to be anymore." So I said, "Well, just tell them you don't drink anymore, that you decided to try it the other way for a while." Here is a guy who, for the money, is going against how he really feels about the whole thing.

Doc Severinsen

Let's turn it around so that the stigma goes on the ones who are the drunks instead of stigmatizing the sober people. The square thing, the dumb thing is to be a juicehead. You get on an airplane at 9:00 A.M. and they want to know if you care for champagne or orange juice. I'm talking 9:00 A.M.! You sit next to some guy who just kissed his wife good-bye, has his little briefcase and his nice pressed suit. He sits down in first class, and they come by with the liquor cart. I see it day in and day out. The guy sits there. "Oh, yes, I'll have a bloody mary, two vodkas." You have a five-hour plane flight, and by the time the guy gets off, he's had four or five of those little bottles at least. He's had wine with his meal. He's had an after-dinner drink. And maybe some food. He has a flushed complexion from high blood pressure to top it off. We're about to land at the airport, and he has fallen asleep in a drunken stupor and missed his chocolate ice cream sundae. In the glide path coming in, he gets the stewardess to give him his ice cream.

He gets off and goes to his meeting with somebody in San Diego, or wherever the hell he is. They go out to lunch or dinner. The guy has two or three beers, a martini, or something. He gets back to his hotel and says, "Aw, what the heck, I don't think I feel sleepy." Why would he feel sleepy? His heart is all pumped up from alcohol at that point. Now he's going to have something to cool down, so he might have a couple of beers and a vodka or a scotch. This is considered normal.

That man should be stigmatized. He should have a red D painted on his forehead, which stands for Drunk. This son of a bitch is going to have a heart attack and wonder, "Why did this happen to me?" God, I feel like grabbing that guy and saying, "You big fat turd, how soon do you want this heart attack? Would you like to have it today? Would it make you feel better?" God, you look at him and you just wonder. And when he does have his heart attack, everyone is going to say, "Poor Freddie. I can't understand it. He golfed, he played tennis, I saw him at the country club Saturday night. He looked fine to me."

Poor Freddie, my ass. He had it coming to him. Somehow we have come to say that this behavior is normal. Go to any country club in the United States on a Saturday night and look at what they call normal. And tell me I'm abnormal. If that's normal, I want to be abnormal.

Jason Robards

A lot of guys are out there working, and they think they're doing just great, but they are all a goddamn bunch of alcoholics. There are not 15 million, there are 50 million alcoholics in this country. That's closer to the true figure. We're talking about half of the adult population. Just look at a professional football game. Ninety thousand drunks are sitting there, and they all go to work the next day.

Billy Carter

I don't think we're getting anywhere. The President appoints a commission, and the same doctors he puts on the Commission on Alcoholism are pushing Valium every day. And saying it's an entirely different thing. Education is a long way from being there. How in the hell can you admit alcohol is a problem when its use is so widespread?

We lock up a kid who has a half ounce of marijuana, but if he gets caught with a fifth of booze in his hand, we laugh it off.

Parents make more alcoholics out of kids than anyone else because they're so scared of drugs. They don't realize that alcohol is a drug. They say it's fine if you drink but don't use marijuana. When I was in treatment at Long Beach, we had a couple of people who were heavy marijuana users. They weren't as screwed up as a hard drinker.

Doug Talbott

Where did yesterday's heroes go? The adolescent of today looks up to two groups of heroes—professional athletes and people in the entertainment world. Yet these two groups have a tremendously high rate of alcoholism and other drug addiction. What's happening today is an epidemic among the adolescents. The kids of today are drug users because their heroes are drug users. There is no question what's going to happen in 1990. By 1990 alcoholism and drug addiction will have surpassed cancer and heart disease as the number one health problem in this country. If America isn't walking or trotting or running, it's galloping into the chemical culture. All Americans are being taught that any kind of discomfort, either physical or emotional, is unacceptable because there is a pill, shot, powder, or needle that will take care of it.

The young people of today are turning to chemicals for instant relief. We are paying the price, and the price is addiction. Alcoholism, Valiumism, Libriumism, cocainism, Quaaludism, amphetiminism, marijuanism, or THC-ism. We're seeing the surfacing of professional athletes and entertainment people with tremendous alcohol and drug problems.

Somebody asked me, "What would you do to turn around alcoholism and drug addiction in this country?" I said, "If I could do one thing with a magic wand, it would be to blow up every TV set in the country. It has destroyed family communication, family togetherness, and love." We've forgotten how to communicate and love, and we're looking for instant artificial release of emotions and instant chemical relief of pain. This is what has gotten the young people of today into such a mess and why I'm so concerned about alcoholism and drug addiction's being so rampant in the entertainment world and the world of professional athletes.

Epilogue

Faith can be the belief in the experiences of other people. On these pages you have met men and women whose lives are examples of dramatic change. The participants do not suggest that they did anything heroic. Nobody wants to be an alcoholic; nobody wants to live in a family that is influenced by alcoholic behavior.

If you can identify with these stories, change your own life. Action requires effort and risk, but it is worth the results.

Individually and collectively the contributors offer their stories and observations as proof that their lives are happier today than ever before. The message to the alcoholic is, "Recognize yourself in our stories; if you do have a drinking problem, do something about it now. We guarantee that your life will be better than you ever dreamed possible."

The message to the families of alcoholics is "Do not accept your life with alcoholism. Seek help for yourself first, then force the issue with the alcoholic. Life doesn't have to be the way it is now."

Everyone in this book offers you hope, and

452

help is readily available.
Have faith.
Have the courage to change.

The publishers hope that this Large Print Book has brought you pleasurable reading. Each title is designed to make the text as easy to see as possible. G. K. Hall Large Print Books are available from your library and your local bookstore. Or you can receive information on upcoming and current Large Print Books by mail and order directly from the publisher. Just send your name and address to:

G. K. Hall & Co.
70 Lincoln Street
Boston, Mass. 02111

or call, toll-free:

1-800-343-2806

A note on the text
Large print edition designed by
Bernadette Montalvo
Composed in 16 pt English Times
on an EditWriter 7700
by Genevieve Connell of G. K. Hall Corp.